DUCK SHOOTING

BROADBILL

DUCK SHOOTING

ALONG THE ATLANTIC TIDEWATER

EUGENE V. CONNETT, EDITOR

Chapters by Frederick C. Lincoln * Philip H. Babcock * Ransom P. Kelley * A. Elmer Crowell * Charles E. Wheeler * Lynn Bogue Hunt * Samuel Bonnell * J. Kemp Bartlett, Jr. * Richard L. Parks * Tracy Hammond Lewis * Frederick K. Barbour * Frederick C. Havemeyer, 2nd * Dr. Edgar Burke * Lou S. Caine * Alan G. Baker * Ludlow Griscom

WITH COLOR PLATES BY
DR. EDGAR BURKE * LYNN BOGUE HUNT

ILLUSTRATED WITH PHOTOGRAPHS AND DRAWINGS

BONANZA BOOKS, NEW YORK

Preface

SEVERAL years ago Dr. Edgar Burke asked me if I would join him in writing a book on duck shooting, saying that before many more years elapsed few of the men who had actually witnessed those memorable old days of market gunning, and the years of superb shooting which followed them, would be with us. He felt that the time had come to gather as much authentic information of those bygone days as possible and make a permanent record of them for future generations of duck shooters.

Having had some experience with the difficulties of writing such a book, I hesitated for some time to comply with Dr. Burke's suggestion. Meanwhile his enthusiasm for the project grew rather than diminished, and in the Spring of 1946 he made arrangements with the present publisher to produce such a book if it were written. He then proposed that a group of sportsmen be invited to write the book, and that I act as editor. Anyone who knows Dr. Burke will readily understand that his enthusiasm was too much for me, and I agreed to proceed with the work.

For several months we corresponded with prominent sportsmen from Maine to Florida and evidently succeeded in transmitting our enthusiasm to such good advantage that before long a distinguished group of gunners were hard at work gathering material for their contributions. Dr. Burke and Lynn Bogue Hunt were painting the color plates which adorn this volume. In a little less than a year I was able to place a remarkable manuscript in the hands of the publisher. I take this opportunity to express my sincere thanks to the authors for the splendid and generous way in which they have made their knowledge available to others. I trust the finished volume will meet with their collective approval.

While the authors claimed to be gunners rather than writers—and, in fact, were selected for just that reason—the reader will discover examples of exceptionally fine writing in the book; but of even more importance, to my mind, is the fact that each and every contribution carries the weight of experience and authority behind it. Not only has the historical background of the many famous gunning areas been recorded, but the present day methods of wildfowl shooting have been carefully described.

As the publisher of a considerable number of American sporting books, I am quite content to sign my name as editor to this volume.

Eugene V. Connett
EDITOR.

Contents

Preface BY EUGENE V. CONNETT, EDITOR   *v*

I. *The Future of American Wildfowl* BY FREDERICK C. LINCOLN   3

II. *New Brunswick* BY PHILIP H. BABCOCK   21

III. *Merrymeeting Bay* BY RANSOM P. KELLEY   45

IV. *Cape Cod Memories* BY A. ELMER CROWELL   56

V. *Long Island Sound* BY CHARLES E. WHEELER   61

VI. *Long Island Pond Shooting* BY LYNN BOGUE HUNT   77

VII. *Great South Bay* BY EUGENE V. CONNETT   86

VIII. *Barnegat Bay* BY SAMUEL BONNELL   105

IX. *Chesapeake Bay* BY J. KEMP BARTLETT, JR.   113

X. *Eastern Shore of Virginia* BY RICHARD L. PARKS   133

XI. *James and Potomac Rivers* BY TRACY HAMMOND LEWIS   161

XII. *Back Bay* BY FREDERICK K. BARBOUR   181

XIII. *Currituck Sound* BY FREDERICK C. HAVEMEYER, 2ND   189

XIV. *Pamlico Sound* BY DR. EDGAR BURKE   202

XV. *Florida* BY LOU S. CAINE   223

XVI. *Louisiana Marshes* BY LYNN BOGUE HUNT   230

XVII. *Making and Painting Decoys* BY DR. EDGAR BURKE   238

XVIII. *Retrievers* BY ALAN G. BAKER   269

XIX. *Waterfowl* BY LUDLOW GRISCOM   288

Index   301

Illustrations

BROADBILL by Dr. Edgar Burke   Frontis

I. THE FUTURE OF AMERICAN WILDFOWL

Atlantic Flyway   6   A Pintail drake   20
Range of the Blackduck   8   The annual waterfowl inventory   21
A family of Canada Geese   20   More ducks on the Potomac   21

II. NEW BRUNSWICK

BLACKDUCK by Dr. Edgar Burke   28

New Brunswick duck country   36   On the way to the blinds   36
On a New Brunswick marsh   36   Blackducks at ease   37
The guide's farm on the shore   Blackducks retrieved by *Bingo*   37
   of the lake   36   Posing for their portraits   37

III. MERRYMEETING BAY

Aerial view of Merrymeeting Bay   52   Poling out cripples in typical boat 53
A goose that didn't get away   52   Waiting for ducks to fly   53

IV. CAPE COD MEMORIES

A. Elmer Crowell in his shop   At Crowell Camp in the old days   56
   on Cape Cod   56   Canada Goose on nest   57
A. Elmer Crowell in 1898   56

V. LONG ISLAND SOUND

Charles E. Wheeler shooting   Pairs of profiles for line shooting 68
   about 1900   64   Indian decoy made of two stones   68
After two hours' line shooting in 1905 65 Pintails and Mallards by
A floating bush blind with boat inside 65   Charles E. Wheeler   69
Boat camouflaged with ice   65   Blackduck made by Francis Burritt 69
Last of the old "lining off" boats 65   Goldeneye drake made by
Bunches of mud serve as decoys   68   Al Sanford   69

Hollow Blackduck	72	Greater Scaup made by Ben Holmes	73
Blackduck and Mallard	72	Old Squaw made by	
Broadbill	73	Captain John Smith	73
Sleeping Greater Scaup made by		Old Squaw from the rig of	
Albert Laing	73	a market-gunner	73
Greater Scaup made by J. W. Selleck	73	Old Squaw made by	
Old Squaw made by		Charles E. Wheeler	73
Charles E. Wheeler	73		

VI. *LONG ISLAND POND SHOOTING*

BLACKDUCK SHOOTING ON WOODED POND, LONG ISLAND, N. Y.,
    by Lynn Bogue Hunt   80

VII. *GREAT SOUTH BAY*

On Uncle Bill's Bog in 1912	88	Henry Gould in double battery	89
On Fiddleton Point in 1912	88	Wilbur Corwin and Henry Gould	89
Wilbur Corwin's camp	88	The midship hatch of the	
Three of Wilbur Corwin's punties	88	*Mabel Jewel*	89
Double battery	89		

BROADBILL SHOOTING FROM A THATCHED PUNTIE
    by Lynn Bogue Hunt   92

A pair of punties hidden on Guli Bar	96	Old style flat bottom puntie	96
Scooter type puntie with		Rigged on West Bog	97
high-crowned decks	96	Two scooter type punties on	
The author shoving to his point	96	Titus Bog	97

VIII. *BARNEGAT BAY*

The Chadwick Hotel, Chadwick, N. J.	106	Blackduck made by the late	
A Barnegat sneak box	106	Captain Charles Parker	110
A shooting box, Barnegat Bay	107	Contemporary Blackduck made by	
Sneak boxes hidden under seaweed	107	John Updike	110
Sneak box with seaweed on decks	107	Broadbill made by Harry Shores	110
Redhead made by the late		Red-breasted Merganser made by	
Captain Charles Parker	110	Harry Shores	110

American Merganser from
   Barnegat Bay   111
Goldeneye made by Harry Shores   111

Canada Goose from Barnegat Bay   111
Canada Goose from the coast of
   New Jersey   111

IX. *CHESAPEAKE BAY*

Canvasback on the Susquehanna   116
Single battery on Chesapeake Bay   117
Double battery on the Chesapeake   117
The end of the day, Chesapeake Bay   120
The author as a boy   120
CANVASBACK by Dr. Edgar Burke

Captain Harry O. Moore   120
Buffle-head from an old "rig"
   at Oxford, Md.   121
Canvasback of cast-iron   121
Canvasback, female, of cast-iron   121
    124

Red-breasted Merganser from
   Hooper Island   128
Old Red-breasted Merganser   128
Canvasback made by Wm. Heverin   128
Canvasback made at North East, Md.   128
Canvasback made by Capt. Ben Dye   128

Broadbill   129
Broadbill, female   129
Canvasback drake   129
Canvasback duck   129
Pintail drake   129
Pintail duck   129

X. *EASTERN SHORE OF VIRGINIA*

A frame blind made of cedars   136
A "drean" through the inner marsh   136
Mud so soft a boat can be rowed on it   136
The author's ducking rig   136
Goose on nest with gander on guard   137
Mallard drakes and ducks   137
Part of a raft of Broadbill   144
Pintails and Mallards taking off   144
Pintail drake feeding in shoal water   145
Mallard duck with young   145
Blackduck from Eastville, Va.   148

Green-winged Teal from the
   Eastern Shore of Virginia   148
Feeding Brant from Cobb's Island   148
Canada Goose made at Cobb's Island   148
Green-winged Teal from the
   Eastern Shore of Virginia   148
Canvasback made by one of
   the Cobb family   149
Broadbills made by A. H. Cobb   149
Canvasback found at Cobb's Island   149
Lesser Scaup from Eastville, Va.   149

XI. *JAMES AND POTOMAC RIVERS*

An unretouched photograph   164
Mallards on the Potomac River   165

Underwater mowing machine   165

AMERICAN WIDGEON by Dr. Edgar Burke   172

XII. *BACK BAY*

Cap'n Billy's Rig   180   A good Canvasback "fly"   184
To kill a Mallard is an   1904 outstanding year at Sand Bridge 185
  uncommon occurrence   181

XIII. *CURRITUCK SOUND*

Canvasback made by one of   The Currituck Club House   196
  the Saunders family   192   A fine lot of Canada Geese   196
Canada Goose standing in rough water 192   Wading ashore from the goose box   197
A typical goose box along the shore 193   Breaking up skim ice by
Typical duck marsh at Currituck   193   rocking the boat   197
Shoal draft boats tied up to   A two-man blind at one of the ponds 197
  the Club Dock   193   Skiffs moored near the Club Dock   197

XIV. *PAMLICO SOUND*

Typical stake blind showing   Canada Goose made by
  entrance door   204   Charlie McWilliams   204-5
The Green Island Club at Ocracoke 204   Brant made in Hatteras Village   204-5
Wild geese picked up starving   204   Battery rigged out at Pea Island   205
Lynn Bogue Hunt in a   Setting out the battery at
  Pamlico blind   204-5   Pea Island   205
A Currituck sit-down battery   204-5   Bound for Pea Island on
This picture shows whole rig set out 204-5   the *Hattie Creef*   205
                                            Setting out for geese at Pea Island 205

CANADA GEESE AND BRANT by Dr. Edgar Burke   212

XV. *FLORIDA*

Duck blind on a mango island   228   Snow Geese and Blue Geese   229
A duck camp on the Homosassa River 228

XVI. *LOUISIANA MARSHES*

DUCK SHOOTING, VERMILION MARSHES by Lynn Bogue Hunt   230
BLUE AND SNOW GOOSE SHOOTING IN THE VERMILION
  MARSHES by Lynn Bogue Hunt   234

XVII. *MAKING AND PAINTING DECOYS*

Broadbill at complete ease	244	Female Green-winged Teal	260
Tying decoy anchor line	244	Male Green-winged Teal	260
Bellport decoy anchor	245	Brant	260
Pamlico Sound decoy anchor	245	Red-breasted Merganser made by	
Paint brushes for decoy painting	245	Captain Parker	261
Mason's Redhead, Premier Model	252	Redhead from a market gunner's	
Mason's Bluebill, Premier Model	252	rig, Ocracoke	261
Mason's Shelldrake, Premier Model	252	Brant, solid wood, made by	
Mason's Blackduck, Premier Model	253	Gary Bragg	261
Mason's Pintail, Premier Model	253	White-winged Scoter from	
Mason's Widgeon, Premier Model	253	Lubec, Maine	261

COLOR PATTERNS FOR DECOYS by Dr. Edgar Burke   256, 262, 266

XVIII. *RETRIEVERS*

Chesapeake Bay Retriever	270	Two dogs retrieved sixty ducks	
A litter of Chesapeake		in three hours!	280
Bay Retrievers	270	Irish Water Spaniels	280
Dead-grass colored Chesapeake	271	Golden Retriever	281
Chocolate colored Chesapeake	271	Curly Coated Retriever	281
American Water Spaniels	274	English-bred Flat Coated Retriever	284
Group of American Water Spaniels	274	Flat Coated Retriever	284
Three Immortals: *Shed of Arden*		Use of dumbbell in training dog	285
Rip; Tar of Arden	275	Golden Retriever	285
Le Noir and F.T.C. *Gun of Arden*	275		

XIX. *WATERFOWL*

Breeding ground	294	Wintering ground	295

DUCK SHOOTING

I

The Future of American Wildfowl

BY FREDERICK C. LINCOLN

CONSERVATION of the migratory waterfowl of the Atlantic Flyway involves all the factors that are common to the other great systems and, in addition, one or two that are peculiar to it. Complete understanding of their far-reaching implications is necessary if the sport of wildfowling is to continue in this region. This is a most important consideration, as it is frequently appalling to note the total ignorance of gunners on such details as the source of the birds that they so enthusiastically pursue, their food and other requirements, and the gun pressure to which they are subjected. In this chapter, the most important factors are summarized in the hope that by so doing sportsmen can be brought to appreciate and to give attention to the problem.

Breeding Grounds. Sportsmen whose seasonal forays for ducks are restricted to a few favored areas along the coast may be startled to learn that the Atlantic Flyway is unique because it has no great breeding ground immediately to the north of the wintering grounds. This surprising statement should be further elaborated.

The important species of game waterfowl of the Atlantic Flyway are the

Blackduck, Canvasback, Redhead, Greater Scaup or "Broadbill," Lesser Scaup or "Blackhead," Pintail, Baldpate or Widgeon, Scoters or "Sea Coots," Canada Goose, and the Atlantic Brant. The Snow Goose (chiefly the Greater) and the Whistling Swan are very much in the sportsman's picture but for nearly three decades neither has been on the list of shootable game. Of the present list, only the Atlantic Brant is confined entirely to coastal areas throughout the year and (except as a stray) is never found in any of the other flyways.

Two populations of the Blackduck and the Canada Goose are involved. One, the smallest, is essentially maritime, while the other has maritime winter quarters but breeds in the interior. Were it not for the relative abundance of these species, waterfowlers of the East would fare rather badly, for from the above list it will be seen that this part of the continent lacks the great diversity of waterfowl that occurs in the West. As has been revealed by banding records, the birds from the interior breeding grounds are the great travelers. Many of those nesting in the northeastern maritime region make but relatively limited migrations along the coast, the southern terminus of their migratory flight being, as a rule, in the vicinity of Long Island Sound and coastal New Jersey. Occasionally a Blackduck or a Canada Goose from the Northeast will fly as far south as North Carolina or Georgia, but such cases are exceptional.

The Blackducks and the geese that fill the bags of hunters in the great ducking grounds of Maryland, Virginia and the Carolinas come chiefly from the interior. Funneling southwestwardly from Ontario to the western end of Lake Erie, some of these birds continue on across Indiana and Illinois to the Mississippi Valley, but most of them, with accretions from Michigan, northern Ohio, and probably western New York, swing abruptly to the southeast, cross the mountains in a nonstop flight and reach the coast in the vicinity of Delaware and Chesapeake bays.

All other important game ducks that winter on the Atlantic Coast come almost exclusively from the great breeding grounds of our North Central States and the Prairie Provinces of Canada. It is true that a limited num-

ber of Ring-necked Ducks are produced in Maine and in the Canadian
Maritime Provinces and occasional pairs of Pintails, Widgeons and Green-
winged Teals also breed in that region, but the number is too small to be of
more than ornithological interest. In so far as the supply for game is concerned, it may be accepted that all the Canvasbacks, Redheads, Scaups,
Scoters, Pintails, Widgeons and Teals that come to the Atlantic Coast are
from the great interior breeding grounds, which also supply the Mississippi
and Central Flyways and, to a limited extent, the Pacific Flyway.

This vast breeding area extends northward from Colorado and Nebraska,
through the Dakotas, eastern Montana, Minnesota, the Prairie Provinces
of Alberta, Saskatchewan and Manitoba, and the great Mackenzie Basin
to the Arctic Coast. Not all of it is used by all species, but it is all of vital
significance to sportsmen of the Atlantic Coast. Unfortunately for the
birds, this region north to about latitude fifty-four degrees is America's
granary, where literally millions of acres are now dedicated to the production of our bread, meat and other foodstuffs. In colonial times, these vast
prairies were dotted with uncounted lakes, marshes and potholes. Thousands of them were small, averaging only a few acres in extent, while others
covered many square miles. All this was ideal country for the production
of ducks, geese and other marsh-inhabiting forms of wildlife. It was truly
nature's "duck factory."

Drainage of many of the lakes, ponds and marshes was inevitable and
has produced valuable acreage for agriculture. Nevertheless, there have
been altogether too many cases where we, as a nation, have treated our
marshlands as we have our other natural resources—acted first and considered later the costly consequences. The country has suffered an incalculable economic loss through the destruction of the natural resources that
were contained in these swamps and marshes. In some states, restoration
of these lands to their original condition is now a favorite project for
"Pittman-Robertson" funds.

Seriousness of the drainage mania that has swept the country may better
be appreciated when it is considered that more than 100 million acres

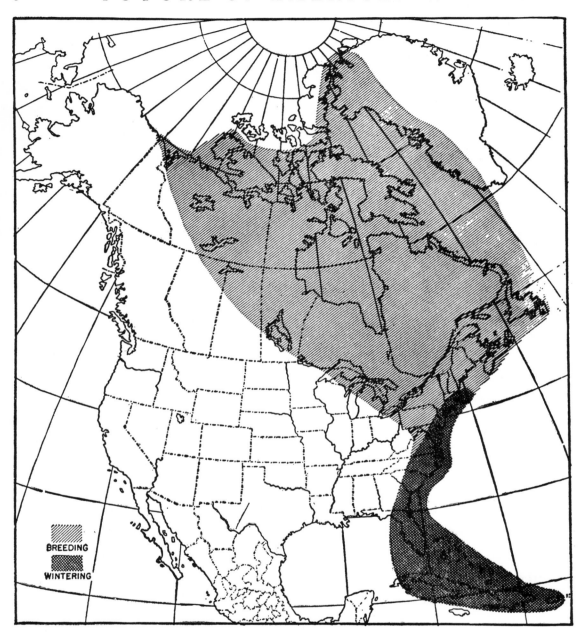

ATLANTIC FLYWAY

The waterfowl breeding grounds of the Atlantic Flyway cover a vast area but in winter the millions of birds are concentrated in a narrow zone along the coast, chiefly from Long Island Sound to the mouth of the Savannah River. Only a limited number spend the winter in the Caribbean region.

have been so treated. This is a region much larger than the combined areas of the Great Lakes, or nearly two and one-half times as large as all New England. With the water drained or draining from such a tremendous territory, is it not proper to ponder on what our waterfowl are doing for places to build their nests and rear their young? The answer, of course, is that they are making the best of a bad situation. Fortunately, the region in Canada north of "the bush" is truly great. There many of our ducks and geese have been pushed for their home sites. Others have utilized such marshlands as have remained in the agricultural regions, although in years of scanty precipitation many of these marshlands become infected with botulism organisms or dry up completely before midsummer and so become veritable death traps for both adults and ducklings.

The northeastern breeding grounds have not been so seriously disturbed by the works of man but, as previously mentioned, they have never been of major importance. Large areas in Maine, Nova Scotia and New Brunswick have remained virtually unchanged from colonial times and on their scattered lakes and ponds, as well as in some of the river valleys, the wary Blackduck continues to find the solitude it seeks for the location of its nest. Within that region there are few great marshlands that could support such a concentration of waterfowl as is common on the prairies. In consequence, the Blackduck has there become a scattered breeder, resorting to the coast as soon as the young are on the wing. Labrador, chiefly in the southern part, produces some Blacks and also some Canada Geese, but the total is not large. This is likewise true of Newfoundland, where extensive investigations by the Fish and Wildlife Service over a period of ten years failed to disclose a single outstanding waterfowl breeding ground.

Wintering Grounds. The waterfowl wintering grounds of the Atlantic Flyway are the marshlands and adjacent waters of the Atlantic Coast of the United States. Some birds do go to winter quarters in Cuba, Hispaniola and Puerto Rico, but present information indicates that the number is not large. This coastal strip, although relatively narrow, is very important, as during four months of each year it supports one of the continent's

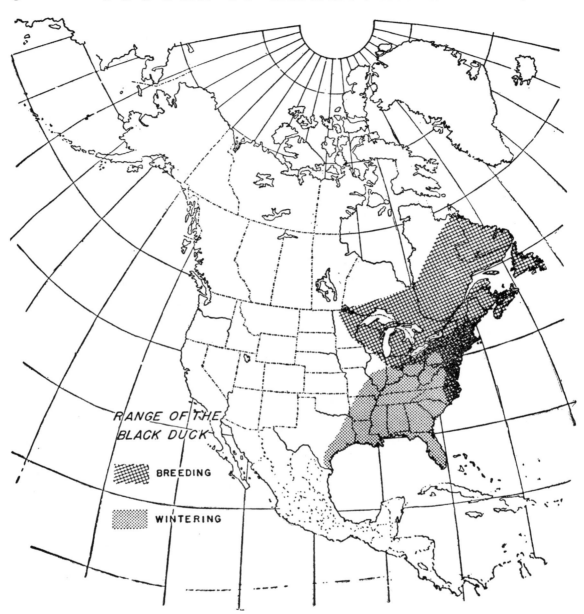

RANGE OF THE BLACKDUCK

The Blackduck has two distinct populations. One, the smallest, is essentially maritime, nesting in Labrador, Newfoundland, the Maritime Provinces of Canada, and New England. The other, which is much larger, breeds in the interior and in the winter is found from Lake Erie and Delaware Bay, south to Florida and the Gulf coast.

largest aggregations of waterfowl. Accordingly it merits more than casual attention.

Stretching in a more or less unbroken zone from the Maritime Provinces of Canada to Florida, this belt of habitat consists of the open, but frequently shallow, waters of the bays and sounds, bordered by a strip of tidal marsh-land of varying width. The marshes are usually formed by the silting up of lagoons or other areas that are protected by barrier sand dunes or beaches, but in some instances, as is the case with some of those on the coast of New England, they result from a gradual subsidence of the land. In the former type, the marsh layer usually is not great, but in the latter there is frequently a layer that will measure twenty feet or more in depth. An outstanding feature of many of these marshes is the natural levee—frequently a shrub-covered strip—that is built up around their outer margins by the action of wind and waves and sometimes by ice. This serves as a natural barrier to hold a considerable depth of water over broad expanses of grassy marsh. It also has the effect of producing a gradation from fresh to salt water, a situation that is particularly common along the Atlantic Coast and accounts for the great diversity of food available to the waterfowl.

While in a natural marsh, undisturbed by drainage operations, the composition of the soil does not seem to be a major factor in governing the distribution of the plant and animal life, it undoubtedly does govern the extent of tide-water movements which, in turn, do govern the distribution of both plant and animal species. In other words, as far as the relative abundance of plant and animal communities in such areas is concerned, water level must be regarded as the controlling factor. This point should be kept in mind when planning improvement or development for waterfowl.

Most tidal marshes have another important physiographic feature, namely, innumerable shallow ponds that are of particular value to migratory waterfowl. The presence of these ponds in a coastal marsh frequently is the deciding factor in bringing to it a large number of ducks and geese.

Food Requirements. Waterfowl in general may be classified as omnivorous feeders—that is, they will, and frequently do, eat almost anything available. With some species it seems to make little difference whether the foods present are pondweeds, wild celery, wild rice, crustaceans or mollusks, as long as there is a plentiful supply. This varied diet is responsible in no small measure for the differences in the flavor of the flesh of the birds. The corn-fed Mallard of the Mississippi Valley is a table bird that ranks second to none, but some Mallards, shot many years ago by the author in northeastern Colorado, that had been feeding on fermented beet pulp dumped into the Platte River by the sugar factories were so rank that they could not be eaten.

Similarly, to the epicure the Canvasback is the most prized of the diving ducks, the general belief being that its delectable flavor results from its extensive feeding upon the buds of the wild celery. Wild celery and other plants, chiefly submerged aquatics, do make up more than 80 per cent of the normal food of the Canvasback, and one of these ducks that has fed on these plants will cause little argument concerning its designation as an epicurean delicacy. Some of these ducks have been known, however, to feed extensively upon crustaceans and shellfish, or even upon decaying salmon. Such birds are unfit for human food.

Most of the game waterfowl that winter on the Atlantic Coast are, at that season, heavily vegetarian in their diet. Some, such as the Canada Goose and the Atlantic Brant, take plant food almost to the complete exclusion of other items. Only the Scaups ("Broadbill" and "Blackhead") and occasionally the Blackduck, show a partiality for animal food, chiefly mollusks. Normally, the great bays, inlets, estuaries and mouths of the many rivers furnish an abundant supply of these preferred foods, both animal and vegetable. Although the Susquehanna Flats are famous for their great beds of wild celery, this plant is found from Nova Scotia to North Carolina, while another form is abundant on the Gulf Coast from Florida to Louisiana. Some of the most desirable pondweeds also make luxuriant growths. A fact widely known to aquatic botanists is that many of the most important waterfowl food plants, including wild celery, widgeon grass, sago pondweed, bushy pondweed and redhead grass, attain their greatest development in slightly brackish waters. The term "slightly" must be emphasized, however, as most if not all of these plants are quickly destroyed by an influx of large quantities of sea water. An object lesson was presented several years ago when the locks were removed from the Chesapeake and Albemarle canals and a tremendous volume of sea water was permitted to flow into Currituck Sound, N. C., and Back Bay, Va. Prior to that time, the beds of aquatic plants were so thick that it was almost impossible to traverse them with a motor boat. With the advent of the salt water the plant life steadily decreased, but when the locks were again placed in operation a progressive regrowth of the waterfowl food plants occurred.

Although the dominant plant in Atlantic Coast tidal marshes is the salt-marsh cordgrass, which is only fair as a producer of waterfowl food, stands of other more desirable plants are frequently found associated with it. Some of these, as the tidemarsh waterhemp and the three-square bulrushes, provide food that is eagerly taken, chiefly by the shoal-water feeders. Where a large volume of fresh water prevails in the marshes, as in the lower reaches of Delaware Bay and the northern tributaries of Chesapeake Bay, there may be locally important areas of wild rice, bordered on the higher levels by the three-square sedges, smartweed, wild millet and other favorite waterfowl food-producing plants.

The last tragic disappearance of the eelgrass is now history and is widely known to Atlantic Coast wildfowlers. This submerged aquatic plant, which grew in dense mats on the mud flats of coastal bays and estuaries, was found on both coasts of North America, and also on the coasts of Europe and Asia. It grew both in full-strength sea water and in the brackish water at the mouths of rivers. Its last diminution on most of our Atlantic Coast began in 1931 and 1932, and shortly after that it started to disappear along the coast of France, from which region the destruction spread to the eastern Mediterranean region north to the coast of Sweden. A multitude of theories was advanced to account for the trouble, ranging from attack by a fungus to that by a bacterium. Extensive laboratory tests were made, but none conclusively demonstrated the causative agent, although most of the evidence points to a mycetozoan—a low form of fungus.

The effect of the disappearance of the eelgrass on one of our most important wildfowl, the Atlantic Brant, was startling. Few birds are so dependent upon a single source of food as is the Brant, as eelgrass constituted more than 80 per cent of its winter food staple. During the first years of the eelgrass scarcity, the population of the Brant decreased rapidly and by the winter of 1934-35 it was estimated that in Pamlico Sound, N. C., there were present not more than two per cent of the number of these birds that had wintered there in 1929-30. Regulatory action was promptly taken by the Federal Government, and the Brant was given complete protection, although this may not have been necessary, as the few birds taken by sportsmen were so thin and emaciated that they were unfit for the table. Following a gradual change in feeding habits, coupled with the year-long protection in both the United States and Canada, the Brant finally recouped its losses and was restored to the list of legal game. The eelgrass, too, made many attempts at recovery and in some years the plants locally made impressive growth, only to die down before the end of the season. Nevertheless, as is usual in all epidemics of whatever cause, the course of destruction was finally run, and at this writing (February, 1947) there is every evidence that the eelgrass is on the road to complete recovery. This is particularly noticeable in brackish waters, but dense growths also have been reported at points in the full-strength sea water of lower Chesapeake Bay.

Pollution. In its direct effect upon our migratory waterfowl, pollution usually means oil. Other kinds of refuse, such as sewage, refuse from rayon, paper and pulp mills, and other industrial and civic wastes, are frequently responsible for the destruction of waterfowl food supplies. But for the direct destruction of the birds themselves, oil is the chief offender and oil pollution is probably worse on the Atlantic Coast of the United States than on any other coast of comparable size in the world.

Narragansett and Delaware bays are at times so heavily coated with oil as to be veritable death traps for any aquatic birds that may alight upon their fouled waters, and this despite two Federal laws, one of which is aimed directly at oil pollution (The Oil Pollution Act of 1924). Enforcement of this Act is a duty of the District Engineers, but as this is only one of a multitude of their responsibilities, and as they have no enforcement personnel, their failure to ameliorate the bad conditions is readily understandable.

The entire subject of pollution has been "investigated to death" by individuals, conservation agencies and by Congressional Committees. Most states are powerless, or at least generally ineffective, in abating a nuisance that if not removed is sure ultimately to destroy our aquatic resources. A Federal law with teeth in it, implemented by conscientious, well-financed enforcement, is the only solution we know that will work.

In so far as the waterfowl food plants are concerned, the subject of pollution is not limited to civic and industrial wastes. Certain injurious plants, either native or introduced, acting as insidious pollutants, may completely destroy great stocks of highly desirable food plants and force the ducks and geese to other quarters, as in the widely known cases of the water chestnut, or caltrop, and the water hyacinth. As usual in such cases, the introduced forms are likely to have the more disastrous effects.

Although several theories have been advanced to explain the immigration of the water chestnut from European to American waters, the exact details are unknown. This plant was first recorded in the Potomac River in 1921, when a small patch was discovered at the mouth of Oxon Run. From that point it rapidly spread five miles up the river and thirty-five miles downstream and completely destroyed the luxuriant beds of wild celery and other desirable native plants.

In the early 1920's the waters of the Potomac below Washington were the winter home of thousands of Canvasbacks, Redheads, Scaups and other highly prized ducks. Today the presence of one of these is a matter for comment among the local bird students. During the course of experimental control work undertaken by biologists of the Fish and Wildlife Service, an underwater mowing machine was developed and the work of clearing the river of these plants was turned over to the Corps of Engineers. Since 1940, all beds, covering some 10,000 acres, have been mowed and it is hoped that this pest has been brought under control. Constant vigilance will be necessary to make certain that no plants have been missed. This alien has also become established in the Mohawk River in New York and is steadily working down the Hudson. A bed about a half mile in extent has been found in the Concord River in Massachusetts.

One report is that the water hyacinth was introduced into the United States in 1884, when the Japanese representatives to the International Cotton Exposition in New Orleans gave some of the plants as souvenirs to visitors. Through this means the waters of Louisiana and Florida received this exquisitely beautiful but pernicious aquatic plant, which in many instances has so choked some of the slow-moving bayous that navigation is impossible. It is apparently of no value as a source of food or shelter for any useful form of wildlife, and although cattle will eat it on occasion, chemical analysis has revealed that its nutritive value is so low that it scarcely balances the energy expended in obtaining it. Where uncontrolled, the plants form such a dense surface mat that the biological pattern becomes totally disorganized. Submerged aquatic plants, important as food for both waterfowl and fish, are killed out by being blocked from the light. Thousands of dollars have already been expended in the effort to control this pest but little progress has been made.

Other plants, such as the widespread cattail and giant cutgrass, can become pests on areas dedicated to the use of waterfowl. Unless controlled, these species quickly will supplant other emergent growth along the margins of ponds and marshes and they may also invade shallow water areas, where they crowd out the desirable submerged aquatics.

Cutting and burning are the chief methods of controlling these plants, but complete eradication from an area may involve temporary drainage and plowing. It is true that both the cattail and the cutgrass provide cover, but other plants will do this job and at the same time furnish an abundant supply of food.

A brief comment concerning the introduced European carp seems appropriate here. While it is true that there is a ready market for this fish among certain elements of our population, it is extremely doubtful if the financial return compensates for more than a fraction of the damage for which it is responsible. From the viewpoint of the wildfowler, the carp is another efficient destroyer of waterfowl food plants, and the destruction is complete. Not only do these fish consume the entire plants, including the root-stocks, but the turbidity of the water caused by their constant rooting prevents re-establishment. With the water chestnut apparently controlled in the Potomac River, it is now a grave question whether the native plants will be able to grow again because, as a result of the intensive activities of the carp, light cannot penetrate the turbid waters. A similar situation exists in portions of the upper parts of the famous Susquehanna Flats and probably elsewhere along the coast.

Hunting Pressure. It is not possible to consider subjectively the problem of waterfowl conservation without including a reference to the pressure that each season is exerted on the duck and goose populations by the hunter. From the viewpoint of predation on the adult birds, there is only one animal of any importance—man. No one will question that a predatory bird or mammal will take a duck whenever the opportunity is presented, but actual case records of the capture of healthy, uninjured adult ducks or geese by such animals are so rare that it is obvious the total damage they do is insignificant.

On the other hand, the total legal take of the hunter is a terrific drain that every honest sportsman will do well to recognize frankly. It indicates the volume of production that must be achieved on the breeding grounds if the ever-growing army of hunters is to continue to enjoy the sport of wildfowling. In calculating the take by hunters, it is necessary not only to count the birds actually brought to bag but also to make some allowance for cripples and lost birds, which are just as positively a drain on this natural resource as are those brought home to grace the sportsman's table. Estimates vary, but a conservative assumption is one cripple or lost bird for every three that are brought to bag.

Figures are tiresome, but in the present connection it is possible to apply them in a way that will graphically illustrate the pressure that is exerted by the shotgun on the waterfowl resource. In 1934, the daily bag limit was twelve birds. That period was at the bottom of the so-called "duck depression," when, at the end of the shooting season of that year, it was estimated the total population of game ducks and geese for the entire continent had shrunk to about 27,000,000. During the 1934 season, on the basis of the sale of "duck stamps," the number of wildfowlers in the Atlantic Flyway (coastal states only) was computed to be a few hundred more than 95,000. If each of these killed his legal limit only once during the season, the total legal take, including cripples and lost birds, would have been in excess of 1,500,000. By 1945, the number of hunters in the Atlantic Flyway had more than doubled (200,000+) but the daily bag had been reduced only two birds (ten permitted).

Using the same method of reckoning as for the 1934 season, it becomes apparent that in 1945 more than 2,600,000 birds were killed. Such figures may seem appalling, but on the basis of studies applied to the entire country, they are believed to be conservative. In considering them, it should be remembered that they represent the legal kill. No allowance has been made for the numbers killed by the bootleggers and the cheaters who shoot at night or out of season, and who use other practices that are obnoxious to the honest sportsman. Possibly the total lost in this way is not great, but it is appreciable.

Conservation in Action. Of all outdoor forms of participating recreation, hunting and fishing are most favored by Americans. The migratory waterfowl resource has been estimated as representing a capitalized investment of one and one-half billion dollars on which the yearly expenditure in harvesting the surplus is at least three hundred million dollars. This estimate is based upon the sums spent for licenses, guns, ammunition, clothing, transportation, lodging and numerous incidental items. It is believed to be conservative. A direct economic return is the forty to fifty million pounds of choice red meat which in itself would be worth from thirty to forty million dollars at the corner butcher shops of the country. There also are the incalculable aesthetic and recreational values reflected in better health, better citizenship and in more abundant living. Although they cannot be computed on a dollar and cents basis, they are very real and America would not be the same without them.

Can they be continued?

The answer depends chiefly upon how earnestly sportsmen strive to understand the many factors that affect their game and then see to it that that understanding is translated into action. The author has endeavored to show the complexity of the problem. It is his hope that this effort has been successful and that his readers are asking themselves what they can do to help.

In anticipation of this question, the following suggestions are offered:

1. *Research.* The first requisite must be to assemble more adequate information. It has become fashionable in some quarters to jeer at research, the scoffers apparently being blind to the fact that the sum total of human advancement is based upon the painstaking and frequently thankless industry of the scientific investigator. Because of the wide distribution of the waterfowl and the great variety of habitats and circumstances under which they live, there is imperative need for more and more trained biologists. On the Atlantic Flyway alone there should be at least two "flyway biologists" and at least three general biologists attached to each headquarters of the two administrative regions of the Fish and Wildlife Service within that flyway. Their objectives should be to determine the waterfowl requirements in every area and then find out how to provide them.

Study of waterfowl diseases and how to combat them is a tremendous subject. When it is remembered that during the summer and fall of 1913 nearly a million ducks were killed by botulism in the Great Salt Lake Valley of Utah, the potential losses from disease became more dramatic. Lead poisoning, caused by swallowing shot pellets, is becoming an increasingly serious problem as the birds are concentrated more and more into limited areas where hundreds of tons of shot have been fired. Not only does the lead ground up by the powerful muscles of the gizzard actually kill, but there is evidence that those birds that recover from mild cases may be permanently sterile.

2. *Enforcement.* It is quite true that waterfowl population losses are not due entirely to legal hunting. This is, however, the one factor immediately controllable and sound conservation must be predicated upon regulating the annual kill to a portion of the increase for that year. Also, a great advance will have been made when sportsmen in general divorce themselves from the fetish of "bag limits." Hunting is recreation and should be kept that way. If the only reason for the trip afield is to get red meat for the table, it is much more economical to patronize the corner butcher.

Even if the present small corps of Federal enforcement officers were to be doubled, the number would still be far too few adequately to patrol the hunting grounds of America. Some states have larger numbers of officers, chiefly for the protection of their upland game. Enforcement of shooting regulations must become a personal matter, and a matter of sporting ethics. A dictionary definition of a sportsman is: "One who competes fairly in any contest, according to the rules and spirit of sportsmanship." The rules in this case are the Federal regulations. Some of them may be of the "nuisance" variety, but if America is to continue to reap the economic and recreational benefits of wildfowling, sportsmen must support restrictions that are imposed solely to insure adequate breeding stocks of birds.

3. *Refuges.* During the past twelve or thirteen years the United States, through the Fish and Wildlife Service, has spent nearly twenty million dollars in acquiring and restoring more than three and one-half million acres of waterfowl habitat. The Service considers the refuge system only about half complete. It needs to be materially expanded, particularly in the winter range of the ducks and geese. Our national wildlife resources may be increased only as we are willing to dedicate lands and waters for that purpose.

Local selfishness, such as was exhibited in the attempt to cause abandonment of the Parker River National Wildlife Refuge in Massachusetts, can have no place in this program. Furthermore, it is a fact abundantly demonstrated that shooting in an area is usually greatly improved after a refuge has become established in the vicinity. Any doubt as to the accuracy of this statement will be quickly dispelled by a trip to any one of several refuges in the Atlantic system. Although a portion of the Mattamuskeet National Wildlife Refuge in North Carolina is open to hunting, the shooting in some years is better in surrounding areas.

The pattern of future wildlife refuges need not follow the inviolate sanctuary concept now embodied in the Migratory Bird Conservation Act. Possibly this law may be amended to permit administrative discretion in portions of refuge areas open to public shooting. Also, it may be desirable to place more emphasis on the development of public shooting grounds adjacent to inviolate sanctuary units. This should have the effect of dispersing the birds and providing more equitable shooting for the rank and file of the hunters.

In the three categories listed, emphasis is necessarily placed upon the national program to which the active support of the hunter should be given. He is the beneficiary or the loser as the case may be, if it succeeds or fails. He also should be particularly alert to obtain the maximum use of water-development projects such as those designed for flood-control, irrigation or hydro-electric projects. Many of these are sure to be carried out, whether wildlife interests object or not. But if sportsmen and conservationists are vigilant and aggressive, the waterfowl and other forms of wildlife may receive proper consideration. Under the Co-ordination Act this is now mandatory for water-development projects that are planned by any agency of the Federal Government. All sportsmen should take an active part in this program for, while losses from drought on the breeding grounds cannot be entirely curbed, they can be minimized through restoration work at other points.

Improvement of waterfowl areas in the Atlantic coastal region can be undertaken. Ordinarily, such projects are likely to be too large for individual effort, but they can be handled by a state under its Pittman-Robertson funds, by a club or by a game association. Usually the problem centers around control of fresh and salt waters and the development of an abundant food supply. Extensive engineering work for water control is not always necessary. Usually the seed stock for food plants can be found in the vicinity. In both these operations, the Fish and Wildlife Service has had extensive experience and it stands ready to advise and assist in such undertakings.

Conservation of the migratory waterfowl of the Atlantic, as well as of all other flyways, can be accomplished and the sport of wildfowling can be perpetuated for future generations of Americans if the scientist, wildlife administrator and sportsman of today appreciate the magnitude of the problem and collaborate in its solution. The time is now, for it may be later than we think.

A family of Canada Geese.

A Pintail drake.

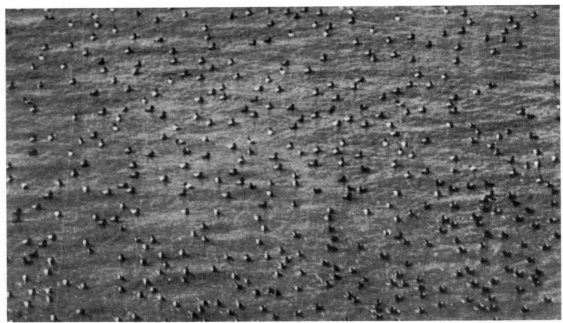

Ducks photographed during the annual waterfowl inventory.

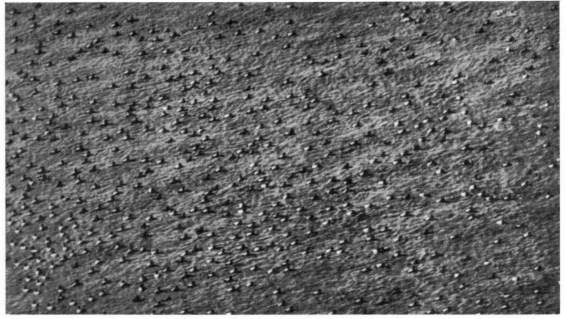

More ducks on the Potomac taken during the inventory.

I I

New Brunswick

BY PHILIP H. BABCOCK

DUCK SHOOTING along the valley of the St. John River in the province of New Brunswick, Canada, is an unorganized affair. There are no clubs, no gunners' headquarters and few wildfowling guides worthy of the name. Such a condition as would permit one to fly in for a shoot of a day or two, to be deposited in a blind from which one could return home, shortly, laden with ducks, simply does not exist. This may or may not appeal to the average gunner. To me it is the most attractive feature of a long list of attractive features. If, on the other hand, you have the time and the desire to work things out for yourself, you can get some fair duck shooting under delightful conditions. And though all duck shooting is a delight, it is this matter of conditions—the sum total of the little unrelated things— that often raises the shooting in one locality high over the head of another.

The season opens September fifteenth, which fact everyone seems to deplore—the birds being so immature—but about which no one seems able to do anything. Following a two-day Fourth-of-July holocaust, the cream of the local duck crop has been eliminated and the bulk of the local duck shooting fraternity retires for the season. Around the first of October come fresh supplies of Blackduck along with Teal and Bluebills funneling down from Labrador, Anticosti, Gaspé and northern New Brunswick. Then later Redlegs and Whistlers arrive, when the real shooting begins.

The laws of New Brunswick require you to have a guide. For feathered game one guide can serve two sportsmen. The word "guide" can be misleading. With few exceptions the guides of New Brunswick are experts in just two things—deer hunting and salmon fishing. The average guide's idea of duck shooting is to crawl a pondhole—of Grouse shooting, to walk a tote road. That goes for those who advertise, too. Of Woodcock most of them never heard until comparatively recently. But they are learning fast. Generally speaking you have to find your own shooting ground—your own covers, your own marsh. But that is not difficult. Don't, however, be so simple as to think your "finds" are going to remain your secret. Guides have a way of getting together and comparing notes. Like as not, next season your discoveries will be public property. One very worthwhile thing which your guide will do for you, however, if he is worth his salt, is to keep you from getting lost—something extremely easy to occur in New Brunswick. Besides this he builds the noon fire, carries and marks down birds and crawls into thickets to flush birds ahead of your dog's point—unless you are one of those fortunate individuals whose dog will do this useful trick at your bidding. In ducking he relieves you of some of the heavy routine work.

By and large the guides are a fine lot, hardly equaled anywhere. There are exceptions, of course. On one occasion one of these "exceptions" fell to my lot, a pale-faced slim youth with a whiny voice—a sort of rural gigolo who played the harmonica and sold hot dogs at country dances. Any qualifications he may have had other than that of possessing the two-dollar fee required for a guide's license still remains obscure.

He met us with a car that had neither top, mudguards or brakes. The descent of steep hills was accomplished by putting the gears in reverse. I didn't know this could be done. But it can and was, albeit the sound was frightening. However, it worked well enough, the only drawback being that we had to coast to a dead stop at the bottom before shifting gears again. In the field we heard our various comments solemnly echoed back to us as though pearls of his own observation. He was quick to catch our jargon, only his timing was bad, very bad. A clever youth! After three days we dismissed him and moved to a happier location. I'm sure he was relieved, for by that time he was thoroughly fagged from walking. And something had occurred to shake his faith in us as gunners.

Deer are an obsession with every man, woman and child in New Brunswick. In the autumn an otherwise normal adult male can be expected to go completely off his head at the mere sight of deer tracks weeks old. On the last afternoon we surprised two does in some open swale between two woodcock runs. They jumped at about sixty yards and went bounding off. Behind us we heard the voice of our guide as he screamed, "Shoot, shoot, shoot!" But we didn't shoot. We didn't raise our guns. From then on, it was quite obvious from his hurt manner he would never forgive us for not filling that fleeing pair with bird shot.

As inland duck shooting in New Brunswick is, as so often happens, some· what inescapably tied up with upland shooting, it might not be too much out of place to discuss the latter for a moment and endeavor to give each some sort of rating. In so doing I shall, of course, be expressing merely my personal opinion. On such a vital matter no two gunners could possibly agree or be expected even to argue and still remain friends.

The Blackduck, when he arrives in the region of the St. John River, is in his prime. Never again will the young birds be quite as delectable. Fresh water fed, stuffed on wild rice and sago tubers that at times will be found protruding from their maws like presents from a Christmas stocking, having endured no long flights, they are at the very peak of gastronomic perfection. This, together with their size and natural aptitude for self-preservation, places them, in my opinion, as the No. 1 sporting bird of the Province. I say this unhesitatingly and I am not unfamiliar with all the superlative qualities of His Majesty the Ruffed Grouse, having chased him over most of New England and well into New York state for the better part of a lifetime. Nor, in my opinion, do Grouse deserve even second place. Instead, I place Woodcock in this position. For it is in New Brunswick and Nova Scotia that Woodcock shooting really excels and becomes a sport far removed from what we call Woodcock shooting in the states.

In placing Grouse third on the list, it is not because of any scarcity except in those years of periodic decline. It is because in New Brunswick they are very much inclined to use their legs rather more than their wings—a habit which increases, markedly, the further you penetrate into the Province until finally there seems little difference between his actions and that of his near relative, the fool hen or Spruce Partridge. Moreover, the covers for the most part do not lend themselves to the operations of a well-schooled team of Grouse gunners. Birds cannot be driven or cornered.

In fourth position I place the other ducks—Bluebills (greater and lesser), Whistlers and Teal. The first two are inferior in size and quality to Blacks. In fact, I have orders not to bring any more home. It's Blacks or nothing. Teal, of course, are rather out of the picture because of their size—and for that reason only. Jacksnipe must be content with fifth rating because of that gentleman's unpredictable habit of being here today and gone tomorrow.

In one respect, at least, the local duck gunners of New Brunswick seem better equipped than many. They have Retrievers, mongrels and cross-breeds, many of them, to be sure, without benefit of selected ancestry or professional training but dogs that find and fetch none the less. Any such is better than none. Through hamlet and town in the ducking area every canine seems to bear the stamp of Spaniel or Retriever. During a half day spent killing time on the waterfront in the city of St. John I saw at least forty-odd unattached dogs wandering about the streets, all of which carried the blood of water dogs. But not always is a sporting or water dog heredity a requisite for accomplished duck work as was at one time most forcefully demonstrated to me by a certain local guide. This man owned what appeared to be a purebred Collie of the working sort you might find at any sheep trials—a farm-raised specimen handy at driving cattle, small, trim and with the usual black body and white collar markings of his breed. A natural retriever with a birddog nose, he could absorb more cold water punishment than it has ever been my lot to witness. All day he would stand in ice water to his middle, sometimes to his neck. Needless to say he had a superb coat. His owner never bothered to provide a stool for him to climb on or to take him in the blind or, in fact, to pay any attention to him whatsoever. It wasn't necessary.

Following a retrieve he would retire behind the blind, find a spot where the grass tops showed extra heavy and edge his way under. And there he would remain absolutely motionless until he saw a duck fall. If from an angle you made a move or spoke to him he wouldn't turn his head, not he. Instead, he'd roll his eyes in your direction, and not too hurriedly either. He was the most duck-conscious canine it has ever been my privilege to gun over. Home at last, after an all-day bout with the ducks, he would be fed in the kitchen and then turned out to curl up in the hay in the barn.

I should like to have seen him spend the night behind the stove but our northern neighbors are not given to pampering those of the four-footed world nor do they pamper themselves. Undoubtedly the suffering he endured affected his health and disposition. He was cross to the point where he was the terror of the neighborhood. He fought with every dog and, being small, got sorely mauled. At eight he was badly crippled with rheumatism and abscesses from old fight wounds. When one day he hobbled after his master on a late season deer hunt, the latter thought it best to make this his dog's last journey. It was with real sorrow that I heard about it and realized I should never again watch the work of this remarkable dog.

Within my limited means I have done considerable experimenting with gun dogs and, although I probably haven't proved anything that wasn't known a century ago by every British handler, at least I have the satisfaction of not having to take the say-so of others entirely for granted. I now know that those dogs of the pointing breeds with a fair coat, such as Setters and French Pointing Griffons, will do a pretty good job on ducks under reasonable conditions. But when the going is really tough you have to call in the specialists. Likewise, in the uplands, if you are willing to sacrifice the "point" you can get satisfactory work from Spaniels or Retrievers. But sooner or later any dog who is worked on the heavier, stronger birds, such as duck and pheasant, is likely to develop a mouth too hard for Grouse and Woodcock. So again you have to call in the specialists to have the work done as it should be done. In theory it is all very fine, and a most reasonable and practical desire in fact, to have an all-purpose dog who can be with you always instead of taking his turn as a part-time companion. But in practice it doesn't entirely work—at least it hasn't for me. In regard to the best specialist for inland duck shooting I do not think the perfect dog has yet been developed. The nearest approach is the American Water Spaniel. In size and color he is ideal. But his coat, as yet, is unsuited for the work when ice is making. Nor do I believe a coat that curls in all directions is of the right sort to give proper protection. When it gets wet it shrinks into close knots until you can see unprotected streaks of flesh.

I believe the present one I own to be a good average specimen. Under severe conditions I have seen him sprawled on the bottom of the boat shaking so violently he could not make his limbs function. It wasn't a case of lack of guts. It was lack of coat. The large, long-legged breeds—Labs, Chesapeakes and Goldens—are unsuited for this work. They are clumsy and troublesome. Small boats are thrown off balance and a frail, hastily constructed blind, such as one uses every day in New Brunswick, has to be rebuilt after every retrieve. The length of leg of these breeds appears to have increased of late—to speed the retrieve in field competition, no doubt. But a few seconds' difference in the retrieve is of no practical aid to the gunner.

Are we destined to have two types, as in the pointing breeds—one for trials and one for gunning? In Nova Scotia I have seen tolling dogs— powerful, heavy-bodied animals with medium to short legs and a coat like a wolverine and something of that color too. Perhaps they would be the answer to the northern wildfowler's prayer or, at least, to a wildfowler on a flooded New Brunswick marsh in November. I wish I knew.

Prior to 1938 I did most of my gunning in New England. Each autumn, habit, circumstance and sentiment sent me back to the covers and small inland marshes of my youth, although it was quite apparent that they had long since been shot out and that gunning over much of New England had deteriorated into little more than a farce, aided by the depredations of disease and vermin. It was apparent, furthermore, that this condition would prevail for a long, long time to come, since we in America seem quite incapable of learning other than the hard way.

New England was, undoubtedly, still the best place on earth to live in but as for gunning—well, it would take more than the exhortations of sentimentalists to convince me that it was morally wrong even to *want* to point your gun at more than two or three birds in an all day's tramp.

Then came the now famous September hurricane of 1938 and in the matter of minutes all my close-to-home covers of southern New Hampshire and eastern Massachusetts, along with those of hundreds of other gunners, were blasted into oblivion. As a countryman, as well as a gunner, perhaps I felt the storm's effect more deeply than some. I know on the morning of the twenty-first I awoke to find twenty-five ancient shade trees lying like jackstraws about my house. Back on the hills lay the orchards I had set out thirty-odd years ago, row on row flat to the ground, or with roots upturned. Beneath the debris lay seven thousand bushels of apples ready for picking. Fortunately, the cream of the crop had already been harvested and was safely stored.

All thoughts of gunning that autumn went glimmering, as I realized that the forests, and with them the old haunts of Grouse and Woodcock, had been turned into a no-man's-land where one could lose his way the minute he left the road, though he might previously have been as familiar with them as with the rooms of his own house.

With ax, tractor, cable and guy wires we set to work, day after day, week after week. Meanwhile, the nights grew colder, the days more brilliant as nature threw her mantle of many colors over the land. Each sunset and sunrise seemed more lavish than the last. Finally, I could stand it no longer and, on an overnight decision, I took my dog and gun and headed for Canada.

This was not the first time I had crossed the border in quest of sport but it was the first time I had done so with the knowledge that I was through with my old hunting grounds for good. No train ever bore a passenger more anxious to escape from reality than did that night sleeper out of Boston. Tied in the baggage car, more accustomed to motor travel than rail, my old Setter Mac refused to be comforted. So, using my lower berth for luggage, I kept him company most of the night while my shooting companions, who had joined me on the train, retired for some rest. This was no hardship for me. I have done so from preference many times. The air is better and there is often a camaraderie among the night shift of railroad men or some slight adventure that helps while away the time. This night was no exception. Sometime after midnight a short stocky brakeman with lantern on arm swung aboard the car as the train drew in to a station. As he passed me he almost stumbled over my dog and turned with an angry oath at the latter. Three times within the next few minutes he passed us, each time glowering and muttering at Mac who, lying quiet and relaxed, all innocent of what was transpiring, gave no response.

Presently, returning from the next car, the newcomer passed us again. This time he suddenly knelt down and in quiet soothing tones stroked my dog for some minutes, uttering words of affection. Then straightening up as suddenly and speaking in a low tone, he apologized for his previous action. "I ought to hate every dog in the world—especially Setters," he exclaimed. "But it's no use, no use. Owned a Blue Belton once and he bit my four-year-old daughter, my only child. She died of hydrophobia." Then after a minute's pause, while he gazed down into Mac's soft, questioning eyes, he recounted to me in detail how his wife had taken care of the child through the violent stage and all and from the shock of which she emerged a broken and aged woman with hair as white as snow.

We had slowed down for the next stop as he concluded and, as suddenly as he had appeared, he was gone. Leaning back, bracing himself, I saw

BLACKDUCK

him swing easily off the slow-moving train and disappear into the darkness, waving his lantern, while I fumbled for words, depressed and shaken by this terrible and moving tale.

As it grew light the flat landscape of northern Maine began to take shape. Lakes, streams, bogs flickered by amid endless forest. The stations grew smaller, mere wilderness crossroads, and the stops more frequent. In between, the good-natured baggage man seemed to have no objections to leaving the sidedoor half open. I shall not soon forget standing in that doorway that breathless frosty morning while the train swayed and rattled on its way, breathing in the cold fresh air as it rushed past and looking out at this scene of endless timber, all standing, undamaged, not a tree down, and all clad in the regal splendor of mid-October. The occasional lonely farmstead stood upright, not a roof missing. It seemed a different world from that which I had just left.

And then before I knew it we were at the border and leaving the land of bad manners behind and entering that of good ones, of simple courtesy and genuine friendliness. This matter of manners has little to do with shooting, perhaps, but it has a lot to do with the pleasure of your vacation. I don't know why Canadians should be so different from us but they are. You first experience it at the Customs. Our officials greet you with a grim or bored stare as though, if you were not a criminal, you were at least a likely suspect. The Canadian Customs' chap, on the other hand, has for you an affable smile. In the natural course of events he may even wish you good luck and a pleasant trip, as he catches sight of your dog or gun. There is nothing set about him, no chip on his shoulder. He is not looking for trouble.

Looking for trouble! Will I ever forget that morose individual on the American side who, early one morning, when I and my companion on a previous trip, were in a particular hurry to reach home before night, removed six Grouse from my bag of birds, claiming I had more than was legal. As he pompously argued with me, official hat on the back of his head, I could see he was utterly unfamiliar with the law but he was obdurate, none the less. Next morning from my home I called up the conservation authorities of Maine and Massachusetts who promptly informed the border official of his error. Several days later four birds arrived with a note from this oaf explaining that he had eaten two! The four he returned had spoiled! I wrote the gentleman that I would have him removed from office if it was the last thing I did on earth. Then, in the stress of other things, I promptly forgot all about it.

Through with the Customs and well into the country, you will from time to time have need to contact storekeepers, garage men and native inhabitants of one occupation or another. All are co-operative and helpful without a trace of salesmanship. And then one day you will arrive on that narrow, back-country road among the hills looking for woodcock cover. Presently, no doubt, you will come upon a set of rather dilapidated farm buildings fitting into a hillside view of broken woodlots, sparse fields and pastures. On higher ground beyond the barns your eye will quickly observe acres and acres of alders, shoulder high, with here and there patches of open ground. And as you shut off the motor, there comes the far-off tinkle of cowbells. It is enough.

You are out of your car and approaching the plowman in the foreground whose magnificent well-matched team seems out of keeping with the discouraged-looking buildings. To your greeting and request for permission to shoot on his land he will probably tell you to help yourself anytime. Not only that, but like as not he may tie the lines to the plow handles and, while his team rests, accompany you to the cover's edge to point out some special spot where recently he flushed a brood of Partridges. And all he asks for this courtesy, this back-country natural graciousness, is that when you return again you spare him two or possibly three minutes of your precious time. Don't hurry by with just a wave and nod. Instead, spare him a few words. He leads a lonely life. He welcomes the chance to stop and chat. If you find rural conversation out of your line, fall back on the weather.

On this trip, which followed the hurricane and which was given over to Grouse and Woodcock, I determined I would investigate the duck situation along the St. John River before another season. A fishing trip to Cape Breton by motor the following summer furnished the perfect opportunity. It was only a slight detour to swing down the valley of the St. John, that loveliest of scenic drives winding along the river's course, up which each season surge one of the great salmon runs of the world.

As a result of this side excursion I made the acquaintance of a farmer whose close-cropped, rocky, rolling acres sloped gently off low hills to a lake on the farther side of which stretched a series of marshes to the far horizon. He was a dairy farmer, if any one word can be found to describe his efforts at making a living, for farming in this country is a struggle that defies the efforts of any single occupation. On high ground, amid the boulders and ledges of his pastured acres, stood a group of unpainted farm buildings whose moss-gray weathered sides blended pleasantly with the landscape.

At one end of the rectangle these formed stood a square, substantial, two-story house. A shade tree or two, a crab apple and a couple of gaunt pines stood nearby. Lawn cutting offered no problem for cattle grazed to the sills. No sign of mechanical monster marred the grounds. Tractor, truck or car were conspicuous for their absence. Instead, the powerful hind-quarters of native bred "chunks" showed through an open door of the barn, behind which hung rows of harness. A grassy driveway of some length led to a country road to the east. In place of the gray stone walls of home there were gray snake fences, almost as old and indestructible as stone, with their natural bars of spiraled cedar. Above the bars of these boundary fences to the north and to the south sprouted the tops of woodcock alders. It was all very simple, all very plain and infinitely appealing to a gunner from New England. For this was New England—New England of fifty or a hundred years ago. The owner of this earthly Eden seemed too to belong. You didn't have to look twice to be sure of him. As luck would have it, he had just taken out a guide's license and, in his quiet unhurried way, agreed to take me on as his first customer.

Accordingly, around the middle of the following October my shooting companion and I arrived on the scene and, after finding accommodations at a nearby farm, prepared to go about the important business of introducing ourselves to the ducks.

Our guide's outfit consisted of a leaky thirty-year-old canoe that he admitted had seen better days, a handful of museum curios he called decoys—which by no stretch of the imagination could ever have seen better days—a borrowed duck boat and a Collie dog—of which I have already made mention.

Our daily schedule worked out something like this: Rising at 3:30 I would let my two dogs out, build a fire in the range, start the oatmeal and rouse the good-natured farm woman who would give the final touches to our breakfast, put up our lunch and go back to bed. While all this was taking place various younger members of this large informal family lay in peaceful slumber all about us, some in the kitchen, some in the hall—anywhere where there was room for a bit of furniture to stretch out on.

It was a two-minute run to our guide's farm where a welcome gleam of light always hailed us from afar. A final cup of coffee, while we discussed weather prospects and plans, and we were on our way, down through the pasture in the dark, loaded with the usual ducking gear. No matter how you plan it there is always endless gear to lug. By 5:30 we would be on our way across the lake. As it grew light, we had only to stop paddling to hear all the sounds of a miniature Currituck—Blacks on the marsh answering each other, Bluebills off shore stirring up great patches of white water as they rose with muffled roar, circling about in restless anticipation of the morning flight.

We usually shot on the marsh until nine or ten o'clock and then moved out to points for Bluebills and Whistlers. But whether it was marsh or point shooting, conditions were the same—it was cold and it usually was wet. That season was a good duck year and the marshes were flooded, with only patches of dead grass tops showing, along with the tips of occasional willow sprouts. We shot singly on the marsh, preferring it that way. We shot in small, flimsy, transparent blinds of willow and marsh grass constructed on the spot wherever it seemed ducks were using.

Often we moved three or four times a day. The most important part of these blinds, the keynote of the whole equipment second only to the gun you carried, was a T-shaped seat you drove down into the mud, using your rear as the implement with which to do the driving. The top of the T (the actual seat) was 8″ by 15″. The lower upright section was an 8″ board sharpened at one end and varying in length from three to four feet, according to the depth of the water and mud.

With the blind up, the decoys out, and the seat in place, you grabbed your gun, an extra coat, your lunchbox and your shell bag and waded into the blind, while the guide and canoe disappeared into the mist. This all seems simple enough until you find yourself standing in two feet of water with your arms full and no place to put anything, including yourself, except a bit of board 8″ by 15″. You try resting things on the blind but it is too flimsy and gives way. Eventually you hang things all over yourself and sit down, your tail within inches of ice water. If you haven't thought to tie string around the loose tops of your boots you will be reminded of that fact the first time you stand up as the hanging lip of each scoops up a cupful of water. But, anyway, you are down and out of sight at last, having fumbled only two or three easy set-ups as they boiled in out of the fog.

During the next few hours you make a mental note of all the simple little things you will bring along next time to add to your comfort, convenience and efficiency—a stout forked stick to rest your gun on, another to hang things on, some sort of cushion for the small unyielding seat, an extra seat to pile things on (this extra seat is essential if your retriever accompanies you). But you never do bring these things—not many of them, at least. If you do, the chances are they are mislaid on the marsh or lost in the darkness at the beginning and end of the day. The truth is there is no room for comfort in all this misery. There is always so much necessary standard gear anyway. You're swamped with it. With the marshes flooded, a condition imperative to good shooting in this section, your blind must be of minimum size. You have no choice in the matter. Fortunately, you can put your legs under water, but you can't your body. If you are tall, and I am tall, you have to lean forward in order to keep down in your tiny latticed hide-out. In other words, you are trying to achieve with a blind what in reality only a sink box or battery could accomplish.

Duck shooting is not noted for its comforts but of all the punishing methods known, and they are legion, shooting Blacks in New Brunswick on a flooded marsh in late October, for me takes the cake. Two hours of this and the cold water has removed all feeling from your feet, then your legs. These in turn draw off the heat of your body. Transparent blinds show less than solid ones but they do not keep the wind out nor do any kind keep the rain off. This all helps to put the finishing touches to your mortified flesh, which after ten or twelve hours of this is mortified indeed. You would be warmer in a duck boat, but seldom can it replace the small blind under the conditions I described for reasons needless to go into here.

However, there are compensations, plenty of them. Some defy words. But just to witness wildfowl moving about over vast silent marshland in winter garb is in itself considerable. And when this somber winter dress is rimmed with lingering patches of crimson forest, like embers of the dying year, and all surmounted by low crested hills, some dark with ever-greens, others of hardwood flaming still, then, indeed, you have no cause to complain—not if it is your privilege, day after day, to watch the miracle of change that comes with each caprice of weather. Bundled up with clothes, burdened with accouterments and doubled up like a rusty jack-knife, your nimbleness and timing are not what they might be. You discover that after you have struggled to your feet, reversed your tortured body in the grip of its submerged mud stance, and let go both barrels, it's quite easy to be thrown off balance so that when you sit down ("fold up" would be a better term) you miss your perch entirely. To say your shooting smells badly is an understatement—it stinks!

But once in a while there is a report like a pistol shot and a small geyser of water rises into the air as one of those glorious Redlegs hurtles out of the stratosphere. Or, a pair coming in slowly, deceived by your counterfeits, checks for an instant right over the decoys, giving you a chance to pot one in midair and nail the other on the flare. The long shot was the more spectacular, but it is a question whether you didn't get more satisfaction from the easy one with its planned deception that you have worked for, frozen for and are prepared to be half drowned for.

When the guide finally returns, your teeth are chattering so that your words are quite unintelligible. He smiles. He knows. But that is not his trouble today. He has been paddling and wading and slogging through miles of marsh putting up ducks for your benefit. He isn't cold but he's a bit weary. Now the dog goes overboard for a cripple or two. You make your way to the point where you join forces with your partner in a single blind. Here that terrible conglomeration of wood and paint, locally considered decoys, are all cast out for the edification of any trading ducks. Strangely enough they work, for these ducks are innocence itself compared to what they will be by the time they hit the New Jersey coast.

Lunchtime is a welcome moment, though, of course, there is no chance to build a fire. But there is hot coffee in the thermos bottles—that is, there is some left, for we have both been nibbling at our lunches off and on in an effort to keep the inner fires burning.

Around 4:00 P.M. we move back to the marsh. Near dark we pick up, spending considerable time over cripples. Under the stars, if the night is calm, we boldly head out across the lake. If stormy we hug the shore. It is nine or after before we get in. It seems a long process stowing things away in the dark, but presently we are headed up the pasture with that welcome feel of firm ground under our feet. We are tired and wet and cold to the point of numbness but we are not conscious of it. We are not conscious of it for just one reason—on each man's back rests a solid burden of damp ducks and with them memories that will remain long, long after all the discomforts are forgotten.

Following our departure for home on one occasion a native gunner paid us the compliment of quizzing our guide as to how those "fellers" get so many ducks, to which our guide made the perfect reply, "They work for them." And so we do, I suppose—just enough, yet not too hard, with the added delight of running our own show. The perfect balance is something hard to achieve—this being one of those "conditions" I referred to earlier.

Back at the farm we relax in the warmth of the kitchen, our labors over. Not so our guide, who has not only the farm and house chores but an ailing wife to minister to as well. He will be lucky to get to bed by midnight. At 4:30 in the morning he'll be ready for us again, chores finished.

Day after day this was the schedule. Some days were fair, more were stormy with high winds and driving rain. On the fourth day we began to wonder how long our guide could "take it," whether he would crack. We never found out, for that evening we ourselves cracked—wide open, with heavy chest colds and chills and fever and, I must admit, something akin to exhaustion. However, three days of rest and kitchen heat under the kind supervision of our landlady put us on our feet again with our enthusiasm a little more under control. From then on, in fair weather, we gunned ducks half a day only and rested the other half shooting Grouse and Woodcock. Stormy days the regular schedule held.

Each year it is the same. In vain we lecture ourselves with the same old phrases, "It doesn't make sense," "At our age we ought—" etc., etc. And then my hand goes out in the darkness and wraps itself around the cold metal of the flashlight. 3:30 A.M. A gust of chill damp air comes in the window. A few scattered drops of rain splash against the glass. Rough weather ahead. Duck weather. I am on my feet. The light is lit—the marsh. There is no other choice.

For the last afternoon I chose our favorite bluebill point. The wind was in the wrong quarter but at least I felt assured of seeing plenty of fowl. With my dog beside me in a comparatively comfortable blind it would be a pleasant way of finishing off the season. I hated to think that it would be all over so soon. I wanted to see the final windup, the last great exodus

New Brunswick duck country.

On a New Brunswick marsh.

The guide's farm on the shore of the lake.

The author's guide on the way to the blinds.

Fish & Wildlife Service

Blackducks at ease.

P. D. Dalke, Fish & Wildlife Service
Posing for their portraits.

Blackducks retrieved by *Bingo*.

of ducks before the freeze. But reason dictated that you couldn't go on forever and, after all, it was better to leave while you wanted more, much better.

During the first hour my young Spaniel made three retrieves, the last with a decoy as passenger. In swimming through the set he had fouled an anchor cord and the attached stool had taken up a position on the back of his neck, where it alternately bobbed, turned and twisted. I was annoyed, as I wanted nothing to occur that might disturb or frighten the youngster in his work. However, though he floundered and tried to free himself for a moment, he soon concluded he was wasting time and headed for that white object out on the lake. Presently, I had the satisfaction of seeing his mouth close on a drake Whistler and in no time he was headed back still firmly saddled with the decoy. As he passed through the set on his return, the anchor grounded and the decoy, freeing itself, came to rest precisely in the position it had recently held. This little act pleased and amused me—rather more than did the subsequent shower bath as my dog climbed onto the seat I had provided for him beside me and shook himself.

Wrapping a coat about him I now relaxed and settled back. An hour went by, then another. Great blue-black storm clouds billowed up, obscuring the sky. It grew steadily colder. Snow squalls were in the making. I took the glasses and focused them on bobbing strings of Bluebills riding the mounting whitecaps out on the lake. A little beyond to the east lay the small snipe marsh at the foot of the pasture I knew so well. Up on the ridge a team and wagon moved slowly along a country road. Beside a set of farm buildings a man and woman were pulling and topping turnips. Those everlasting turnips! Feed for the cattle in winter.

Moving the glasses north again I swept them slowly over some of the familiar grouse and woodcock covers of the past two weeks. Then on to wooded hills and the far horizon. Surely Hammond would have approved this land. J. H. Hammond and his golden era of shooting! Hammond, the "Nestor of American Sportsmen," that "most expert of expert wing shots" who wrote that "one day among the forest-crowned hills of dear New England was worth weeks on the treeless plain." They slaughtered the game in those days but one could hardly be blamed for wanting just a little of it. The Golden era! Mixed shooting! Well, this was as near as I had ever come to it.

For a moment I felt almost grateful to that wind that had blasted me out of the old grooves and ruts of the past. And now once again, I moved the glasses slowly along the horizon, moved them until the faintest suggestion of a blur arrested my attention, a darkening smudge that rapidly grew into thin pencil lines, one behind the other, stretching across the sky.

Ducks! Blacks! Hundreds of them! Thousands of them! Incredible sight! On they came—four or five thousand at a guess. Lines of a mile in length, bending, straightening, ever changing. Migrating Blackducks! The last great vanguard before the final exit. As they arrived directly overhead, the pale late afternoon sun broke through a rift in the clouds for an instant, glinting on their wings—wings and bodies that at their height looked no bigger than those of Teal. No sound came from them—or did there? Just the suggestion of a whisper. But who can trust one's ears at such times?

Soon the great lines had vanished to the south, leaving with me that sense of exhilaration that must have stirred in the soul of gunners on a marsh since time immemorial. There is a note akin to sadness too—of loneliness, and longing, the pull of the far horizon. Always this miracle seems fresh and undimmed. Thus fell the final curtain on my first ducking expedition to New Brunswick.

Ah, Canada! Young and innocent, full of visions and hopes. Take heed of your neighbor across the way. Be warned by the errors of my great country where lawlessness, greed and ignorance have nullified the efforts of conservation. Today you desire your share of manna. You are out for the tourist-sportsman trade. Your bulldozers are on the march, crushing, tearing, leveling their way across your vast wilderness. Behind come the gravel trucks and behind these will come the pleasure cars mile on mile, with their money bags, their gadgets and their loud-voiced occupants.

Have you reckoned the cost? Have you thought of our polluted streams and vanished and vanishing wildlife? Listen, Canada! Listen to the words of the late John Phillips, whose untiring efforts at wildfowl conservation deserve the everlasting gratitude of not only my country but yours as well. He is speaking of his beloved shooting ground, Currituck, and the essence of his thoughts are uniquely applicable to Canada today . . .

"Currituck, the land of happy dreams! May your shores ever resound to the clamor of wildfowl. Long of a winter evening may the wild Swans, all rosy pink in the sunset glow, wing their appointed way, softly calling from the sky. Long may there be a harbor where he who loves thy wide horizons may lie 'alone to hear the wild Goose cry.' Hold yet for a little while the march of progress, O you rushing millions, that the last of the happy hunting grounds shall not perish from this changing world."

As the years roll by we have from time to time improved on our guide's equipment. On the man himself it would be hard to improve. No professional in the matter of guiding or gunning—something he would be the first to admit—he has, nevertheless, a blend of qualities which makes his very presence always a help, always a pleasure. For knowing him and his family you are the better. New Brunswick folk are old-fashioned about Sunday. They take their Sabbath seriously. They believe that it should be a day of rest in more than words only. Shooting and fishing are prohibited. Thus it always came as something of a surprise, especially after his arduous week, when we learned in the general course of events that our guide had spent the early hours of that day not in prayer but in overhauling our temperamental outboard just to be ready for Monday—an occupation that quite often calls for something else than prayer.

So, too, later in the morning, would come another surprise, like as not, as on his way home from church and introducing the visiting preacher he would thrust his head in at the door of our farmhouse with the announcement, "Boys, there's a mighty raft of duck off the mouth of the creek. Better come down later." And so, later, down we would go to his farm and, since we couldn't shoot at ducks, we would look at ducks—standing by the hour with him on his veranda, passing the glasses back and forth between us. Verily, the value of a good guide, like a good friend, is hard to appraise. But, as I was saying, to his meager outfit we have contributed, and to which statement I might add in the language of the street "and *how!*"

Boats, outboards, decoys, blinds, dogs. What else is there left? Time was when we made the trip by train. Then it was a station wagon, then a car and trailer, now two cars are needed to move all this paraphernalia. And at this writing it appears that by another season nothing short of a transcontinental bus will see us through.

But, though we groan and moan and laugh too, over the matter of all this gear, let no man think we do not appreciate the fact that it plays a very important part in the fascination that is duck shooting. One or two special items that have been worked out from trial and error might be of interest to a newcomer to this northern shooting. I have no doubt there are more and better ones. These have simply been evolved from personal experience on the ground.

From the U. S. Army surplus camouflage material made for use in the jungle of the southwest Pacific, you can make a most excellent blind to keep out the wind and give yourself more freedom of movement. The material has a green background on one side, brown on the other, so that by reversing it you have the proper color for early or late season. Cut two strips three by six feet. (It is more convenient to handle in two sections rather than one.) Put grommets in the corners and midway on the long sides. Stitch a double row of strips, top and middle, same material, to form loops, both sides, for grass. Four stakes and some string complete the blind—three feet square, just right for yourself and dog.

If you want to speed the setting up to almost a matter of seconds, and time is often precious on a marsh, tie snaps to the grommets and have permanent stakes with loops top and bottom. Roll the blind up on the stakes and you have a handy rig that, on the right day in the right place, will be worth its weight in gold. A hood of this same reversible material is useful, to be buttoned on your coat. Have your tailor copy the pattern of the GI field jacket hood. The standard waterproof clothing of rubber coat, rubber trousers cut off at knee and hip boots are not enough. Besides this, you need a pair of armpit waders—not the light-weight fishing sort, but the heavy, black rubber type worn by wharf repair men and the like and in the enormous foot of which can be worn a sheepskin shoe. These will keep you really dry and fairly warm. Of course, you can't move around with them on and if you fall into deep water you'll probably go to the bottom and stay there.

And now, having done all this, the only thing left is to grow a beard or blacken your face, as did the market gunners of the Chesapeake in the olden days. And remember, when it came to ducks, those gentlemen, as the saying goes, knew their onions. One and all declared a colored man could kill twice as many ducks as could a white. I'll leave it to you.

As to creature comforts in New Brunswick, back in the country you are about as likely to find a bathtub as you are to encounter a white moose. If you have arrived at that time of life when bathing in a mountain stream in October has lost its allure, then there is just one thing to do at week's end, if you feel too untidy for comfort. Go to St. John or to Fredericton, whichever is the most convenient from your field of operation. Either one offers a pleasant and not too long drive beside the river. At Fredericton the old Winsor Hotel understands gunners and will tend to your needs satisfactorily, following which you can stroll along the side streets of this peaceful and picturesque old town on your way to Neill's famous hardware store —dispensers of sporting goods and sporting information—en route marveling at the ancient elms, than which there are no finer, I am sure, in North America. Here, too, among the merchants of Queen Street can be found the famous Stanfield woolen underwear—100 per cent pure, without which no native gunner would dream of facing the late fall elements. I recall an occasion when the upper portion of a set of these superlative nonshrinkables was returned to me by an irate washer woman with these terse words pinned thereon: "I consider this a sweater, not an undershirt!" There is, too, another commodity of 100 per cent purity, which has been known to be used by duck hunters, especially after a long day on the marsh. Fredericton has a liberal supply.

I like Fredericton. I like everything about it—the great river out front, the quiet streets, the lazy, restful, easygoing atmosphere. Perhaps my choice indicates a slovenly nature. Perhaps, in this modern world, it rates as a "hick" town. Be that as it may, to me it appeals. At the far end, beyond the Cathedral, on a hill back from the river, stand the handsome stone buildings of the University. As I leave town and head east I half unconsciously look up the street leading to that hill and its seat of learning. Sometimes I turn and go up the street. But often as not the hour is late, I am in a hurry and have to be satisfied with a glance, promising myself more time on the return.

Up on the hill at his desk sits a farm boy who was. We met many years ago under somewhat different circumstances. It was midsummer and I had only recently taken possession of my farm. For several days I had been putting in hay and, with the weather continuing hot and fair, everything had gone well, albeit slowly, for I was alone, the hired man having departed as soon as I had a good lot of grass down and really needed him. Dusk was approaching as I started on the last load that last day. To the south thunderheads had gathered and the low threatening rumble of an approaching storm echoed through the heavy atmosphere. I tried to hurry but not even the threat of rain with all it meant to a weary haymaker could stir my tired limbs to quicker action. Suddenly the heads of my team came up sharply, their ears shot forward. I looked up to see a white-shirted figure climbing the wall. He carried a fork and with long brisk strides he crossed the field to where I was. It was my next door neighbor's eldest son, a boy in his late teens. Flashing me a quick grin, he mumbled something about not liking to see a fellow haying alone, and then he went to work. With a few deft sweeps the tines of his fork would gather the scattered and fallen wisps from the load and then all in one motion they and a tumble of hay would be lifted, turned and deposited in just the right place on the wagon, followed by another before you had time to turn around. There was no clumsy derricking effort with fork held as a fishpole. Instead, he was right in close, with no motion or effort lost. You needed only a glance to see he was one born with "timing" and plenty of it. It was a pleasure to watch him, still more to work with him. I was grateful to that farm boy that evening, a feeling that has lingered through the years and continues to this day as he sits at his desk on the hill where he happens to be dean of the Faculty of Civil Engineering and Applied Science at Canada's oldest university. It so happens, too, that he has long since become an expert with gun, rod and golf club. How expert I shall not attempt to inform you here, but you would be surprised. I am not surprised though, not when I recall the smooth easy rhythm of that pitchfork in the dusk of a certain sultry summer evening long, long ago.

So that is one reason (there are plenty more) why, if I don't turn at his street I promise myself a visit later—a visit to catch up on an old friendship and to learn the latest of Grouse, Woodcock and the great family of wildfowl from the very best source that I know. And as I leave Fredericton behind and head down along the river road, it's just possible I may smile a little to myself as I ponder on the vagaries of life and the strange tricks that Destiny plays with our lives.

At the Admiral Beatty Hotel in St. John it will be very easy for you to imagine you are at the Ritz, only the food will be rather better. Later, you had better take in the marine supply house of Thorne, Ltd., down near the waterfront. Here you can buy a salmon line, some weights for your decoys or some especially fine china to take home to your wife as a peace offering—an enchanting store. Following this, a short walk along the harbor front will convince you that nothing is to be gained by dallying too long in this singularly bleak and dingy shipping port.

But whether it is Fredericton or St. John, it will be a happy sojourn. Always you will be among amiable and pleasant people—Scotch, Irish, English. This is another of those "conditions" I referred to earlier.

Having made a few suggestions regarding the shooting of ducks in a certain infinitesimal section of this vast continent of North America, I am now prepared to offer something on how to save ducks, on the theory that no one should write about killing them, no matter how amateurish it may be, unless he is prepared to offer something on saving them—like a good forestry program whereby no man may cut down a tree without planting another in its place. So I am now going to suggest to you, my reader, that the first thing tomorrow morning you go to your lawyer and tell him you would like to change your will. Tell him you wish to leave a substantial sum of money to your favorite preparatory school (if you have no favorite, any school will do), the interest therefrom to be distributed each year as prizes—first, second and third, for the three best theses on Conservation, to be written by members of the senior class. The winning essays are to have the proper publicity (if you are hipped on ducks, you can earmark it ducks only).

Can you imagine the interest aroused in that school on this vital subject by your offer of, say, $100, $50 and $25? Can you imagine the boost to conservation if similar offers could be made to all the graduating classes of all the schools all over the country? Can you picture the research work that would be done on this most essential national problem by all these competing thousands and the resulting knowledge of incalculable value that would accrue where utter ignorance now prevails? Can you see the light of inspiration that would be kindled here and there in some brilliant young mind at its most impressionable age? Can you— You can't? You think it bunk? Sheer nonsense? Well, have it your own way. Meanwhile, my conscience is clear.

And now I'll bid you adieu. If ever you head across the border, may the ways and manners of those "backward" people offer you as much relief and satisfaction as they have given me. And when it comes to shooting, may "long powder and straight" be yours, and above all, may your retriever be a good one. It's another way to save ducks.

I I I

Merrymeeting Bay

BY RANSOM P. KELLEY

MERRYMEETING BAY is in south central Maine. Two great rivers, the Androscoggin, coming from New Hampshire, and the Kennebec, coming from Moosehead, join with the Eastern, the Abbagadassett, the Cathance and the Muddy rivers to form an irregular, shallow bay eighteen miles long and a mile to three miles wide. This fresh water bay has a five and one-half foot tide two hours later than at the mouth of the river twenty miles away. Within half an hour's flying time are many large salt water bays on Maine's deeply indented coast line. In the winter the Bay is frozen over from early December until early April. Two-thirds of its area is exposed at low water and is much broken up with small channels and guzzles. In the summer and fall the flats are covered with heavy vegetation, mostly wild rice and bulrushes but almost any known duck food that will grow in fresh, cool water can be found on either the mud flats or sand bars or in the guzzles. Much of the shore line is wooded although there is considerable farming on the intervale lands on the west shore of the Bay.

The Merrymeeting area offers twenty thousand acres of the finest conceivable habitat for wildfowl and is singularly blessed, in that it lies at the intersection of two of the three main Maine flyways of waterfowl, and so close to the third that many birds from the coastal flyways work the Bay. From the meager banding records at hand, the first flyway leads from James Bay in a northwest-southeasterly direction across the St. Lawrence near Quebec city, Lake St. Francis and Lake Megantic in Quebec; thence through the mountain pass at Chain of Ponds, across the Belgrade Lakes to Merrymeeting, approximately one hundred miles from the international boundary, two hundred miles from Quebec and six hundred miles from James Bay. This flyway is fed by birds from the Umbagog area. The second flyway, running north northeast and south southwest brings the birds three hundred miles from the mouth of the St. Lawrence, Labrador and Davis Strait, across the St. John River near Maine's northern tip, through Square Lake and on across to the Penobscot Valley. This flyway crosses near Pushaw Lake into the Sebasticook watershed, which leads them directly to Merrymeeting. The third and last main flyway comes along the coast, and the birds, after passing outside Mt. Desert Island, cross Penobscot Bay and the low country south of the Camden hills, many of them entering the bay area through the Eastern River, although some come in directly from the sea and many more that have stopped to rest in the coastal bays join in with the local birds that are trading back and forth into the Bay.

While gunning at Merrymeeting you soon learn that if a local gunner says "duck" he means a Blackduck *(Anas rubripes tristis);* and "goose" means a regular Canada Goose *(Branta canadensis canadensis),* for these two birds make up the bulk of our hunting. Quite common also are the Blue-winged Teal *(Querquedula discors),* Green-winged Teal *(Nettion carolinense)* and the American Pintail *(Dafila acuta tzitzehoa).* Our common diving birds are the Greater and Lesser Scaup *(Nyroca marila* and *Nyroca affinis),* the Ring-necked Duck *(Nyroca collaris),* the American Golden-eye *(Glaucionetta clangula americana),* and the Buffle-head *(Charitonetta albeola).* All three Mergansers *(Lophodytes cucullatus, Mergus merganser americanus* and *Mergus serrator)* or Shelldrake are frequently seen. Mallards *(Anas platyrhynchos platyrhynchos)* are taken and seem to be less wary than the Blacks, particularly the females. During the last ten years I have taken occasional Barrow's Golden-eye *(Glaucionetta islandica)*, Baldpate *(Mareca americana)*, European Widgeon *(Mareca penelope)*, Shovelers *(Spatula clypeata)*, Redheads *(Nyroca americana)*, Canvasbacks *(Nyroca valisineria)*, Eiders *(Somateria mollissima dresseri* and *Somateria spectabilis)* and various kinds of Scoters *(Melanitta deglandi, Melanitta perspicillata* and *Oidemia americana)* which, when taken in migration before they get to the coast, are delicious eating and are not at all fishy. Wood Ducks *(Aix sponsa)* are seen occasionally and are usually passed up if recognized in time. The only Cinnamon Teal *(Querquedula cyanoptera)* I have ever seen in the Bay I encountered while working a bunch of geese; we let them go and didn't get any geese.

The Canada Goose has again become very common in Merrymeeting. Last fall during the entire open season there was not a day but what we saw one or more flocks passing through. The height of the flight seems to be between the middle and the last of October. I have taken Lesser Canadas *(Branta canadensis leucopareia)* and one Hutchins's Goose *(Branta canadensis hutchinsi)*. Snow Geese *(Chen hyperborea hyperborea* and *Chen hyperborea atlantica)* occasionally stop in and I have definitely identified one flock of Cackling Geese *(Branta canadensis minima)*. Brant *(Branta bernicla hrota)* are often seen in the Bay after an easterly storm.

The American Coot *(Fulica americana)* or Crowbill, as he is locally known, visit us in large numbers and it is interesting to watch them form a circle and bluff out a Bald-headed Eagle. The eagles are usually very numerous at the start of the duck season and are not at all well liked. These birds are also very effective in keeping Pheasants from becoming too numerous in the open farming country on the western shores of the Bay. Grebes and Loons are also occasional visitors.

Early histories of Maine mention large quantities of waterfowl in Merrymeeting Bay and some of them claim that the Indians brought rice seed

to the area from the midwestern part of the country. There are many conflicting local legends, the most commonly accredited of which claims that
Captain Jack brought the first seed to the Bay in the 1840's. During the last
fifteen years the Fish and Game Department has introduced many fresh
strains of aquatic plants in the Bay. Giant bulrush seems to be crowding
out the wild rice in some areas. It is particularly noticeable in the Big Cove,
Bluff Head Cove and many other places, that the wild rice is most thrifty
where the geese have concentrated in the spring. The geese in their feeding habits dig up quantities of bulrush roots and while so doing do a nice
job in planting the wild rice seeds left over from the previous fall.

The market gunners at the turn of the century were active in Merrymeeting. Most of them used flat-bottomed, single scull boats and their
methods of operation were very effective. Their boats were usually fourteen or fifteen feet long and about sixteen inches deep at the deepest part.
They were rigged for rowing and some of them carried a light mast and
sails which could be stowed. They were sculled with a short, four foot,
crooked oar through a leather-bound scull notch set well off-center in the
stern. They used no decoys but traveled around the Bay looking for flocks
of feeding or resting birds. They often spent an hour or more working a
flock of birds until they got them setting just right. A double eight or six
shot in a strap took a heavy toll and then a second gun was used in the air.
One of the famous early hunters carried a double six, two tens and two
twelves, all muzzle loaders. In later times the modern repeating guns replaced the muzzle loaders and double floats became more common.

By the middle 30's Merrymeeting was at its prime as a sportsman's paradise. The market gunners had turned to guiding. Bill Darton had had his
try at gunning with the use of stationary floating blinds. After an abortive
attempt to outlaw the gunning float in a short but bitter fight in the legis-
lative halls at Augusta, permanent floating blinds were outlawed. Double
scull boats became the usual method of gunning.

In any area different gunners have different methods, but Merrymeeting could be roughly divided into two distinct areas, "Down the Bay" and

"Up River." Up river the gunners are apt to gun in the same set, day after day, and flat-bottomed boats are most generally used. Down the Bay, below Browne's Point, the gunners are apt to roam more and use bigger round-bottomed boats. Let's gun a day in each place.

For our up river day let's gun with Captain Harold Houdlette on Green's Point, at the mouth of the Eastern River. After a leisurely but ample breakfast we walk a few hundred yards down the shore to a little brushed-in shelter. The flats in front of us are just covered with water, as it is two and one-half hours before high tide. For the next five hours we will have good water to gun. It being early in October, the weather is comfortably warm and a light southwesterly wind gives promise of ideal conditions. Through the rice and bulrushes a mowed path runs westerly four hundred yards to the Kennebec River channel. There are two pools mowed out of the bulrushes, each about thirty yards in diameter, one on either side of the main path. They are reached by branch paths and a heavy fringe of grass has been left at the ends of the paths. The Captain has just returned from setting a dozen blocks and five sets of shadow decoys in the southern or windward pool.

Above our heads we can hear the repeated roar of passing flocks of ducks and as the light grows brighter we can see birds by the thousands flying down river. At legal shooting time, the Captain tells us to be prepared to go out on a scull. As there are several boats gunning nearby we don't want to waste any more time than necessary. The boat is hauled stern first on the beach beside the blind. It is a fourteen and one-half foot flat-bottomed craft, with a ten foot open cockpit thirty-four inches wide. The sides and bow are decked in and covered with grass. The Captain's gun lies across the thwarts behind a shooting board, which is a moveable shelf with grass tacked on it. My gun is put in the bow along the starboard side, and on the floor boards there is a rug for warmth and dryness. A low whistle from the Captain makes us watch over the decoys where a flock of eight big Blacks are circling. Once they almost land; two birds are below the grass; but shooting up-wind flares them; however, they circle again. This time as they circle four birds drop into the leeward pool and the other four go off down the Bay.

Following the Captain's instructions, I climb into the boat and after sitting down in the bow, I work forward, lying on my back until my head is so low that I can just see over the bow of the boat. My gun stock is under my right elbow, my right hand handy to the safety, my left hand comfortably on the forestock. The barrel of the gun rests on the combing and the muzzle sticks out eight or ten inches at a very low angle. After seeing me properly stowed in the bow, Cap pushes the boat off and warns me to keep perfectly still until he tells me to sit up and shoot. The birds, he tells me, should be just to the left of the bow when the crucial moment arrives.

Using a four foot crooked oar thrust through a scull hole in the transom, Cap, who is also lying flat on his back with just his head cocked up, slowly, but very steadily, propels the boat out the mowed pathway towards the pools. Time never passed so slowly and every instant I expected that the ducks would discover that something was wrong or would be frightened by someone shooting nearby. At last we turned off into the right hand channel and the boat seemed to be going so slowly that I doubted if we were moving at all. I had stripped off my heavy top clothing before leaving the shore, but I discovered that I was sweating profusely and I could hear my heart pounding so loudly I was afraid the ducks could hear it and think it was an Indian war drum. Just as the bow entered the thin fringe of grass separating us from the pool, the Captain swung the boat to the right and slowly came to a stop. About twenty yards from me I could see a pair of birds. One of them seemed to be looking right at us but he soon dropped his head. At the Captain's word, I sat up.

The birds looked at us for a surprised second and then jumped into the wind. I swung onto the right hand bird and carefully covered him, but it was my third shot that brought him down. Captain Harold very nicely one-two-threed the others. I had the feeling that I had been shooting where the bird had been because my sitting position slowed my swing. We picked up the birds and went ashore.

For the next four hours we had interesting shooting. The singles, the pairs and small flocks decoyed beautifully and from then on the Captain left the shooting to the bow man. Our execution was not good, but by eleven o'clock we had a reasonable number of birds.

There was a nice set of goose blocks in the channel, a gunshot or more from the mouth of the mowed path. The tide had left us, and as I questioned the Captain as to what came next, a bunch of geese appeared high in the north. It was apparently a family of six who had come a long way, for without circling and hardly opening their mouths, they lit in the broad river channel beyond the goose blocks. After quickly changing to heavier loads, I took my place in the bow and the Captain slid the boat out over the mud. The grass on each side of the pathway concealed him from the birds. As we reached the open water he slid into the boat and we started down river after the geese. The birds in the meantime had drifted away with the tide and were perhaps three hundred yards from us. We worked down the edge of the channel, using the channel bank for a background, until we were below the geese. Then he slowly swung out into the river and headed toward the birds. The light southerly breeze was on our quarter and we were headed down the sun-path toward the geese. They paid no attention to us until we were within one hundred and fifty yards of them and then they turned and headed for the goose decoys. We crowded them faster and faster, until we were sixty yards from them, then, at the warning call of the gander, they quickly turned into the wind and, after spreading out to get wing room, they jumped towards us. Between us we were able to stop three goslings. When we paddled back to the mouth of the path, we found a mere trickle of water coming over the mud. We walked in and hauled the boat after us.

After lunch and a council of war, we went back to the shore blind. The Captain had three suggestions. First, we could watch there and walk to any birds that lit in the pools; second, we could push the boat out to the channel bank and set our decoys in the open water, using the brushed-up boat for a blind; or third, we could take his dog in the brush for Partridge and Woodcock. The wind had dropped to an "Irish hurricane," and there was hardly a cloud in the sky, and we figured with full bellies it would be more comfortable to nap on the shore and follow the first plan.

After an hour, without seeing a bird, three Mallards appeared from nowhere and lit in the northern pool. Two of us walked out within easy gunshot of these birds and we had the satisfaction of adding them to our bag. When we got ashore we counted up and figured we had enough for one day. We picked up our gear and headed for Browne's Point, five miles down river.

The next day at Erle Browne's we found that each of us would have a guide for the day. There were nine boats going out from South Point this morning and we found the boats to be quite different from the one we had used the day before. These boats were each a little different and were sixteen feet long and round-bottomed. Some had a little decoration on them and others had none. They were painted a drab color. When I got in the bow of Erle's boat I found considerably more room, and that the rails were a little higher. As we left the shore and took count of stock we found that we had in the boat our guns, two lunch boxes, two shell boxes, two pairs of binoculars, our rain clothes, twenty-one cork decoys, eight sets of shadows, a large bundle of twenty-three pieces of arbor vitae brush, and a spare seven and one-half foot oar. I noticed that Erle was poling the boat at a good rate of speed without too much apparent effort.

As we headed down the Bay we made quite a flotilla; but four of the boats kept along the shore to the westward and Erle told me that they were headed for Bluff Head Cove. Another boat turned off in a guzzle and the guide said he thought he would set Pogge's Hole. We turned into the Big Guzzle and the fair tide pushed us up through very quickly. This guzzle branched three ways, just before it reached the Abbagadassett channel. Two boats took the south branch and one went to each of the other branches.

The boat behind us set its decoys in a pool at the guzzle's mouth. We continued to the southward a couple of hundred yards. Our eight sets of shadows we set on a trawl along the outside edge of the bulrushes. Then

Aerial view of Merrymeeting Bay shooting grounds.

A goose that didn't get away.

Poling out cripples in typical boat. Note shooting positions.

Some lunch while waiting for ducks to fly.

we pushed into the grass fifteen yards and set out block decoys partially in the pools and partially in the bunches of rice and bulrushes. Then we turned back, and ahead of us I could see the other three boats finishing their sets. The four boats pushed back down the main guzzle for about four hundred yards where we rendezvoused in a small side guzzle.

The air seemed to be full of ducks and many large flocks were headed out to sea. We could see other bunches landing in the open water sanctuary a couple of miles away. Before long one of the guides told us to keep still, and a bunch of twenty or more Blackducks started swinging the decoys. They would start to settle in one set and then flare and move on to the next. There was a moderate southerly wind blowing which put a nice ripple on the water and made the decoys look more natural. Finally a pair of birds dropped into our decoys and four swung back and lit in the northernmost of the four sets.

Erle started out for our birds and another boat came along in back of us. As we went booming up the guzzle with a fair tide, Erle explained to me that, according to the unwritten law of the Bay, it was "our scull" as our birds had lit first, and that the other boat would scull his birds but not shoot until our birds jumped. As we broke around the corner I saw a bird swimming into the grass and heard Erle mutter: "That's good; I hope they'll stay there." The birds had apparently lit to our shadows and swum into them. Not finding them to their liking they had started into the grass to see the other decoys. As we swung in by the shadows Erle told me to be ready as he didn't know just where the birds would be. Suddenly he told me to "take 'em" and as I sat up he jumped to his feet to back me up. One bird broke to the left and the other to the right. As my right-hand bird folded I heard the splash of his, hitting the water. I looked to our left to see how the other boat was making out and could see three dead birds in the air at once. They were nearly out of sight before we heard the five shots that cleaned up that flock. We quickly picked up our birds and paddled back to the other boats, and during the next six hours there was something doing every few minutes for one or the other of the boats. The tall tales

that were told as we waited for more birds to appear would have shamed
Baron Münchausen.

It was noticeable that time after time a few birds would decoy from a
large flock and the rest would go back to open water, unmolested. One flock
of twelve lit between our decoys and the next set. We made a successful
two-boat scull on this flock, and between us we stopped seven birds.

When the ebbing tide threatened to leave the guzzle dry, we picked up
our decoys and set the shadows just outside a big bunch of bulrushes. Outside and beyond them, and a little downwind, we bunched our block
decoys. At this time there was about eight inches of water over the mud.
We put the arbor vitae brush in brush sockets along the combing of the
boat and pushed into the big bunch of bulrushes where we soon grounded
out. The decoys lay well to the left of the fore and aft line of the boat, with
the furthest one about thirty yards from us. For the next hour nothing
further happened, and the other three boats which were downwind from
us had remained quiet. Then some singles and pairs appeared, but these
fell to the downwind boats. As I composed myself for a nap, a remark from
Erle called my attention to six big Blacks headed our way from the river
channel. Without a single circle they plopped onto the mud just outside
our decoys. Erle gave the word and I sat up and tried to shoot with a face
full of brush. My bird finally pitched down into the Abbagadassett channel. Erle sat there laughing at me; he had made no move to reach for his
gun. We dragged the boat back out of the bulrushes and slid her over
the mud to the channel. The bird that I had shot was a cripple and the
strength of the ebb tide took us well down the Bay before we eventually
picked him up.

A mile or so beyond us was a large raft of Blackducks that had drifted
out of the Sanctuary. Erle got me down so low in the boat that only once
in a while could I see the water thirty yards ahead of us, and, after putting
a good application of vaseline on the sculling oar, started the long scull
after the rafted birds. When we were within a few hundred yards of the
birds, Erle struck a slow and steady pace. He had instructed me to hold

tight, no matter what happened, until he gave the word to shoot. The rafted Blacks were having a grand time, playing and splashing water; but when we got within a hundred yards of them the nearest ones jumped and flew a short way. For an hour we kept sculling and sculling, the birds refusing to let us get close enough. As a big bunch moved up the Bay another quarter of a mile, I asked Erle if it was any use and he told me that if we kept at it long enough we might get close enough. At last a pair of big "red legs" seemed to pay no attention to us and let us get just as close as we wanted. I had the good fortune to get the pair, and after Erle had rested a moment or two, we took the flood tide back towards our decoys. As we picked up and started home he told me that he had been hoping for a flock of geese to alight in the open water while we were down there; but that it was still a little early in the season for them to be really flying.

Merrymeeting today is terribly overcrowded with gunners and many of them are gunning entirely from floating blinds. Last fall the second day of the season was foggy in the morning and when the fog lifted I counted forty-five boats around me. We had a very small kill for the year as the birds were soon driven out and spent their days resting in the ocean. At night they were in, feeding by the tens of thousands. Legislation is now pending to restrict the use of outboard motors and we are hoping that as times become more normal there will be a more reasonable number of gunners in the Bay.

I V

Cape Cod Memories

BY A. ELMER CROWELL

I WAS born in 1862 and have lived here all my life. When I was a boy I was very much interested in birds, and as I grew up the interest grew with me. At the beginning of my shooting, an old woodsman made me a bow-and-arrow gun. In fact, he made me two guns with very strong bows. I had a needle in the arrow and with it killed many small birds, such as Blackbirds, Robins and Doves. I was right-handed, but shot from the left shoulder because I could not squint my left eye, so became very good at it. I remember my uncle saying one time, "Elmer, you will make a good sharp-shooter—I know, because you handle the gun right." When I was twelve years old my father gave me a new twelve-gauge shotgun. Then, I was some boy! He put an overcharge powder in the gun and lashed it to the fence and tied a string to the trigger and stood off aways and pulled the trigger. He did this to be sure it would not burst. She did not. From then on I was some sport. The next fall I killed my first Blackduck. That was the beginning of my real shooting.

At fourteen years of age, my father bought a large tract of land on the south shore of Pleasant Lake in East Harwich, with a fine sand beach which

A. Elmer Crowell at work in his shop on Cape Cod.

A. Elmer Crowell in 1898.

At Crowell Camp in the old days.

N. Y. Zoological Park

Canada Goose on nest.

was ideal for my duck decoys. I had only six live decoys the first season. I made nine block decoys and put them off about thirty yards in the lake. I had fairly good luck that fall—killed ninety-seven Blackducks and a few other ducks.

The next season I had twenty-eight live decoys: I pinned six on the beach and kept the twenty-two for flying from the blind. The blind was a board fence about thirty yards long, and when well brushed with small pine and oak limbs looked very much like the background. I had very little trouble in getting the birds near enough to shoot. That season I killed one hundred and eight Blackducks and many small ducks.

When I was in my teens, there were many farms around my house and Quail or Bob Whites were in goodly numbers. They were sure to be in the rye fields. A friend gave me an English Setter, and she was a lovely dog with a fine nose. On damp days I took to the fields and brush. My best bag of Quail was fourteen in one day, but the average was six or eight in a day's shooting. Grouse were not plentiful here at any time—the covers were thick and it was hard to get at them. Today there are hardly any, just a remnant left; also the Quail have thinned out.

The farms have all gone to waste timberland now—very few are still here. The farmers gave it up and began to grow cranberries. And all cedar swamps had to go under the hammer.

The most I ever shot in one day was nine Grouse, and on many an all-day hunt would get but two or three. Jack Snipe never were here in any great numbers. I shot as many as seven in a one-day hunt late in September and October. Golden Plover were not plentiful here in my time, although I have shot quite a few. My father told me that when he was a boy he saw two men who had shot, one morning, a bushel basketful of Golden and Blackbellied Plover, but in 1884 they were scarce here. When I was shooting for market on shore birds, the Yellowlegs (the lesser and greater) were the most plentiful. I made many good bags, with a few Jack Curlews and other shore birds.

There were a few Eskimo Curlews left. We called them Doughbirds, as they were so fat sometimes when shot in the air they burst open when hitting the ground. But today they have gone for good—I never see one.

The next season I had forty live decoys and tried out a new way of handling my ducks. I sank a pole with a ring in the top and ran a line through it back to the blind, which made an endless line. I tied four live ducks to it and pulled them off in the pond about thirty-five yards. It was about two weeks before they were broken in so I could pull them out without their making a flutter. After that they were all right.

Then I began to fly them from the blind. It was some job to get them back to the blind at first, but in a few weeks they were broken in fine. They would fly out to the runner and light with the four ducks made fast on the endless line and they would follow them to the beach. So when a flock of wild ducks came along we filled the air with decoys and the wild ducks would light right with them. After that, it was easy to pull them to the beach or within shot. That was the first time it had been done with any success.

That season I bought my first hammerless shotgun, ten-gauge, weight nine pounds. I used it for shooting at large bunches of ducks; also geese. That season I shot nine wild geese—I had no geese decoys; they were shot from the air while going over the blind. The next fall I had five live geese decoys but did not have any geese to fly. I had them pinned on the beach, which did not amount to much, but I killed fourteen geese (mostly in the air in flight) and a good number of ducks, so all in all it was a good season.

The next season was a poor one. The ponds were all dried up—no feed for the ducks. The shooting was very poor.

The next season was my banner year. Everything was right for the birds —good feed in the ponds, and plenty of water. I saw more birds in flight than ever before, but hard to stop them. The night shooting did not amount to much as they were on flight at night and did not stop in the lake. I killed one hundred and sixty-four Blackducks and forty-three Ruddies and many small ducks.

The next fall Mr. Charles Hardy and others had the Three Bear Camp built on Pico Point, and I had the care and handling of the decoys. I bought a large number of live geese from a friend in Hanover, Mass. It made, with what we had, about fifty in all. This blind was about a half mile from mine to the west. We had a large beach made out into the lake and pinned twenty geese on it. Then we built pens on the hill back of the blind, attached electric wires to them, and ran the wires down to the blind. We had four boxes on the inside of the blind with electric buttons.

When we saw a bunch of geese coming we pushed the buttons and the trapdoor would fall down and out would come the flyers. They would fly out over the lake, and sometimes they would join the bunch of wild ones and bring them to the beach. It was a success and we had good shooting for a number of years. At that time we began to bait the small ponds with corn, and two years later we baited in front of our blinds at the lake. It stopped the Blackducks from going south, so the ponds were full of ducks; the shooting was great. But we could not sell them in the markets, as the law cut it out. Soon the law cut out the live decoys, and that was the end of good shooting here.

In 1898, Dr. John C. Phillips of Boston and Beverly, Mass., came to see me about running his camp and new blind in North Beverly at Wenham Lake. He had just built a fine camp there and wished me to show him how to handle ducks and geese decoys. We had some good shooting there. I remember on one day in December we killed thirty-nine Geese and twenty-two Blackducks. Later we ran a camp at Oldham Pond in Hanover, Mass., on the south shore, for geese. The goose shooting was good some years. It was not much of a pond for ducks. I gunned there a number of years. Then I gave up hunting for a time and began making decoys out of wood. I was with Dr. Phillips ten years.

Dr. Phillips gave me a four-gauge shotgun to shoot on long bunches of geese and ducks. The cartridges were so long we called them Roman candles. We made many a good shot with it.

I made wood decoys for ten years. Then I began to make song birds and shore birds for ornaments; also ducks. I soon had all the work I could attend to. You will find them from coast to coast and in Europe and France. I made them in sets of twenty-five ducks, twenty-five song birds and twenty-five shore birds.

After a few years the old fever came back to me, so I bought an automatic sixteen-gauge shotgun. When my son came back from World War I, I bought a tract of land on Bushey Beach Pond and built a blind for him. We gunned it there for a few years. We baited it with corn and had good shooting most of the time. One year we had a heavy flight of Pintail ducks. The pond was full of them each morning when we got there. In about four years the law cut out baiting, so we gave up the blind; and I sold it to a Fall River man, Dr. Ralph W. French. A few years later it was sold to a Boston lawyer. Now it is closed.

I worked at making decoys nearly forty years. Then I had to give it up as I had rheumatism in my fingers and could not hold my knives tight enough to carve. I have not done any work for three years now, but my son is making them from my patterns and has all the work he cares for.

I am eighty-four years old and my mind wanders back to the good old days when there was no law on birds. They were the days for me!

V

Long Island Sound

BY CHARLES E. WHEELER

THE story of wildfowling along Connecticut's shore of Long Island Sound must of necessity begin in the pages of Connecticut history where it is recorded that "Ye wilde ducks and geese were so plentifulle as to darken ye Sunne when they arose from ye mud flats and marshes." It is also recorded that "Ye feathers made goode beds and heade rests."

The killing of wildfowl during this early period was prompted more by a need for food than by a desire for sport. Consequently the toll taken was comparatively small.

Different methods were used by those pioneer gunners, such as stalking, pass shooting and ambushing. In many instances the gunner would crawl a considerable distance to get within range of his target. It was quite a common practice then to take a stand behind a cedar bush on a beach between the Sound and the marshes, just at dusk or during a blow, and get several shots at birds passing over. But the most popular method was to lie in ambush in the sedgegrass that edged all the creeks and sloughs in the marshes and await the evening flight of ducks. The gunners often stayed well into the night, getting several shots and usually a pair or two of ducks.

The Indians of that period did most of their wildfowling during the day and were known to set up stones along the shore, a small one atop a larger one, for decoys. These were very practical. It is quite evident that the Indians used bows and arrows and scored many misses, proof of which is had in the number of arrow points found by the oystermen and clam-diggers of today, who ply their trade along the shores.

Learning a lesson from the Indians, the settlers made crude wooden decoys and built small, shallow punts or scows for marsh shooting. Muzzle-loading flintlock guns replaced the bows and homecast slugs were used instead of arrows.

Refinements were made through the years, both in methods and equipment, until about 1870, when such men as J. W. Selleck and Commodore Francis Burritt of Norwalk; Captain Burr Smith and Captain George Allen of Saugatuck; Captain George Hine, Edward Laing and Ephraim Wakeley of Stratford; Captain George Smith and Clark Baldwin of Milford, came into the picture with the newfangled double-barreled, muzzle-loading, per-cussion cap scatter gun which used small shot instead of slugs. These men were capable gunners who designed and built some very practical boats for point, rock and marsh shooting. Their decoys too, were by now much better and some of them compare most favorably with the best handmade "stools" of today. All of these men gunned through the 70's and 80's and have recited to the writer many highlights of their interesting experiences in wildfowling during that period.

After them came such noted gunners as Charles "Cappy" Wicks and "Ash" Bond of Stratford, "Jimmie Lew" Miles and Captain George Green of Milford; Eugene Shepard and Henry Murray of Branford; Doctor "Len" Sanford of New Haven and many others through the Thimble Islands, east-ward to the Rhode Island border.

Every shore town with rocky points, breakwaters, beaches, inland creeks, islands, reefs, ponds and potholes had its full quota of duck hunters, guns, boats and decoys. There were sportsmen, commercial gunners and just plain killers. There were all types and styles of boats and decoys and there were guns which might be classified as "shootin'-irons," "gas-pipes," "fusees" and "cannons." They ranged from twelve-gauge to four-gauge—smaller sizes were not yet common among duck hunters. There were muzzle loaders, breech loaders and, in the early 1880's, the Winchester pump or lever action repeating shotgun came into vogue. Heavy loads of black powder and No. 4 and No. 2 shot were used in these guns, until the market gunners found out that their kill was greater by using smaller shot and lighter loads.

Perhaps the most popular gunning boat of that day was a small, shallow, flat-bottomed skiff, partially decked over so that sedge or rockweed might be draped over the deck as a camouflage. These boats were anywhere from ten to fourteen feet long, three and a half to four and a half feet wide, and just deep enough to conceal the hunter when he stretched out on his back in the boat, with his legs forward under the deck. These boats would float in about three inches of water, slide easily over soft mud and could be used as a sneak boat in the creeks, poled through the sedge or cattails or hidden in the reefs or rocks along the shore.

Many stories are fresh in the minds of the old gunners of today that were told to them, when they were boys, by the old gunners of yesteryears. The stories were about hazardous trips in these little boats to and from the many reefs and islands well off shore from the mainland.

In those days it was not difficult for an experienced gunner to gather a fair bag of really good birds almost any day. There were Canada Geese, Brants, Mallards, Blackducks, Pintails, both Blue- and Green-wing Teal, both greater and lesser Scaup (Broadbill), Whistlers, Old Squaws, American and Red-breasted Mergansers (Shelldrake), Buffleheads, an occasional Baldpate and both Whitewing and Surf Scoters (Coots), all in quantities in keeping with the food supply. This fluctuated somewhat and with these changes came the ups and downs in wildfowl visitations. In other words, when there was an abundance of food, the birds were plentiful and they stayed here. When the crop of food was light, it was cleaned up quickly and the birds moved on farther south in search of better feeding grounds.

Since the disappearance of eelgrass and brantweed, the Geese and Brant pass by, stopping only occasionally to rest.

The pollution of river and harbor waters by municipalities and industry has been a very definite factor in the destruction of small fish, shellfish, crustacea and plant life which constitute the food supply for our water-fowl and shore birds.

Wildfowling purely for sport increased quite rapidly and a new style of hunting came into vogue known as line shooting. This was practiced by groups of several gunners who would anchor their boats in a line between two islands, between an island and a sandbar or between an island and the mainland. A distance of about two gunshots was left between boats and the gunners tried not to shoot when a bird was in line with another boat. But many a man has been sprinkled with shot from a neighbor's gun while lined off with the gang.

Line shooting was fun and many an old "Skunkhead" Coot would try to cross the line at the east end, be turned by a shot, run the gauntlet of five or six guns and finally get across the west end amid the shouts and jeers of the gunners who gibed each other about their marksmanship or "shootin' iron." Large bags were often taken by this method and many cripples left to become the prey of the gulls.

Mention has been made of stalking, pass shooting and ambushing as methods used by the old-time duck hunters of this area. Under stalking may be included a method known as poling or pushing, which consists of poling a light skiff through the grass, the shooter in the bow and the poler in the stern. By this method the gunner was pushed up to within range of the fowl and had a real sporty shot, at an unknown angle, as the birds flushed from the sedge or cattails. Still another method of stalking was known as sculling. This might well be called a killer's method, because when conditions were ideal, fowl were slaughtered by market hunters.

The boat used for sculling was a low, flat-decked type with a coaming around the cockpit and a sculling hole out through or over the stern. Ice and snow were piled on the deck and around the coaming to give the

Charles E. Wheeler shooting from battery about 1900.

Clarence Bacon, Dr. Charles Porter, Cliff Morton and Charles Lanfare after two hours'
line shooting in 1905.

A floating bush blind with boat inside.

Sculling a boat camouflaged with ice.

The last of the old "lining off" boats left.

appearance of a large cake of ice drifting with the tide. The hunter, dressed in white coat and hat, lay on his back or side, with his feet forward under the deck. He operated a curved sculling oar over his shoulder and out through or over the stern. This method of approach had to be done very carefully lest the ducks be frightened by seeing a cake of ice rocking badly in quiet water or drifting unnaturally against the tide or wind. When properly done the birds were entirely unafraid. Great rafts of Broadbills have been known to separate to let the make-believe ice cake drift between them. Instances of Blackducks trying to climb out on the ice were not uncommon. The hunter usually carried two guns, one of large bore, possibly an eight or a four, and the other a twelve. The big gun was used for the first shot while the fowl were on the water and, in case it was a double-barreled gun, the second shot was used as the birds jumped. This resulted in stopping a large number of birds, many of which had to be shot over with the twelve-gauge.

The record kill for this area was made with a double-barreled, four-gauge gun owned by the writer, when eighty-one dead Broadbill were gathered and forty-six cripples were shot over with the twelve, making a total of one hundred and twenty-seven birds. Other kills with this gun of upward of fifty birds were not uncommon. Broadbill paid the heaviest toll, as they sat closely together in great flocks, thus offering an excellent target. Large kills of Blackducks, Geese and Brant were also listed in the record of this "killer."

Ambushing included all methods wherein the gunner secreted himself in the surrounding cover of grass or rocks, either in a boat or on land. It should also include the use of a boat known as a sinkbox, another known as a battery, and a floating or staked-out bush blind.

The sinkbox was a very low, decked-over affair with just room enough for the shooter to lie down. It had water compartments which, when filled, sank the boat down nearly level with the surface of the water. The smoother the water, the lower the box was sunk. In case the wind breezed up and it got rough, the gunner lightened his boat by pumping out some of the water ballast. Sheet lead coamings were used around the edge of the box in which the shooter was hidden. These lay flat on deck in calm water and could be turned up in sloppy weather. This type of boat was painted lead color and could be used in the open a long way from shore. It was surrounded with a large setting of decoys and usually was attended by a boatman who retrieved the kill, although some gunners picked up their own kill, in which case the water compartments were not fully filled and the boat could easily be handled with oars.

The battery was a much larger outfit and had to be carried in a large skiff or aboard a sail or power boat. It consisted of a box to accommodate one to four gunners, built in the center of a floating deck which, in the case of a one-man rig, would be about twelve feet long by six feet wide, with a folding canvas wing on each side and a canvas head wing across the bow. When all spread out it covered an area of about eighteen feet long by twelve feet wide. It was anchored on the shooting ground with bow and stern anchors, a large setting of decoys was anchored around it and sufficient lead or iron decoys were placed on the deck to settle it down to the level of the water.

The edge of the shooting box was lined with a lead coaming which could be turned up in rough weather. The whole was painted a lead color and, when deeply sunk in the midst of a few hundred decoys, was very well hidden and birds came in as gentle as chickens. This rig could be used in the open in quite rough water and had to be attended at all times by a boatman whose job it was to flush distant flocks and pick up the kill.

The largest battery of record for this area was a four-gun rig, with a deck twenty-five feet square, upon which a man could walk. This was surrounded with three to four hundred floating decoys and another hundred were fastened to the deck at close intervals, making the entire outfit look like a veritable island of birds. It was set out in the bay just before opening day and was left there for the entire season. The gunners lived aboard a cabin craft, which was the tender during the day and the hotel during the night. Thus they were on the job from daylight until dark every day. When shipments of fowl had to be made, the tender did the trip ashore at night. This rig was finally outlawed.

There were two types of bush blinds, one a floating device, rectangular in shape and large enough to conceal a skiff or duck boat. It was made of two by six plank with holes bored at close intervals to hold peabrush or cedar tops cut about three feet long. This blind was anchored at one end only, so it would swing with the wind. It was left on the feeding grounds throughout the open season. The surrounding area, within gunshot, was kept well baited so that the fowl became accustomed to the blind and fell an easy prey to the gunner with a good rig of decoys. The other type of bush blind was a staked blind. This, too, was rectangular in shape and of the same size as the "floater," the difference being that the brush was cut longer and stuck into the bottom of the bay instead of into a floating frame.

Still another method of hunting waterfowl practiced to quite some extent can hardly be called stalking, as that term implies sneaking up on the target, nor can it be called ambushing, as that suggests lying in wait for the game to approach. It might be called chasing, as it was done by running down wind to the birds in either a sail or power boat. It was generally known that ducks took wing against the wind, so it was quite a popular sport to sail up to windward of a flock of birds, swing off before the wind and sail directly toward the flock.

The birds were momentarily bewildered and would start swimming away, but would soon turn and head into the wind, preparatory to taking wing. All this time the boat, with one to four guns aboard, was getting closer quite fast. Finally, the birds jumped, some swung right, some left, affording good shots to all guns and the kill was all too many. Later came the small power-driven boats. With these the gunner would maneuver slowly and quietly until his boat was directly up wind from the birds, about two gunshots away, then with a quick helm he headed directly toward the flock, drove full speed ahead and in a matter of seconds was within easy range of the now frightened ducks. As they flushed, the slaughter began, for by now the repeating shotguns were popular duck guns. The cannonading was terrific and the casualties equally high in killed and wounded. In both sail and power boat hunts the faster the boats and the more guns aboard, the greater the kill. Some hunts really were shameful.

Pass shooting was practiced all along the shore wherever a beach separated the Sound from inshore marshes. Sandbars extending from islands to the mainland or from the mainland a considerable distance out into the open ocean were also used by the pass shooters. Breakwaters, too, afforded places where fowl passed over rather than to fly out around the end, and gunners hidden in the rocks would bang away at birds as they traded to and from their feeding grounds. Many guns have been terribly "strained" by shooting at birds two or three gunshots high.

It has been said that "Hen" Murray of Branford Point killed a Coot from Spectacle Rock that was so high and it took so long for it to fall, that it actually stunk by the time it struck the water.

Another long shot is credited to Dr. Charles Porter of Branford, who was gunning on Taunton Rock one afternoon when a Blackduck flew over, too high for an ordinary load. So "Doc" slipped in a load of Double O buckshot and swung his old "gas-pipe" out about ten feet ahead of the duck, shut both eyes and pulled the trigger. He watched the bird for several seconds and finally saw it crumple and start falling. He stepped into his gunning skiff and rowed ashore at Pawson Park, arriving there at about the same time the duck hit the ground. "Doc" admitted that it was a fairly long shot but nothing like that one of "Hen" Murray's.

Pass shooting is still very popular from Penfield Bar in Fairfield and from Charles Island Bar in Milford. It is not at all uncommon at either place to see ten or a dozen gunners scattered along the length of the bar at low tide and many a stay-late has gotten his tail wet while wading ashore after the tide had risen three or four feet.

Ambushing is still the most popular method of hunting wildfowl for both the men and the boys. Every evening finds gunners tucked away in the sedge or reeds that skirt the shores of creeks and ponds, with a few decoys set out in front. Every sunrise finds a gun or two hidden away at about every popu-

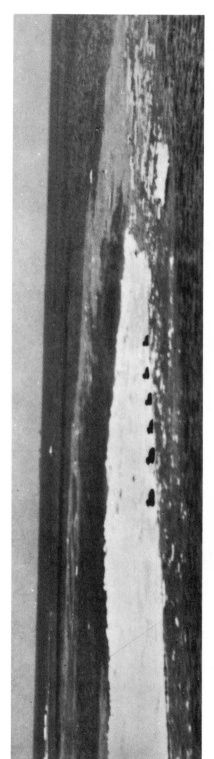

Bunches of mud on edge of icy shore serve as decoys.

Indian decoy made of two stones.

Pairs of profiles for line shooting.

A pair of Pintails by Charles E. Wheeler.

A pair of Mallards by Charles E. Wheeler.

Goldeneye drake, made by Al Sanford,
Saugatuck, Conn., in 1882.

Blackduck, hollow wood, made by Francis
Burritt of Norwalk, Conn., in 1885.

lar place on points, among the rocks or on the breakwaters, all with varying rigs of decoys and boats but all bent on having a day's fun—like the Irishman who told his friend what a fine day he had while duck shooting. "But did you get any ducks?" asked his friend. "No," says Pat, "but, begorra, I give 'em wan helluva serenadin'."

And so the persistent hunt for wildfowl went on every day of the open season. Many thousands of fowl were slain—in fact, it seems almost a miracle that enough survived running the gauntlet from north to south and back from south to north to constitute breeding stock for another crop.

As time went on there were refinements in equipment and an increase in the number of shooters, which resulted in a much larger kill each year. This suggested drastic restrictions in the interest of conservation. The first real big step in this very right direction was taken by Connecticut when her legislature enacted a law in 1901 providing for a closed season on waterfowl from January 1 to September 1. Other states were quick to recognize the value of the start made by Connecticut and followed suit with legislation prohibiting spring duck shooting.

In 1913, Congress passed the so-called Weeks-McLean law. This was the first attempt to federally prohibit spring shooting of waterfowl and paved the way for the passage in 1916 of the Act providing for a convention between delegates from the United States and Great Britain to draft a treaty for the protection of migratory birds in the United States and Canada.

The conclusions of this convention were ratified by the two nations and later, in 1918, the Migratory Bird Treaty Act was passed and the treaty ratified. This Act superseded all state laws and from the day of its passage the work of rebuilding one of our great natural resources really began on a nation-wide basis.

Supplementing this came a similar treaty with Mexico, in 1937, the Migratory Bird Hunting Stamp Act, the Lacey Act, the Co-ordination of Wildlife Conservation Activities, the Federal Aid to Wildlife Restoration Act, and the establishment of several Federal Sanctuaries. Many regulations were adopted having to do with the sale and transportation of wild-fowl, the use of guns larger than ten-gauge, the use of boats propelled otherwise than by oars, the use of blinds or floating devices made to conceal the hunter, if more than one hundred feet from shore, the use of repeating guns of more than three shots, the use of sinkboxes or batteries, the use of live decoys, the shooting over baited areas and the shooting before sunrise or after sunset.

These treaties, laws and regulations all had for their purpose the restoration of our wildfowl and certainly put a very definite crimp in the old-timers' methods. But the old-timers also realized it was high time that something be done to save the remnants of our wildfowl population from the fate of the Passenger Pigeon. So an overwhelming majority of them approved the plans and got on the band-wagon.

To Secretary of War John W. Weeks of Massachusetts, and to United States Senator George P. McLean of Connecticut, co-authors of the Weeks-McLean Bill, belongs the everlasting credit for sponsoring the principles of conservation and restoration which resulted in the aforesaid regulations and ultimately in the outstanding example of international co-operation which now exists between the United States and Canada and which for thirty years has been a determining factor in the success of this great movement.

The recording curve for wildfowling in Long Island Sound areas swung down to a very low point during 1916 and 1917, which condition, together with World War I and its restrictions, put a stop to most of the gunning and temporarily checked the development of the youth of that period along wildfowling lines.

This respite in killing gave nature a chance to heal her wounds and soon the fruits of more birds reaching their breeding grounds became apparent and the wildfowl curve began a slow but definite upward climb. Immediately after the Armistice a renewed interest was shown by gunners, both young and old, and the increased sales of guns and ammunition resulted in an increase in the kill of wildfowl. But the study of conservation had been launched, the seeds of restoration had been planted, had grown and were now bearing fruit.

The swing upward continued, slow but sure, until 1940, despite the ever-increasing number of shooters, as was evidenced by the additional number of hunting licenses sold. This recovery proved beyond a doubt that stopping spring shooting, providing more and larger breeding areas, protecting the brood stock during their breeding period and reducing the bag limit were the major factors in the restoration of our waterfowl and that the future success of the plan, over a long term of years, would depend upon the application of these common sense principles, plus the enforcement of minor regulations.

Naturally the production curve zigzagged a bit at times, because of adverse nesting conditions. This was reflected in a wavering kill curve which sounded a warning to the administrators to be on guard. And the warning came not a minute too soon, as the production curve zigzagged downward much faster than the kill curve. In fact, the kill curve actually wavered upward a bit.

This was dangerous and the controls were set to correct the slippage. Bag limits were reduced and the open season shortened, with the result that temporary improvements in production were recorded, which proved conclusively that the strict adherence to the principles of the Migratory Bird Treaty could and would save our wildfowl.

Credit must be given to various organizations for their interest in and continued support of conservation activities, but to a nation-wide army of sportsmen and conservationists known as "Ducks Unlimited" is due the thanks and commendations of a nation for having financed and administered an international program of restoration, entirely supplemental to other national and international conservation activities. This most worthy movement, although comparatively young, has already been instrumental in reclaiming thousands of acres of valuable breeding areas, preventing the exploitation of other similar territory, launching an intensive educational program of wildfowl conservation and compiling a most valuable record of migrations, flyways and population of wildfowl on an international scale. All this has resulted in getting the shooters of North America conservation-minded and on the right track toward a come-back.

Summing up, wildfowling in Long Island Sound from the days of the bow and arrow and Indian methods to this day of most modern firearms, ammunition, boats and decoys, it must be said that while methods of hunting have not changed much, the increase in the number of gunners, plus the improvements and refinements in all equipment, has made for a tremendous increase in the kill. While recent conservation studies and activities have turned the production curve upward a bit, our future watchword should be "Eternal Vigilance" lest we, as custodians of this wonderful natural resource, violate our obligation and turn it over to the next generation in such a badly depleted condition that the youngsters of tomorrow will have to visit a museum to see what a "Honker" or "Puddleduck" looked like. *What a tragedy!*

DECOYS

Decoys have always been a factor in wildfowling ever since the Indians placed stones along the waterline of the shore or used bunches of mud on the edge of icy shores to toll the birds within range.

There has always been a question between gunners as to whether or not there was any real difference in the attracting power of a rig of motley, ill-shaped blocks and a setting of decoys that really looked like ducks. Some claimed that birds would come to any kind of a flock, while others asserted that ducks could tell the difference and would decoy much better to a bunch of well shaped, nicely painted decoys. Of course, there is nothing that resembles a live Mallard as much as another live Mallard. But inasmuch as live decoys are tabooed, the next best thing is something that resembles the live bird and it has been the experience of the writer that in actual competition with several rigs of inferior decoys, the ducks chose to come to the bunch of superior decoys.

Hollow Blackduck.

Blackduck.

Blackduck.

Mallard.

Blackduck.

Blackduck.

FROM THE PERSONAL RIG OF CHARLES E. WHEELER OF STRATFORD, CONN.

Sleeping Greater Scaup (Broadbill) male, made in 1870 by Albert Laing of Stratford, Conn.

Greater Scaup (Broadbill) male, made in 1875 by J. W. Selleck of South Norwalk, Conn.

Old Squaw, female, made in 1900 by Charles E. Wheeler of Stratford, Conn.

Greater Scaup (Broadbill) female, made in 1876 by Ben Holmes of Stratford, Conn.

Old Squaw, from the rig of a market-gunner from Essex, Conn. Period 1880-1890.

Wooden Broadbill from the rig of an old market-gunner in Essex, Conn., 1880-1890.

Old Squaw, made by Charles E. Wheeler, won the Grand Championship award at the New York Sportsmen's Show.

Female Old Squaw, made by Captain John Smith of Mt. Sinai, Long Island, N. Y., in 1888.

There must be a very real difference in the eye of an approaching duck between a flock of nondescript, long-necked, poorly made and painted blocks that jump and pitch, roll and toss in a tideway or a bit of ruffled water, that look scared and actually do scare a wild bird, and a setting of well shaped, properly painted, steady riding, gentle posed decoys that really impress a bunch of birds with the quiet and safety of the situation.

Two experiments were made by friends of the writer, one in which a flock of fifty poorly made associated species were used in one setting and another group of fifteen high grade cork decoys were set about seventy-five feet to one side of the others, so that birds leading up toward the two rigs had a chance to decide for themselves which group to hail to. The result was that all lone birds, pairs or trios went directly to the small bunch of good-looking decoys and the larger flocks chose the open water between the two settings, but favored the good-lookers.

This friend wrote later: "I would not have believed it, had I not seen it. Guess those cork decoys of yours must have had sex appeal."

In the other instance, another friend wrote, "There are plenty of ducks here [Cooper River, South Carolina] but they are wild and if I am to get my measure of them, I'll have to get some better stools than I am using."

The writer sent him a few good ones to try out and later received a letter saying, "I had some bang-up duck shooting, better than the other fellows down here. My neighbor directly across the river . . . seems to think that I have some special kind of molasses and can't understand why all the ducks come to me. The real reason is . . . that I have the right kind of stool (yours) and it didn't take more than one look at his to know why the ducks pitch into my lot."

There are many other similar instances in which good decoys have proved their superiority. Today the men who really get birds when competition is tough are the ones most particular about having better decoys.

The desire to have better decoys is evidenced by the efforts of sportsmen to make their own, and in a very definite move on the part of the machine-made decoy manufacturers to produce a better and more efficient decoy.

To the true sportsman, there is something to wildfowling besides killing a lot of birds and there is a certain satisfaction that comes as he views a nice setting of decoys, often his own handiwork, and notes how gentle the incoming birds scale in on stiff wings and stick out their feet as if putting on the brakes. This approach, over high-grade decoys, makes for cleaner kills and fewer cripples to skulk away and die.

LINE SHOOTING

Since the advent of power boats, line shooting from boats is a thing of the past, although lining off on a sandbar at low tide is still done to quite some extent.

In the old days, the "gang" were polled the night before at the country store, usually around a pot-bellied stove, and the conversation went something like this: "Did you notice that lovely sunset tonight?"

"Yeah, guess we'll have a good day tomorrow; probably a light air o' wind off the land."

"What d'yuh hear about ducks?"

"Lots of ducks. Jim Pete told me today there are plenty of Coots and quite a few Old Squaws, all feeding in the run back of the Beacon."

"How's the tide?"

"Couldn't be better—high tide just before day, so if we leave at five o'clock we'll take the first of the ebb tide and be all lined off before sun-up."

"How about the rest of you fellows—will you go?"

"SURE."

And so the party was made up, all agreeing to meet at the Lower Dock at five next morning to row down to the mouth of the river to line off across its mouth.

The writer recalls being one of just such a party, back in the early Nineties. There were seven boats of us, all rigged about alike, as far as the gunning skiffs were concerned. Some of the boys carried a few profile decoys, mounted on lath triangles in groups of three, or on flat boards in pairs.

These were anchored so as to trail off with the tide astern of his boat. Some used one or two exceptionally large stools with the idea that they could be seen a long way off and would start the approaching birds toward his particular point in the line.

Some gunners preferred the east end of the line, some the west end, and some the center. Positions were determined by drawing numbers and a small pool—a quarter or half dollar each—was made up for high gun. After the usual arguments over distance between boats, we got lined off and as the sun first stuck his head up over the eastern horizon, the call was passed along the line, "Git down! Lay low!" and here came a bunch of Coots from the east'ard. They got abreast of the middle of our line and then swung in toward the feeding ground, back of the Beacon. It looked as if No. 5 (Rad Smith) would get the first shot and as usual Rad got nervous and couldn't wait until the birds were near enough, but "riz" up and blazed away with both barrels of his old ten bore.

He didn't touch a feather. They turned off and hauled in again between No. 7 and No. 8. Here they got a real reception from Herk Smith, who had a new Scott ten and was a very good shot. He tripped up one with each barrel and turned them toward Anse Dart, who had an old-fashioned lever action pump gun—and did he pump it! He just emptied it, killed one dead and straggled down two others. So it went throughout the forenoon.

There were long kills, easy misses and cheers or jeers for Tom, Dick or Harry as their individual performance merited.

Each boat had a buoy on the end of the anchor line so that it was not necessary to pull up the anchor when going to retrieve a bird—just cast the line off a cleat, throw the buoy over, gather the bird and return to the buoy and make fast to the anchor line.

Chasing cripples was the cause of more arguments than all else. "Why don't you kill 'em instead of just slowin' 'em up?" "Get back in line—you're spoiling our shots!" and many more such caustic remarks. All of these rolled off the chaser like water off a duck's back. He had thoughts of that pool and another duck meant one more toward that goal. His come-back was all in good fun and forgotten as soon as it was time to leave, so as to have a fair tide home.

While rowing home, the alibis, excuses and ribbings were something to hear. One gem was a confession by Chick Welles, who said, "I don't know what ailed me today—I just couldn't hit a cow in the behind with a snow shovel."

Another would lay it to the ammunition—a new load that he was trying. Another would claim that his gun didn't fit because of his having too many clothes on. But the real pay-off came when they reached the dock and the several bags were piled up on deck and counted. One would have six, another seven. One would say, "That big Skunkhead [Surf Scoter] should be in my pile—he fell twenty feet before you shot." Then the other would retort, "Whatinell are you talking about? You just scared him so as to make my shot tougher."

The pool was paid to the high gun and it was up to him to see that Bill got a pair of Coots, Bill being sick and unable to go. And so a day lining off with the gang is over and with a "S'long, fellers," each one pulled away for home.

V I

Long Island Pond Shooting

BY LYNN BOGUE HUNT

WHEN this writer was a yearling and gunning the streams, millponds and potholes of southern Michigan, Blackducks were about one in twenty to Mallards and in a smaller proportion to Pintails, Teal and Wood Ducks.

A Blackduck in the bag was to him a thing to brag about at the gatherings in the local grocery store. His first one was bigger and heavier than any duck he had ever knocked down. He didn't know exactly what it was, so he took it to old Mr. Griffin, the town taxidermist.

"No," said the aged man, "it's not a very dark Mallard hen. It's a species of its own. It's a Blackduck drake and quite a prize hereabouts. Notice his very red legs. He has just come down here from Canada, where this variety breeds. Better mount him. You will not get too many of his kind."

The youngster was learning taxidermy from this old master and he mounted the duck in the best style he could manage. He wasn't a very thorough bird-stuffer and the moths got his specimen in time, but the memory of that first Blackduck has stayed with him and he has never seen one in the air since without a twinge of the old thrill when his first one jumped out of the cattails of his favorite pothole.

After many years of gunning, Blackducks continue to command his utmost admiration and respect. It is his belief that these ducks are growing in wisdom and wariness from season to season. They decoy with more caution. They pass suspicious places with more intelligent circumspection. The least movement, the least disarray of the blind or of the stool and they will have nothing to do with it. Away they go to the despair of the poor gunner who wonders what he has done wrong now.

His first experience with Blackducks in moderate numbers was in a heavy northwest gale on the western end of Lake Erie. Mallards and Teal were coming over from the Canadian side at the mouth of the Detroit River. Even Canvasbacks, Redheads and Bluebills were streaming off the lake to take refuge in the cattail marshes inshore behind him.

Among all these were more Blackducks than he had believed existed. The Blacks were scraping the sky while the others were just skimming the bulrushes where the gunner thought he was well hidden. He was, too, as far as the other ducks were concerned, but the Blackducks that went over knew he was there and he will never forget one big black drake that trimmed ship overhead, slowed down a bit, deliberately cocked his head to one side and took a good look at the poor hopeful far below.

When this young man took the bit in his teeth, deserted a living job on a Detroit newspaper for that Mecca of all ambitious artists, New York, he settled himself there, began peddling his wares and looking over the shooting possibilities. He picked Staten Island as a place to live, where rents were cheap and he could enjoy the never-ending glory of the ferry ride to the city. In spare time he haunted the marshy shores of the island and discovered, to his amazement, Blackducks galore. No Mallards, no Pintails, no Teal—just Blackducks, except for Scoters and Old Squaws off shore. And all this in a borough of the great city only a few miles away.

Later, when he was better established as an artist and had more time, he discovered the Blackduck possibilities of Long Island, with its endless bays and marshes, its wooded streams and, best of all, its little ponds lying in the pine woods to the east. Here were Blackducks in, to him, vast numbers, living in their chosen environment—the woods with plenty of fresh water and an ideal background for their color. A guide whom he came to know well said: "Blackducks like the woods." The whole truth, tersely put.

The youngster learned in time from his own observation and from guides and baymen that Blackducks and Broadbills (Bluebills in Michigan) are the staple ducks of Long Island. Canada Geese and Brant were staples too. Pintails, Widgeon, Teal, Redheads and a few Canvasbacks were to be found, but only in especial places.

Well, Blackducks were good enough for him, so he began to haunt the bays and woods of the island in ducky weather and to learn that these birds yield only to the careful, cautious and duck-thinking hunter. He learned that the Blacks cleared out of the timber and the marshes before dawn and went to sit on the ocean where they would be safe all day, to come inland again to feed when it got so dark that the only evidence of their return was the whistling of their wings overhead and occasional glimpses of dark forms tearing through the gloom.

"Now how did they hit upon that?" he asked himself. "Of course, Blackducks have been gunned for generations on Long Island and all down the Atlantic Coast, and they must have found their safety-at-sea by bitter experience and long ago."

One of the finest scenes in nature this writer ever beheld was this departure in the gray light of early day. It was at Little Egg Harbor in New Jersey. It was just possible to identify them as they came out high from the dark mainland. As they crossed the beach they began swinging in great circles like gulls, as they drifted off shore in the westerly breeze. One more Blackduck surprise—that they could soar like gulls if they were so minded.

Blackduck weather is stormy weather on the Atlantic shores. Then he heads for the woods. In this environment the Blackduck is not at all conspicuous. In fact, he is a bit hard to see in the shadows of the shorelines when he is on the water, and when he comes in against a woodsy background he is rather a ghostly mark. No trouble at all to see a Mallard or a Sprig in the same setting, but a Black blends so well with the woods that if he were stationary on such a backdrop, I think many gunners would fail to make him out.

Eighty per cent of the writer's Blackduck shooting has been in the woods of eastern Long Island. Here the blinds are firmly built of wood and thatched with inconspicuous brush on the four sides and the roof. A seat runs across the rear and at the front, below the opening where the gunner looks out, is a shelf for the shells. This opening comes below the line of vision as the gunner is seated. When he gets to his feet to shoot, he has about sixty degrees right and left to swing his gun and since the front edge of the roof is well within the front wall of the blind, he has freedom to shoot overhead when occasion demands.

A small stool is used—six or eight decoys are ample. This is placed about twenty yards out, with careful regard to the direction of the wind and the direction from which the ducks are likely to come in. The blinds are windproof and even with a cold gale roaring through the treetops it is pretty snug down below. Little flaws of breeze through the timber ripple the water, giving the decoys lively action. The only thing you lack for complete contentment is Blackducks pitching in over the top.

Blackducks never seem to come through the timber as Mallards often do. Blackducks do not seem able to maneuver in timber as well as Mallards and Wood Ducks. The Blacks come through a lead to the water or pitch down with a grand rush from the treetops. You see a bunch coming high as you watch through the topmost twigs. They see the stool or answer the caller or are just coming home anyway, bow their wings, tilt their bodies forward, draw back their heads and come side-slipping down at terrific speed, to level off to leeward of the stool and come on in. If the wind is at your back the ducks aim to hit the water just outside the decoys and when you get up to shoot they sky-rocket out of there, right and left and sometimes right over your head. Tremendously exciting and not easy shooting.

BLACKDUCK SHOOTING ON WOODED POND, LONG ISLAND, N. Y.

If you are shooting across the wind you rise to shoot just as they start to settle over the stool and you get beautiful side and going-away shots as they tower out. Also exciting and difficult. But when circumstances oblige you to shoot facing the wind and they come down over your head from behind, then you really have it—fast, tough shooting and if you get your limit that day, you can give yourself a good ruddy grin in the mirror as you shave before dinner.

The writer has done some shooting at Blackducks with guides who have established blinds of their own on open-water points and islands in the bays of the south shore of Long Island. They are pleasant and competent people and he has had excellent gunning with them. But this type of shooting is rather tough going. A start before daylight from wherever the guide keeps his equipment, sometimes breaking the ice in the canal leading to open water. Then after the stool is set, a big one compared to that used in the woods, sitting in a blind that is not windproof by any standards, or lying on shoulderblades in a puntie, shivering between shots, then picking up the stool and the long cold journey home.

This got the better of him as years went by. His shooting of more recent years has been on controlled properties where the Blacks are regarded as worthy of all the consideration a fine game bird should have. They are granted a good big sanctuary on the property where they are never molested. If a big bunch comes in, no one shoots into it. Instead, the gunner sits back in the blind and waves a handkerchief. Some of the ducks see that and away they go except for two or three who may fail to get the signal and drop into the stool.

When the bulk of them are well away the gunner gets up, jumps the ducks out of the stool and gets a couple if he is that good. The big flock has not been frightened and will come again another day. The practice in such shooting is never to fire at a bunch of Blackducks of more than six. This is good conservation and, selfishly perhaps, keeps the Blacks living on the place.

This hunting disregards the legal shooting hours by never being in the blinds before eighty-thirty or nine o'clock, so the heavy early flight is not disturbed. The shooting is over at about four in the afternoon, earlier if the limit has been reached. Thus the Blackducks enjoy an undisturbed return to their feeding grounds each evening, knowing they are secure for the night. Nothing is so demoralizing to any kind of ducks as very early and very late shooting. Gunfire, especially when it is almost completely dark, generally will drive Blackducks out for the rest of the season.

This sort of gunning is considerate of the ducks and satisfies the conscience of this duck hunter who wants, above all things, to see fair shooting continue for himself and for all those who inherit his love of the out-of-doors and the things that take him there.

A day such as one he had at a tiny pond in the woods was his top day with Blackducks and will remain so as long as he has a memory. There were two of us, a guide and a Chesapeake Retriever. When we got to the pond there were a couple of Wood Ducks there and about half a dozen Blacks. They promptly got out. The guide put out the stool and we settled down to await events. It was a bright day with a lively southwest wind blowing, just right for the ducks to drop in through a good lead at the northeast.

After about an hour the first one came, high, into the lead, wings set and tearing down fast. We had settled who should take the first single and that man took him very neatly as the duck changed his mind and started out as fast as he came in. A half hour brought a pair swishing down in the same high-speed fashion. They both stayed with us and the dog, sensing the quality of the day and the shooting, did his proud part by bringing in both ducks by the necks at the same time. The ducks continued to come, sparingly, but just right until we had fifteen down without a single miss.

The sixteenth duck ruined us. We had planned to quit early so we could get some flounder fishing, but we did want that sixteenth duck and that perfect score. This Blackduck was the first and last that I have seen rattled. When we got up to take our deliberate turns at him, he flew right in our faces and went away over our heads through the barrage without losing a feather. Or maybe he wasn't rattled at all but had taken a lesson from some of the Ruffed Grouse that lived in the surrounding woods. You know how a Grouse in a tight corner will ruin you by flying straight in your face. Maybe that Blackduck was the smartest of all that smart race.

Another memorable day with Blackducks came about like this: we had a freeze the night before and we waited for the sun to get fairly high, so we didn't get to the pond until about ten o'clock. The pond was frozen except for a spring at one end, fifty feet or so square. There were at least a hundred Blacks in that open water and no one knows how many Green-wing Teal. Anyway they were whacking each other's wings as they swarmed out. "They will be drifting back in about an hour," said the guide. They didn't drift back in an hour nor in an hour and a half. So we sent the guide to see if the ducks were using the tidal river where it had not frozen.

By the time he got back the temperature was colder and our pond had closed up almost completely and we went to a blind on the stream. We got a few shots there. Around two-thirty the wind came southwest and the air warmed considerably. "Maybe," said the guide, "by now that spring in the pond has opened up a bit. It can't be much slower shooting than here any- way." So we went back to the pond and, sure enough, it was now half open water but no ducks were in there.

We waited and we waited and we waited. The pond was now completely clear of ice but on this late December day the light in the woods was drain- ing away, when, suddenly, six Blacks slammed into there from nowhere. We got three of them. By the time the dog had them in, more came in small bunches until we began to worry about the number we had down. They came so fast we had lost all count. The legal hour was close at hand when we quit but the ducks were still pouring in. They swooped over the guide as he was picking up and when we got out to the car Blackducks were still spinning overhead for that pond.

Came a day in another season when, from open water everywhere, the mercury dropped in the night to eighteen and even the tidal river was solid ice in the morning. But on this place there is a narrow brook with, at its source, some big springs. The banks of this stream are steep and very heavily wooded. The Blackducks were trading about high overhead looking for open water. Said the guide, "I know where there'll be some ducks today and there'll be more coming if it gets colder. We'll give it a try."

This was quite a journey and plenty of snow was coming on the north-wester. The tires of the car squeaked in the icy snow as the writer had not heard since he lived in the Mohawk Valley as a small boy. This was real old up-state winter weather. We had to drive north a mile, west a mile, and south two miles or so to get to the banks of the brook where the springs and the blind were.

When we got into the timber the snow was drifted so deeply it was a question for a while whether we should make it. It was bitter cold and the snow clung to the trees but the ducks were there in the springs, all right, and came boiling out as we pulled up. We scarcely had the stool in the water before they came winging back in such numbers that we spent most of the time shooing them out. Bad luck occurred for those who dropped into the stool or came in legitimate numbers. The mist from the springs froze on the decoys so they looked like Christmas tree ornaments but the ducks didn't mind. They came in just the same.

We got our limit early and got out of there for the comforts of the fire-side. On the way out a Whitetail doe crossed ahead of the car in the snowy woods about in the manner of the hare in *The Eve of St. Agnes,* when he "limped, trembling, through the frozen grass."

The next morning the temperature had dropped to eight below. One of our party had killed no ducks at the stand assigned to him. None of the others would stick their noses out in that frigid blast, for it was now blowing harder from the northwest under a dirty sky full of snow. This man had no clothing for such a day but we rigged him out among us, and the writer, always the crazy duck shooter, volunteered to take him to the blind where we had shot the day before. The heavy underwear, lumberjack style, from Nova Scotia; the feather-lined shooting jacket and the alpaca-lined pants felt like nothing on at all by the time we reached the blind, but we stuck it out for an hour and got the man some ducks to take home.

We shot one at a time. We had to take turns trotting up and down back in the woods to keep our feet from freezing. Some of the ducks, down across the stream, we had to leave there. We hadn't the hardihood to ask the guide to retrieve them and he made no motion toward doing it on his own.

"These winter hawks (red-shouldered) and the foxes will get them and I ain't the man to take them away from those poor devils in this kind of weather," was his extenuating comment.

V I I

Great South Bay

BY EUGENE V. CONNETT

GREAT SOUTH BAY extends for some thirty miles along the south shore of Long Island, formed by a narrow stretch of sand dunes separating the bay from the ocean. It averages slightly under four miles in width, the southerly third being shallow sand flats. The northerly part has a depth of some eight feet, except along the shore. Shallow parts afford excellent feeding grounds for "tip-up" ducks, while the deeper parts are popular with such diving ducks as Broadbill.

Up until the time that all eelgrass disappeared on the Atlantic Coast, the shallower flats of the bay abounded in this excellent wildfowl food. In the deeper parts are found small duck clams and other food in which the diving ducks delight. I am glad to report that eelgrass is once more becoming abundant in the bay, a fact which partially accounts for the many Brant that spend the fall here. When Brant can get a diet of eelgrass, the young birds are about the best eating wildfowl I know of. When they have to resort to "cabbage" for food, they become so strong in flavor as to be almost inedible.

The water east of a line run from Howell's Point in Bellport across to the Bellport Coast Guard Station on the ocean beach is known as Bellport Bay.

It is with this part of Great South Bay that I intend to deal in some detail. A description of the gunning in Bellport Bay will, with the exception of scooter shooting, serve to describe the methods used in the rest of Great South Bay. It will, however, have the added advantage of depicting the best shooting in the bay and a situation which, to the best of my knowledge, exists nowhere else in the United States.

In 1693, Queen Anne granted a large tract of land known as the Manor of St. George, in what is now Brookhaven Town, to Colonel William "Tangier" Smith, brother of "Bull" Smith of Smithtown, who also received a grant on the north shore of the island. Colonel William Smith was Ambassador to Tangier at one time in his life—hence his nickname and the name of a large section of his grant. Not only was the land of St. George's Manor given to Smith, but the bottom of Bellport Bay, together with the fishing, fowling and oystering rights in the bay. Miss Jean Smith, a direct descendant of Colonel William, still occupies the original Manor House, and the original Queen Anne grant may be seen by visitors.

In 1767, the Smiths and the Town of Brookhaven formed a partnership for the joint control of the bay bottom, with the oystering and gunning rights, which rights have finally rested in the control of the town. Brookhaven Town has leased these rights—at least the gunning rights— first to certain individuals and latterly to an organization known as the Pattersquash Gunners Association, Inc., which today has the lease. Any bona fide voting resident of Brookhaven Town may join this association for a fee of ten dollars a year. In addition, a limited number of associate members are elected each year for a fee of fifteen dollars, these members being mostly land owners whose official voting residence is elsewhere.

I am fortunate enough to have been an associate member for some years past, but I also shot in Bellport Bay during the years when the lease was held by Wilbur A. Corwin, who operated an excellent camp on the beach near the Bellport Coast Guard Station. I first gunned with Captain Will in 1916, having shot in the open waters west of Bellport for ten years or more before that. In those earlier years one spent the greater part of the night on such well-known points as Fiddleton, Blue Point or Long Cove Point to cope with that ancient rule of "first come, first served."

In looking at two old photographs taken by me in 1912 of the late George B. Turrell, I marvel that with such decoys we ever killed many birds. But we did make quite respectable bags of Blackducks in spite of our rig.

From time to time strenuous efforts have been made in the courts to prove the old Smith grant gunning rights illegal, but each time the courts upheld the terms of the grant, and the gunning rights of Bellport Bay have remained in the hands of Brookhaven Town. We therefore have the most unusual situation of a famous wildfowling ground being owned by the public and open to the public in every respect, except as to the shooting rights.

For instance, although I own waterfront property on the bay, I cannot shoot on that waterfront unless I am a member of the Pattersquash Gunners Association. And as I am a legal resident of New Jersey, I cannot become a member of the association except through the good will of the board of governors in electing me an associate member from year to year. This situation, which I am sure is unique in this country, results in the preservation of the quality of the shooting in Bellport Bay.

The association makes its own regulations as to the hours of gunning, by-days and methods of shooting—all within the framework of state and federal game laws. At present, for instance, gunning is forbidden until 8 A.M. and stopped at 4 P.M. in order not to drive too many Blackducks off the feeding grounds. Scooter shooting, which will be described later, is not permitted. One may not shoot at a flock of Blackducks containing more than eight fowl. Indiscriminate shots at ducks which may be out of gunshot are quickly censured.

I recall an incident which, fortunately for me, ended happily. Five Pintail flew over my hide on the Northwest Point of Big Ridge, at a height which I suspected might be out of gunshot. The gunning had not been productive that day and I was very anxious to get some birds. Moreover, I had a new English gun which had shown itself capable of knocking a bird out of the air at long range, so I took a chance on the two leading drakes. That

On Uncle Bill's Bog in 1912. A better hide. The late George B. Turrell and the author killed eight Blackduck that day.

Three of Wilbur Corwin's punties moored to posts. 1920.

Wilbur Corwin's camp. The back porch where Ike Smith exploded the beans and Henry Gould opened the oysters.

On Fiddleton Point in 1912. Mason decoys and a poor hide.

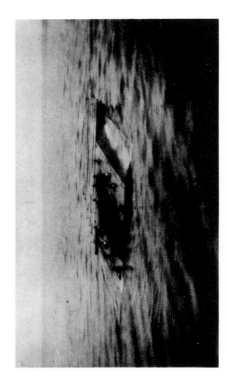

Double battery. Note hinged wings and canvas stretched on battens at the bow. Lead strip around the cockpit could be turned up.

The midship hatch of the *Mabel Jewel* where the battery was carried.

Wilbur Corwin and Henry Gould anchoring the battery. 1920.

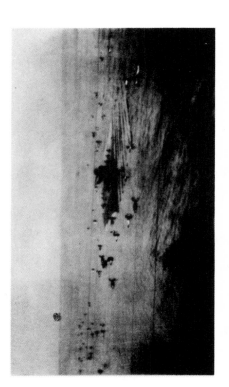

Henry Gould in double battery. When the other gunner got in the left side, it would sink to water level. 1920.

evening, when I shoved in to the clubhouse where the watchman lives throughout the season, he said to me: " 'Gene, it's mighty lucky for you that you killed those two sprig out of that bunch that flew over you. They were 'way out of gunshot, and I was all set to report you to the governors."

The Bellport gunning grounds comprise a group of low-lying islands or "bogs" near the southern or beach side of the bay. These bogs, unfortunately, seem to be getting smaller each year, due to the action of ice. In fact, in my time two of them have disappeared altogether, namely, Titus Bog and Meserole Bog. The names of the best points are: Little Ridge, Gull Bar, Northeast Point of the Big Ridge, Northwest Point of the same, John Ryder Bog, Inlet Point, Inlet Point Bog, West Bog, Goose Point and Quanch Island.

There is also the Lead Bog, Sheldrake Bog and Southeast Point of the Ridge, the latter three not being considered as good as the others. When there are more than eight rigs gunning, each end of Little Ridge is used. We therefore have fourteen points that will accommodate two men each. The clubhouse of the Pattersquash Gunners is located on Pelican Island, most easterly of the bogs, there being a channel into the landing stage at this point.

In former days, when the Corwins had the lease of the gunning rights, their headquarters were near the Coast Guard Station at the westerly end of the bogs, where another channel runs in through the flats.

The Corwins' gunning camp has been operated by the same families since at least 1861, both for sportsmen and market gunning, for an old puntie built for Joseph Henry Titus carries that date and is still in the possession of Wilbur A. Corwin, son of Wilbur R. Corwin. The house originally was the Quanch Life Saving Station (the government brand is still on the attic stairs), and stood about 550 feet east of its present location. It was later moved to Quanch Island, where it stood for fifty-two years, during the latter part of which it was used by the Bellport Gun Club, Inc., until 1895, when Captain Wilbur R. Corwin, who was superintendent of the club, bought it and moved it back to the beach on land which he owned.

The original house was bought from the government by Bob Petty, Sheriff of Suffolk County, for use as a hunting lodge for himself, Dan Petty and Wilbur R. Corwin. Living room furniture was bought by Bob Petty and Captain Corwin from the underwriters in New York City when it was salvaged from the steam and sailing ship *Ben Franklin,* which foundered off the beach to the southeast of the present camp location.

When I first shot with Wilbur A. Corwin in 1916, Will employed three other guides and a cook, so that four men could gun under ideal conditions, each with a guide. Our party would arrive at Bellport on the evening train, be driven down to the town dock, there to be met by Will and the *Mabel Jewel,* an old clipper bow South Bay sloop, with a large hatch amidships and a winter cabin aft. The hatch provided an ideal spot on which to carry a battery, and the cabin welcome warmth, if not too much comfort, to the men tending the battery.

Duffle and guns on board, we cast off to sail across the bay to the camp, where Captain Ike Smith was soon asking us whether we wanted our eels cooked "round or split." Meanwhile, Henry Gould, who was no mean cook himself, would be busy on the kitchen porch opening local oysters. In those days baymen ate their oysters in a big, heavy coffee cup, in which some eight or ten oysters were shucked. A generous dash of vinegar was poured over them, with perhaps a dash of coarsely ground black pepper. I can recommend this as a superlative way in which to eat Great South Bay oysters.

After a delicious and tremendous meal, guides and gunners sat around the living room, talking ducks and shooting until much too late an hour. Not until I acted as a guide for Will several years later, when one of his regular men had a broken leg, did I realize how the guides longed to go to bed early, for they were routed out about four o'clock to put fresh hay in the punties and get everything shipshape before the "sports" had to get up.

Breakfast finished, each gunner left in the pitch dark with his guide, the latter standing on the stern deck and shoving the puntie over the flats to the point where they were to shoot. Parenthetically, the first morning I was acting as a guide, I hit the soft spot in the drain between Quanch Island

and Goose Point and gracefully landed on my back in the water! A fine start for a budding young guide. A second puntie with a full rig of stool had been left on each point to be shot that day, and it was only a matter of minutes to rig out.

Will's stools were rigged either two or three on a bent galvanized rod, so that they could be set out or picked up in less than half the time required by individually anchored decoys. I have never seen this method used elsewhere, and can vouch for its handiness.

The punties in those days were flat-bottomed, with not much crown to the decks. Watertight hatches were used over the cockpits when under way, and the gunner sat on the hatch with the guide standing on the afterdeck to shove. In rough weather the inside of the boat was thus kept quite dry. If stools had to be carried, they were stacked on the forward deck, their iron rod mountings making it easy to stow them securely. These flat punties could be pulled out on the bare bog and if the tide marks on the seaweed were not disturbed, birds would stool perfectly in spite of the fact that the punties lay entirely unconcealed. The gunners had to lie quite flat in them and keep still, of course.

Today, with the high-crowned and deeper scooter punties used in Bellport, it is thought necessary to hide them in the grass, or lie beside the edge of the bog in the water. For the past several years cedar blinds have been stuck up on some of the points to afford better hides. I question the necessity for these blinds, having for years gunned successfully in exposed punties. However, these blinds do serve to break the cold winds, and the ducks do not seem to mind them.

As the morning wore on Will would unwrap a bulky package and hand me a tremendous baked bean sandwich. Faced with such an article in a New York restaurant, one would say it was simply impossible for a human being to swallow so huge an affair. But lying on West Bog or Little Ridge on a December morning the last mouthful vanished with regret.

As a matter of some historical importance, let me tell how Captain Ike Smith baked beans. He filled a very large dishpan about half full of beans (remember, he was cooking for eight or nine hungry men). These he covered with water into which a generous dose of soda had been thrown. He put this huge dishpan on the stove and brought the contents to a rousing boil. Then he stepped outdoors into the cold, drained off the water and tossed the beans into the air. Whereupon each bean exploded, and in doing so lost its power for evil.

Back into the kitchen, where more water was added and large pieces of salt pork were introduced. The pan was then put in the oven and, except for a look once in a while to make sure that the beans were not drying out too much, the pan was left for the better part of twenty-four hours. This, I maintain, is the best way in which to cook baked beans—bean-hole addicts and others to the contrary notwithstanding.

Captain Ike also made a clam pie that should be recorded for posterity. He chopped up a mess of hard clams with their juice, added crushed crackers, milk and *plenty* of butter and black pepper, with a little salt. This was baked in a deep pan with a light, thick crust, well browned. As Will Corwin put it: "This is IT!"

The following day, if the bay were not too rough, we might go battery shooting. Will's batteries were double boxes in which two men could gun. Two guides would stay on the *Mabel Jewel* to tend the battery. As I have said, the battery or "machine" was carried amidship on the *Mabel,* and a large stool boat was towed behind her. About one hundred and fifty decoys were used, the battery itself being surrounded with them and the rest tailed off to leeward in, roughly, a pear-shaped pattern.

On the decks of the battery lay a number of iron Broadbill stools which, together with the weight of the gunners, sank the battery to water level. I have timed Will Corwin and Henry Gould with my watch, and can state that they have set out the entire rig in twenty minutes. Furthermore, they have picked it up—ready to set out again—in nineteen minutes.

As a number of other guests at the camp have timed this performance, it may be accepted as fact. As Will put it once: "Henry was a little stout

BROADBILL SHOOTING FROM THATCHED PUNTIE

and a little short, but he was the best of the lot." Fortunately, I am able to show a picture of this peerless pair starting to set out a battery.

If the wind kicked up a sea, the lead strip tacked around the cockpit was turned up a few inches to keep out the slop. The canvas apron, stiffened with battens, which lay on the water to windward of the box, kept the seas from breaking over the machine. And the two hinged canvas wings at the sides also helped to keep it afloat as the water roughened. There came a time, however, when it was no longer possible to lie in a battery if the wind really blew. Then we put in to camp and went point shooting.

Will wisely provided gun rests in all of his punties and batteries, and he insisted that they be used. They were nothing more than a stick across the foot of the cockpit on which the barrels of the gun must be rested, thus preventing the muzzle from getting inside the boat or battery box. There have been cases of men shooting their feet off in a battery when their guns went off by mistake. With the gun barrels on the rest, an accidental discharge went off harmlessly in the air.

I speak of this wise precaution because my gun once did go off for no reason at all, and that simple little gun rest prevented the charge from blowing off my foot and demolishing the end of the battery. On the other hand, a man shooting in a battery off Bayshore, about that same time, was not so lucky. The battery sank, his foot was blown off and he was drowned.

It was not unusual in my time to kill a limit of twenty-five Broadbill in a battery at Bellport, sometimes before noon. This was true of battery shooting in other parts of the Great South Bay. Nor would it be much of a trick to do it today, were battery shooting permitted. West of Smith's Point, and east of Amityville, battery shooting used to be permitted. Beyond these limits, the bays narrowed down too much to make battery shooting reasonable.

Today scooter shooting is permitted west of Bellport Bay and east of Amityville, and some excellent gunning is enjoyed. Gray scooters, with high coamings around the cockpit, are anchored more or less as a battery used to be, and with a proper rig of stool good gunning for Broadbill is enjoyed. The scooter rig is tended by a motor boat, just as we used to tend a battery with a sailboat in the old days. (A crab net is used to scoop the dead fowl off the water.) When the gunner knocks a bird down, he stands up and signals to the tender. In this manner the men on the tender can keep track of where dead birds are to be picked up. If fowl are stooling freely to the rig, the tender will keep away as long as possible, so that the flight will not be disturbed.

Lying on West Bog one day, a good many years ago, with Will Corwin, he told me of a day's battery shooting which Captain Charles S. Hawkins had in 1878, gunning for market. (Joel Barbour mentions this historic occasion in his book *Duck Decoys,* which I published some years ago, and Will Corwin has pointed out to me that Joel did not have his facts correct. The following account is taken from a letter which Will has recently written me.)

Captain Hawkins lay in a single battery and was tended by Captain Wilbur R. Corwin. For many years these two men gunned for market together, Captain Hawkins shooting and Captain Corwin tending the rig, the latter function being almost as essential as the shooting. They must have been a great team.

On the day to which I refer, these two men returned to Bellport with six hundred and forty ducks, mostly Broadbill, which they shipped to New York at twenty-five cents a pair, F.O.B. Bellport! Captain Corwin "kept account of guns fired on the cabin slate, which was fastened to the sliding hatch, and always looked for and picked up plenty more dead ducks than he counted guns fired," to quote his son's letter.

A notable bag of birds was shot by Judge H. A. Bergen on Titus Bog (named for Joseph Henry Titus). This was in the days of the Bellport Gun Club. Guided by Richard B. Hamel, the Judge killed sixty-four Broadbill, ninety-eight Blackduck and one Gadwall between 9 A.M. and 1 P.M.! This record is taken from the Bellport Gun Club camp register and is signed by Judge Bergen. This register, by the way, was presented to the club by

Sydney Dillon Ripley, the then treasurer of the club, and is now in the possession of Wilbur A. Corwin.

When the bag limit was twenty-five ducks a day, Wilbur states that many, many days they would take up the battery at eight, nine or ten o'clock in the morning, with the limit of fifty birds for the two gunners. When Wilbur's father and uncles, R. B. Hamel, John and Ed Corwin, gunned for market "the one-day bag to ship to market for one of them in an ice hole used to be ninety-seven Redheads," Wilbur writes me. "I do not mean that happened too often, but it happened to each of them. And when I was a boy John Petty did it once off in the ice hole northwest of Fiddleton Flat."

About 1897, I remember sailing with my parents from Bellport to Smith's Point in Barney King's big catboat. A flight of ducks went over that literally darkened the sun. I presume that they were Broadbill, and I hesitate to guess at how many tens of thousands of birds I was looking at. In comparatively recent years I have watched a raft of Broadbill getting off the water and they looked like smoke from a prairie fire drifting up off the surface of the bay. That particular raft must have been a mile long and contained 10,000 birds.

The method of estimating the number of fowl in a raft used by the Federal Government is as follows: "The formula for estimating the number allows one duck per square yard. Since it is obvious that no raft of ducks is actually a parallelogram, but instead, it tapers off at the ends, and has open spaces in the general mass, we always subtract one-third from the original figure . . . It has been tested several times by aerial photography and the actual count in the pictures has shown that the estimate by eye is close." I have quoted this from an article by Dr. Frederick C. Lincoln in the *Audubon* magazine.

Thus a raft of birds a mile long—I have seen such a one—averaging one hundred feet wide, would contain 11,734 birds. On the basis of this measurement, and assuming that birds in flight might be counted in a similar manner, the clouds of them which I saw from Barney King's boat in 1897 must have contained in the neighborhood of several million birds!

I realize that this sounds fantastic, but I am assuming that a cloud of birds sufficient to darken the sun, would perhaps be half a mile by at least a quarter of a mile in size. Such a flock, estimated by the formula I have quoted, would yield 2,323,200 birds. It is my firm belief and recollection that the flock was larger than I have stated.

When I was much younger and hardier than I am today, I indulged in ice shooting. One shoved over the ice, in a white gunning scooter with iron shod runners, to a water hole; threw out a dozen Whistler stools and, dressed in white overalls, lay in the scooter waiting for birds to arrive before an icy, cutting northwest wind caused rigor mortis to set in. These scooter stools were lovely pieces of work, made thin and light to fit under the deck, but they were very effective.

Ice shooting was rugged work on a cold day, and the returns were not too plentiful when I did it. On the other hand, some of the best shooting I ever had was when there was a lot of ice in the bogs, and one could lie on a point with some open water for the stool. Seldom have I failed to have a good Blackduck shoot under these conditions. But that is not what I mean by ice shooting out on the open bay in a white rig.

I have also shot in a pile of ice cakes on the shore and killed a few geese. But goose shooting in the Great South Bay is fortuitous; quite a large number of geese fly over during the season but it is an occasion when one kills a decent bag of these grand birds. Brant, on the other hand, are present in large numbers. Again it is a banner day when one kills a good bag of Brant —or rather was, when the law permitted a good bag. It is a fact, however, that Brant collect in large numbers in the bay.

And now for a brief description of a typical present day shoot in Bellport. The club ferry, namely Everett Brown's power boat, leaves the town dock at 6:30 on a November morning. It is still dark, but a faint paleness seeps across the sky over Smith's Point. Eight men arrive and get aboard before the boat leaves for Pelican Island, where, thirty minutes later, they climb ashore and carry their duffle to their punties, a line of which are drawn up on the south side of the island. Everyone is busy for ten minutes sponging

A pair of punties hidden under the edge of the bog on Gull Bar.

Scooter type puntie with high-crowned decks and iron-shod runners on bottom.

The author shoving to his point in the early morning.

Old style flat bottom puntie, showing how stool are carried. Oar and sail in the cockpit.

Rigged on West Bog. This hide would look better from the water than from where this picture was taken.

Two scooter type punties on what was left of Titus Bog a few years ago. This bog has since disappeared.

icy water out of punties, pushing them to the water's edge, and stowing guns, lunch, ammunition and water bottle aboard. Soon the call comes from the clubhouse: "Time to draw! Hands up for rigs!"

The gunners move to the steps of the house and one of each pair holds up his hand so that the number of rigs can be officially counted. This morning there are five rigs, as one man will shoot alone. So five Kelly pool pills are put in a small basin and each rig draws one. The man with number one gets first choice of points; number two gets second choice, and so on.

Meanwhile, everyone has been whispering to his partner about the wind and the possibilities of this point or that. Everett Brown brings the club register to the door and as each pair choose their point he enters their names in the book. At night their bag will be recorded in detail, and in this way exact records are kept from year to year.

Number one has chosen West Bog, which brings a sigh of relief from number two, who has been itching to get the outside of the Little Ridge. Number three takes Goose Point; number four chooses Inlet Point, and the last man takes Gull Bar, somewhat disconsolately. He will probably turn out to be high gun for the day! I say that because, this past season, last choice was high gun on numerous occasions.

When drawing is over they go to their punties and shove off for their points. Before long one sees two men off each point setting out their stool, and a few minutes before eight o'clock, when shooting starts, no one is to be seen. But some fifty Blackducks are apparently sitting off the end of the points. As they shoved out to their points the gunners stirred up flock after flock of Blackduck, Pintail and Widgeon which had spent the night among the bogs. Sometimes a bunch of Broadbill get up, but they are more likely to stay in the deeper water.

Perhaps seven or eight hundred birds have flown out over the bay, some to alight in the open water, some to wing their way to fresh water ponds and creeks and still others to fly across Long Island to rest on the open Sound for the day.

Whether we are to have good shooting now depends almost entirely on the weather. If it blows hard, the birds will move around, and many should come back to the comparatively quiet water among the bogs. If it is mild and still, there will be a little shooting during the first few hours, and then nothing doing until the last half hour, when birds will start drifting in for the night. On such bluebird days, we can always pick up a few oysters, walk around on the bogs in the hope of jumping a Blackduck or Teal from some little "drean" or pond hole, or just sit up in our punties and chat.

Today it is blowing and before long the welcome sound of muffled shots comes rolling over the water from Goose Point. A quick glance in that direction reveals four Blackducks flaring wildly into the air, while two are spinning crazily to the water. Everyone snugs down tighter into his puntie, although he knows perfectly well that Blackduck are not so foolish as to stool right after being shot at.

Out of nowhere a pair of birds come pitching into our rig and it has happened that after four shots are fired at them, they scurry off unharmed —except for hurt feelings that they should be greeted in such a manner when dropping in to join friends. However, this time they stay with us, and are soon reposing peacefully on the stern of one of our punties.

The wind blows harder and a mean-looking sky is making up in the west. We hear shots on this point and that and we see men shove off in their punties chasing winged birds. Others merely wade out into their stool and pick up birds which have been cleanly killed. The first drops of rain start to fall. Now the queer thing about a duck hunter is that instead of bewailing the fact that he is in for a miserably uncomfortable time, he is happy as a lark. The worse the weather gets, the better his shooting should be. All that counts is that the birds will fly.

When a cripple is down one is lucky to kill it within wading distance of the point. Otherwise, it means launching a puntie and shoving after the wing-tipped bird. First, a furious chase and then a shot. The bird keeps on. Another chase and another shot. I have seen it take half an hour to gather in a wing-tipped Blackduck and I have seen the day (too often) when it cost ten shells to get a bird.

Just as you shove back to the point, your companion yells: "Get down! Here they come!" And that is all the good that does. Birds always seem to head for the stool when one man is picking up dead or crippled birds. You pull out your puntie, panting and sweating from your long chase, while your companion gets out of his and dances up and down on the bog, swinging his arms to warm up. Next time he will do the sweating, as we take turns at this cripple chasing.

Finally, lunchboxes come out and just as you are pouring a hot cup of coffee from your thermos, somebody whispers: "Get down! Mark east!" In come a pair of Widgeon. And so the day wears happily on, until it is time to pick up. Sometimes we are more than ready for this task. Sometimes we wish the clock would stop for a few minutes, as the birds are moving. With stools stacked on our afterdecks, we may step our masts, if the wind is fair, and sail back to the shack. Otherwise, we shove over the flats with our nine-foot shovin' oars, and are mighty glad when we push the bow of the puntie on Pelican Island, stick our oar in the bog and tie the puntie painter to it.

Hatch covers are fastened down and duffle and birds are carried to the shack where the watchman makes a record of each man's kill. In a few minutes everyone is aboard Everett's boat and he is collecting the dollar ferry fare. Before you left the shack in the morning, you paid one dollar shooting fee. So this fine duck shooting costs you ten to fifteen dollars a year, plus one dollar for each day you shoot, plus ferry fare. Where can you beat that? Soon the "Ducks Unlimited" can is passed around and everyone puts in five cents for every bird killed. At the end of the year the association usually doubles the total of this collection out of its funds and sends its contribution in.

One more tale of a day that wasn't exactly typical. It was December, with a skim of ice on the flats. When the ferry left there were only Everett Brown, Kellogg Dominy and myself aboard. When we reached Pelican

Island a sheet of ice stretched off to the bogs. Keg and Everett said they would go to Little Ridge and I chose Gull Bar, it being the shortest shove.

We would push our bow onto the ice, rock the puntie and thus break a path ahead of us. It was tough work for a city man like me! I made Gull Bar at last, huffing and puffing like an old steam engine. Just to the east was a large water hole, and I soon had my stool set out in it. Then the big red-legged Blackducks, with a stray Mallard, began coming in.

What a shoot! Before noon we were on our happy way back to Bellport with the limit each. I remember another day when we spent the whole day in Everett's motor boat, stuck in the ice, and unable to reach Pelican Island. Well, that's duck shooting, I suppose.

One is likely to learn a good deal about rigging out and gunning in general if one shoots in Bellport Bay, as there are no guides today, and you must do it yourself. I have shot with guides, acted as a guide and done the thing for myself. I'll choose the latter style any day.

A typical rig of stool for Bellport Bay shooting consists of twenty-five Blackduck. I use four Pintail and five Widgeon with the Blackduck. Some gunners use half a dozen Broadbill instead. Others carry from two to five goose stools. With two gunners to a point the total rig of stool is impressive —some sixty or more decoys, which is quite generous for point shooting.

It is my practice to set out the decoys with plenty of open water patches among them. The light fowl may be placed either at the head of the rig or in the middle. It is noticeable that with really carefully painted light fowl stool (Dr. Burke painted mine) both Blackducks and the others will almost invariably flutter down to them.

I completely agree with both Dr. Burke and "Shang" Wheeler that it pays to have your decoys look as much like live fowl as possible to make them, particularly in the coloring. I would prefer oversized bodies to under-sized. However, the size of decoys must of necessity be somewhat controlled by the method used to transport them to the point. When racked up on the stern deck of a South Bay puntie, they cannot be as big as when stacked in a large stoolboat. And if carried in a scooter when ice shooting, they must be smaller and slimmer yet, so that they may be stowed under the decks.

A word as to the length of anchor ropes. All our water is less than waist-deep. On the average it is knee-deep. With a sufficiently heavy lead mushroom anchor, the anchor lines should be not more than seven feet in length. This may not agree with Dr. Burke's ideas, but after he has tried to pick up a rig from a tossing puntie in heavy weather, each stool being picked up on the end of the long shoving oar in which a notch has been cut to catch the line, he will realize that any longer length of line is an abomination. The same is true when you are wading by the stern of your puntie and lifting decoy and anchor onto it.

I have a dozen Blackduck stools which I bought some years ago from L. L. Bean of Freeport, Maine. Everyone who has ever shot over them has conceded that they are most lifelike-looking decoys. The modeling of the decoys themselves accounts for much of this opinion. But the way in which mine swim around is perhaps half the secret. By fastening the lines on to the bottom of the stool several inches back from the forward end, the decoy will sail back and forth with the wind and tide in the most lifelike manner imaginable. But each one must be given plenty of space to swim in, or trouble will result.

In setting out stool for point shooting in Bellport Bay, it is important to place them so there will be no bog in front of the ducks as they decoy. Blackducks apparently feel more comfortable when there is plenty of open water ahead of the stool. It is equally true that the ducks should not have to fly over the bog to reach the tail end of the decoys. In mild weather it is well to spread the stool out with a single bird in the lead at the head. Leave plenty of openings between stool down to the tail, where a fairly closely bunched group may be placed. In heavy weather they should be pretty tightly bunched together, as they will show up better in the rough water if so placed. In still weather they may be set farther from the gunners. In heavy weather they may be closer.

There is a very marked difference in the behavior of native fowl which have been shot at and those new birds which have just come into the Bay. The former will exhibit definite "bog shyness," while the latter will tumble into the stool like chickens, if everything is rigged right—and the birds feel like it! It is evident, therefore, that after severe weather and heavy storm conditions the shooting will be much better than when the absence of such weather has failed to bring in new birds.

Day after day in mild weather, I have watched hundreds of birds fly out of the gunning grounds upon the approach of the gunners shoving to their points in the morning. Day after day I have seen these birds fly back into the gunning grounds as the gunners shove home at night with almost no birds moving during the day. In the absence of heavy weather and new birds, the shooting is inclined to suffer seriously.

In our point shooting we expect to see Blackduck, Pintail and Widgeon stool reasonably well. Broadbill, as a rule, will fly over the rig at high speed without actually stooling. Brant do the same, seldom in good range. The Pintail appear to be the most cautious about dropping in, often circling around high in the air before deciding to come in. More often than not they merely fly off after a careful inspection.

In my opinion more shots are lost because the gunner moves, by reaching for his gun upon the approach of birds, or turning his head to watch them, than because he is not lying flat in his puntie. Iron resolve is required not to twitch a muscle when your companion whispers, "Don't move! Three on the right!" Every instinct is to move the head for a better look and to reach for the gun as it lies across the gunwales of the puntie. Such movements often cause the birds to flare and leave for other points.

The manner in which the punties are hidden is of the greatest importance when birds are shy. In low tides it is difficult to prevent the bows from sticking out a foot or more over the surface of the water. It is better to have the entire boat in the water against the edge of the bog, rather than the bow in the water and stern cocked up on the bog.

A quarter of a century ago the prevailing design of duck punties on the South Shore of Long Island was a flat bottom with a slightly crowned deck. They were pulled out on the bog stern first, and the gunner shot over the bow. The crown on the forward deck was high enough so that the gunner's rubber-booted feet could be stuck upright under the deck without crowding. Sometimes a lighted lantern was placed between the legs in really cold weather! The afterdeck was flat in order to hold the rig of stool.

The modern type of puntie is "scooter built"—that is, the bottom boards run lengthwise, instead of transversely, and oftentimes a pair of iron-shod runners is bolted to the bottom, as the original scooter puntie was developed for use on the ice. These punties have moderately rounded bottoms and high-crowned decks. They are warm in cold and windy weather, and the gunner can hide in them easily. The high-crowned afterdecks do not lend themselves well to carrying a generous rig of stool. However, these scooter type punties, many made by the late Benjamin Hallock and Lewis Howell of Moriches, are slowly but surely replacing the older flat-bottom type.

Most punties are equipped with a small sail, generally a spritsail rig, which can be folded up and left in the boat. Usually one can sail at least one way to or from the point and this is a very pleasant manner of traversing a mile of water. Otherwise, one shoves the puntie with an oar about nine feet long, round in cross section, except for lower three feet, which is somewhat wider and flattened in cross section. The lower part affords sufficient surface to serve as a steering oar when sailing or when shoving.

Captain Frank Corwin of Brookhaven, L. I., makes the finest oars I have seen and does it as a hobby. One is fortunate to own one of Captain Corwin's oars!

The modern scooter type punties are certainly easier to shove than the older style, but many gunners still prefer the latter because of the larger cockpit openings, the wooden hatches and flat afterdecks. The new type hatch cover is simply a piece of canvas with four grommets on either side into which lengths of cord are fastened. These are then tied through galvanized iron rings fastened to the thatching battens, which run down each side of the deck. Under these battens salt meadow hay is stuffed tightly, to serve as an effective camouflage for the boat. The photographs will make most of these points clear.

In high tides at some points, it is impossible to wade when picking up stool. This task must be performed from the puntie. Here is a simple but exceedingly useful trick: Cut a sharply incised notch about half an inch deep four or five inches up from the lower end of the shoving oar. Then when you pick up the anchor line of a decoy it catches in this notch and is easily brought aboard the puntie. If the wind is blowing very hard, an anchor is a great help in picking up decoys. Anchor the puntie to windward of the stool. As you pick them up, let out line and drop the boat back until you have gathered them all in. Even when the depth of the water permits wading, this is a useful trick to hold the puntie as you are picking up.

Thin floor boards with quarter-inch battens, thus raising the top of the floor board about half an inch above the bottom of the puntie, are a source of considerable comfort, as one always gets a certain amount of water in the boat when getting in with wet boots—assuming the puntie doesn't leak a drop. A simple flat board of proper dimensions serves as a back rest when propped up against the end of the cockpit. A kapok cushion on which to rest the end of the spine may be considered effete by some hardy souls, but I prefer to be effete rather than have my terminal facilities get so sore I can't gun the next day!

One more simple gadget that has its great uses at times is a wooden or iron stake several feet long, with a few feet of light line attached to the upper end. This is stuck in the ground and the line fastened to a ring in the stern to hold the stern in position when the tide floats the puntie.

V I I I

Barnegat Bay

BY SAMUEL BONNELL

THE Barnegat Bay region consists of a series of smaller bays, rivers and marshes extending just inside the Jersey coastline from Bay Head in the north to Cape May in the south, a distance of approximately one hundred miles.

These shallow bays of salt tidal water, which becomes brackish where fed by countless rivers and creeks, are protected from the Atlantic Ocean by long narrow stretches of beach and dunes, cut by numerous inlets.

The width of these bays varies. In some places, it is better than two miles, while in others the marshes and sedges have reached out and divided the waters into innumerable thoroughfares and channels, dotted here and there with small islands. As if tiring of this effort to choke off the bay, the marshes farther along recede, allowing the waters to broaden out once more. This process repeats itself until the southern tip of New Jersey is reached.

For years, and probably for centuries, this coastal strip has been one of the great concentration points for migrating wildfowl. They are no longer found, however, in the great quantities of former days. This isn't to say that ducks aren't still in fair abundance, but the odds are constantly lengthening against them as, bit by bit, their former wintering grounds are en-croached upon by the march of civilization.

Marshes and sedges are being filled in and great areas of bottom dredged up to make way for real estate developments and resorts. In short, the hand-writing is on the wall for many parts of this famous gunning region. True, the Federal Government has established sanctuaries which will help to preserve the species, but, to the wildfowler, the curtain is slowly being rung down.

In spite of this depressing aspect, Barnegat Bay, with its legends, folk-lore and traditions, still awakens in countless gunners the memories of happy hours spent on its waters and marshes—memories of a day when the shift-off came, the Geese were coming in over the dunes, the Brant were uneasy and on the move, small bunches of Broadbill were trading up and down the bay, and, toward late afternoon, the Blackducks started.

The species of wildfowl found here in the greatest numbers are Canada Geese, Brant, Broadbill (Greater Scaup) and Blackduck. Also prevalent in lesser quantities are Baldpate, Pintail, Teal (blue- and green-wing), Wood Duck, Green-leg Blackduck, Golden Eye, Bufflehead, Old Squaw, Ruddy Sheldrake and Coot.

Occasional flights of Redheads and Canvasbacks are still seen but not nearly as frequently as in days past. These species of diving duck were at one time very abundant in the upper bay, before the advent of the Manasquan Inlet and Bay Canal. Opening of this waterway in 1925, as part of the inland waterway system, brought salt water into the head of the bay, formerly fresh to brackish, destroying the natural feed of wild celery and grasses enjoyed by these ducks.

This is a source of sorrow to old-time gunners who tell me they used to see Redheads in such numbers that they practically blotted out the rising sun as they swept upward from their feeding grounds in the early morning.

Those were the days when Grover Cleveland, a famous sportsman in addition to his other achievements, frequently enjoyed gunning in this area. He used to make his headquarters at the Chadwick Hotel, at Chadwick

The Chadwick Hotel, Chadwick, N. J. Painted in 1901 by Gerard Hardenburgh.

A Barnegat sneak box, with spray hood and stool rack in place.

Sneak boxes hidden under seaweed, 1915.

Sneak box with seaweed on decks.

A shooting box sunk in the marsh, Barnegat Bay.

Beach, a famous landmark until it was destroyed by fire thirty years ago. Since Cleveland's day, Democrats, like Redheads, have thinned out considerably in the region.

Returning to the Wood Duck and native Blackduck, these two species make their home here the year round, the former nesting in or near the cedar swamps along the adjacent rivers, the latter in the marsh and sedges.

The native (or common) Blackduck, with olive-colored legs, is a bit smaller than his big, black, red-legged Canadian cousin. It's a lucky gunner who bags one, for this Blackduck, living in close proximity to civilization throughout the year, is doubly cautious and will generally give the most carefully prepared blind a wide berth.

The eelgrass disease that swept up the Atlantic seaboard about two decades ago had a harmful effect on the wildfowl in these parts, the chief sufferer being the Brant, who made this plant its main food. Other species were affected as well and many of them moved on to feeding grounds farther south. Some, however, stuck it out, maintaining a precarious existence until the spring flight north.

It is heartening to note that in the last few years the Brant, which at one time was at the point of extinction, has staged a tremendous comeback and is now in considerable numbers in the bay region. The eelgrass, likewise, is staging a comeback, sizeable patches having appeared in the last few seasons, together with other grasses.

When a gunner thinks of Barnegat Bay, he's likely to think of the Barnegat sneakbox, which originated hereabouts and is probably the best-known duck-hunting boat in the country. It's the boat most generally used for wildfowling in the bay, either in its original design or modified according to the whim of the gunner.

The original sneakbox is a broad-beamed, shallow boat, varying in length from twelve to fourteen feet, with a beam of approximately four feet. It is round-bottomed, with a slightly rounded deck rising a little above the waterline, and carries a draft of roughly six inches. A hatch is amidships with a cover that can be locked in place for stowing duffle. The boat is generally equipped with a canvas sprayhood, forward of the hatch, which can be raised or lowered. Decoys are carried on deck, stowed in racks aft of the cockpit on the stern.

For ice-shooting, a pair of runners is laid parallel along the bottom, and the boat is painted white. Some models are built with a centerboard and carry a small mast and sail, which can easily be stepped and unstepped.

By and large, the sneakbox is a splendid seaboat and can ride out very heavy blows. In former days, they were rowed to and from the gunning grounds but now, with the advent of power, they are generally towed.

Where permanent blinds have been set up, the usual practice is to leave the sneakbox at the gunning shore, using it to store decoys and duffle as well as for setting out, picking up and gathering birds.

The sneakbox is also an excellent boat for jump shooting and can easily be rowed, sculled or poled through the marshes and thoroughfares where conditions are favorable for this kind of shooting.

But it is where permanent blinds do not exist that the sneakbox is at its best. The gunner rows, or is towed, to his favorite spot, sets out his decoys, pulls the boat in among the reeds, grasses it down with sedge grass, reeds or seaweed, makes himself as comfortable *as possible,* and awaits what the gods have to offer.

In many sections of this region, that is the only practical way to gun as the sedges and seadogs are sometimes under considerable water, because of winds and tides. Also, many of these marshes and beaches offer the gunner but little concealment among their short reeds and grasses. The sneakbox, with only a few inches of freeboard, blends with the surroundings and doesn't show above the skyline.

Most of the bay shooting nowadays is done from points and coves of the marshes. In former years, however, before the outlawing of batteries and sinkboxes, a considerable amount of gunning was done by that method.

Conditions generally determine the type of blind used. While the sneakbox remains the favorite for most sections, in others the sunken box or barrel, buried with the top a few inches above the level of the marsh or sand-bar, is preferred. These vary in construction and size, holding from one to five men, and can be made of wood, concrete or steel. A good tight cover and pump are requisites for this kind of blind.

Where points or coves have tall reeds or bushes running to the shoreline, the conventional sit-up blind is in general use, ranging from just a squat or hide in the natural cover to elaborate wooden frames thatched with rushes and with floors, seats, shelves and even stoves. This type of blind is equally useful for pond hole, river and creek shooting, although in the rivers and creeks considerable gunning is also done from pushboats in the river marshes, using either the good old sneakbox or a lighter and smaller double-ender of the dugout type, either poled or sculled.

DECOYS

As the Barnegat sneakbox is a product of the region, so are the decoys. To reduce the weight of equipment to be carried by the sneakbox, the decoys were specially constructed in two sections, to permit their being hollowed out. Size being another factor, your local decoys are not only lighter but proportionately smaller than those used elsewhere. By way of compensation, weights are affixed to the bottoms in the form of flat lead pads, and the heads are made slightly larger in proportion to the body so that the decoy can make a better show on the water.

The local decoy maker has never had any trouble finding materials, as cedar swamps abound in the region and small sawmills are within range of most communities. The waste slabs of white cedar can be had for the carting away.

Outside of those sections which the Federal Government has purchased for sanctuaries, the better part of the marshes, sedges and islands are now controlled by individuals—both natives and visiting sportsmen—or by gun clubs, estates and land development companies. This doesn't mean, how-ever, that the casual visitor can't enjoy a day's shooting. Most of the communities dotting the bay have guides to take out the visiting gunner and arrangements generally can be made for the day, week or season.

In many instances, marshes have been in families for generations, with the guiding and management handed down from father to son. The livelihood of a great many of your baymen depends on the gunning in conjunction with other seasonal bay pursuits.

However, it is interesting to note that your true bayman is a breed that is dying out with the times, the real start in his decline dating from the abolition of market gunning in 1918.

Although we deplore the slaughter that went on in the days of market gunning, we should give the old market gunner his due. It was he who developed wildfowling as we know it today and many of his methods cannot be improved upon. Such tools of his trade as the sneakbox and decoys adapted to various localities serve the present-day sportsman as faithfully as they did his commercial predecessor.

The writer well remembers the bustle that used to spring up around the small boat yards and landings as the local gunners prepared for the season. Decoys and sneakboxes would be receiving their allotment of paint, "shootin' cabins" being placed on the old clamming catboats, stove pipes adjusted, and so on. At the first touch of frost, or when the first rumor spread that fowl were in the bay, off they would go to the shootin' ground.

In this particular locality, the rendezvous was the winter anchorage back of North Point of the beach in the shadow of historic Barnegat lighthouse. There, back of the sedges, sheltered by the dunes and bayberry, was a motley array of shacks made of driftwood and old wrecks, while moored against the banks were the catboats with their attendant boxes and a sprinkling of scows with cabins built on top, houseboat style.

Some gunners preferred to trek to the shootin' grounds in the old beach wagons, which, loaded with gear and supplies, would come creaking on their broad-tired wheels down the old dunes roads.

Frequent excursions back to town to ship ducks and take on supplies broke the monotony, if you could call it that, of gunning.

Very old hollow Broadbill, made at Tuckerton, N. J., by Harry Shores.

Redhead, male, made about 1865 by the late Captain Charles Parker of Parkertown, N. J.

Contemporary Blackduck covered with "painter's flock," to prevent shine. Made by John Updike, Green Bank, N. J.

Hollow wooden Blackduck, made about 1860-65 by the late Captain Charles Parker of Parkertown, N. J.

Red-breasted Merganser, female, hollow, made before the Civil War by Harry Shores of Tuckerton, N. J.

Red-breasted Merganser, hollow, made before the Civil War by Harry Shores of Tuckerton, N. J.

Goldeneye, male, hollow, made before the
Civil War by Harry Shores of
Tuckerton, N. J.

Goldeneye, female, hollow, made before the
Civil War by Harry Shores of Tuckerton, N. J.

American Merganser, from Barnegat Bay. A
fine example, maker unknown.

Canada Goose, from Barnegat Bay, N. J.
Made in 1900.

Canada Goose, maker unknown, from the
coast of New Jersey. Obviously very old.

Canada Goose, from Barnegat Bay, N. J.
Made in 1890.

They tell a story around these parts of one of these old-time baymen named Howard and his son Samuel.

Howard was sitting near the stove in the old Squan House with several of his cronies one morning when young Samuel stepped in.

"Samuel," said his father, "looks like it's makin' for a no'theaster, so I and Jim here are agoin' to gun the pond on the upper marsh tomorrow. Now my gun is down in the cabin of the *Nancy,* tied up to the bank in the beach channel near those old cedars just this side of Nor'west Point, and I want you to go and fetch it. You'll find the key to the cabin door in the cockpit."

Samuel, being a dutiful son, started off, knowing full well he had twelve miles of marsh and dune to cover with the weather makin'. Late that evening, Samuel arrived back at the Squan House and found his father in his accustomed seat by the stove. As the boy brushed off the snow, the old man asked, "Got my gun, Samuel?"

"No," said Samuel. "I couldn't find the key to the cabin door."

"Humph," said old Howard. "Did you look in the cockpit?"

"Yes," said Samuel, "but all I saw there was a hatchet."

"That, my boy," said his father, "is the key." And, turning to his cronies, he sighed, "I'm afeerd that boy will never larn nothin'."

Mention of the Squan House, a pleasant old inn that has recently, and lamentably, been pulled down, brings to mind the many taverns and hostelries scattered through the bay area which were gathering places for visiting and local wildfowlers. Some of the most memorable, such as the previously mentioned Chadwick, are gone now, while others are but shadows of their former glory. There are even sad cases of chromium fittings and juke boxes invading the once mellow retreats of thirsty gunners. A few, however, still carry on in the old tradition, little changed by the passing years.

The old names must awaken fond memories in many a sportsman: the Ocean House at Toms River, Eno's at Forked River, the Sunset Hotel in back of the Barnegat lighthouse at Barnegat City, the Harvey House at

Harvey Cedars, the Tuckerton House at Tuckerton—these are but a few of the many oases linked to the past and present of gunning on Barnegat Bay.

Perhaps the writer has dwelt too glowingly on the past, and too gloomily on the present. Certainly Barnegat will be a concentration point as long as ducks fly, so here's hoping that our children and our children's children may continue to enjoy this grandest of sports on its historic shores and waters.

I X

Chesapeake Bay

BY J. KEMP BARTLETT, JR.

SWEPSON EARLE, in the preface to THE CHESAPEAKE BAY COUNTRY, tells us that the shoreline of this great bay covers between four and five thousand miles. He quotes Captain Charles W. Wright in his pamphlet on Chesapeake Bay, *The Mother of Waters,* as saying that "from the capes to the head of the bay is one hundred and seventy nautical (one hundred and ninety-five statute) miles." Flowing into the "Mother of Waters" are forty-eight tributaries which combined have one hundred and two sub-tributaries, called branches, ranging from two to fifty miles in length. The combined length of the navigable waters comprising the bay, its tributaries and branches, is over one thousand, seven hundred and fifty statute miles.

Beyond these navigable waters lie marshes, leads, guts, ponds and sloughs, rich in wild rice, oats and pondweeds. Viewed from the air this vast stretch of water, reaching its rivers and streams back into the low flatland, looks like one vast green and blue pattern of lacy, lush wetness. What wonder that waterfowl, after winging across prairies, plateaus and mountains, glide with arched wings down to the welcoming surface of this vast winter resting place!

113

One frosty morning in late November I hunted with my "Jim dog" over the high corn and stubble fields of *My Lady's Manor,* in Baltimore County. All that day flock after flock of swan, evenly spaced, threaded their way south. Each wedge-shaped line followed the same course at the same high level. As they came to a point in the sky where they could look down on the upper reaches of the Gunpowder and Bush Rivers, with the broad stretch of the bay beyond, they seemed to fly with a new life, calling from flock to flock. It was a joy to behold their eagerness to reach their journey's end.

On another November day in another year I was in a blind on Boxes Point. The ducks were there and the shooting was good, but we missed the swan and wondered if they were not about due to arrive. About noon they came, at first long white lines of them, high in the north, coasting over the center of the Chester River and gliding down to the broad open water off Ringolds Point and the flats out toward the bay. As they landed, they seemed to break up into separate families—Mr. and Mrs. with their two or three blue-necked, high-voiced babies, and the sleek white yearlings following. The greeting and welcome they yelped back and forth to each other was wonderful to hear. They seemed to be exchanging gossip and telling their experiences of the trip, as well as showing their offspring the local landmarks and waterways. I was glad I was there and wished I knew whence they came, what cities and valleys they had looked down upon, what courses they had followed and what experiences they had been through.

The ducks, of course, come first. Wood Ducks—"Summer Ducks," father used to call them fifty years ago when he would row me up a cove back of grandfather's Talbot County home to try for a shot at one flying over the treetops to the river—are with us in small numbers the year around. While trout fishing in May last year in the Green Spring Valley, I actually saw a female Wood Duck light in a tree about fifty yards from the stream, awkwardly waddle down a limb and pop into a hole in the tree that I had once taken a coon out of several winters before.

We used to shoot Wood Ducks in September and there was a branch of brackish water running into the Choptank River where, if you carried a canoe across several fields and through the woods, you could paddle through the docks and sunflowers at high tide and knock over one or two as they jumped out of the low marsh. The trip was a long and slow one in a horse-drawn cart and we had to spend the night in a barn, sleeping on dried corn blades, which cracked and crunched throughout the night as we sank lower and lower through them toward the barn floor. I recommend it only for a fourteen-year-old boy or a fly tier who really needs a drake Wood Duck skin for his favorite trout flies.

The Blackducks stay with us also the year around nowadays—not the big orange-leg fellows that come in the fall, but still it is nice to have them around flying over the marshes at sunset and cruising by the lawn in the morning with their broods of olive down.

Early in September the Teal are here. They are around the marshy islands at the head of the bay, for all the world like flocks of pigeons. We see them too while shooting Rail on the Patuxent marshes. Except for an occasional shot in the early days of November, we never get a chance at them now, but in the first decade of this century they made great sport on the flats. We used to have a stool of blue-wing decoys and we would set them out at the edge of an island covered with reeds, into which we would shove the boat. I remember the flocks rising and twisting as they came around the shore, flashing white in the sun as they wheeled, and then gray as they swung toward the decoys. I cannot seem to remember ever shooting many, but I know I missed them time and time again. About five years ago I purchased a 410 pump gun and to test it I took it to the blind with me one day. A small duck came booming across the river and over the edge of the decoys. The little new gun folded him up, and when Nelson Cully, the guide, brought in the beautiful green-wing drake, he said, "That's a cute little duck and a cute little gun."

The rank and file of our ducks—indeed, the squadrons and battalions of them—begin to arrive in early October and keep coming until about the middle of November. We believe that the cold weather in Canada starts them on their way to us and we know that when the first freeze comes to the upper bay the "good ducks" start coming down to the Eastern Shore points.

A few Baldpates and Sprigtails herald each new season. We welcome the first Blue Peters, for we believe they hold the ducks on our shore. Then comes the build-up. Each morning the concourse seems to grow, and word spreads to the club members. The duffle bag is taken out of the attic, the shells are looked over and the boots are brought from the closet. In a few days all are piled in the front hall. Then comes the day when the back of the car is filled, the office is closed and we are off to the shore.

In a locality so long famous for its duck shooting one would expect to find that many of the points, bars, rivers or marshes would bear names that identified them with wildfowl or gunning. The fact is, there are few of such names. Swan Point is, of course, obvious, and swan still congregate there in numbers that resemble surf from a distance, but it is more of a fisherman's mecca than a gunner's. Hunting Creek, in Talbot County, suggests it was once a favorite shooting ground, but that must have been long ago, for it would be hard to visualize many good blind locations there now. Then there is that delightful little lagoon on the Western Shore, south of Sandy Point, that bears the charming name of Goose Pond.

A story of a night shot that was taken there many years ago was told to me by Judge Moss, whose ancestors lived at White Hall, on the shores of which estate Goose Pond borders. One evening, a hundred or more years ago, the geese were congregating there and making such noise as to be heard by the guests in the Manor House. Old Mr. Moss loaded his gun and, going out through the kitchen, called to a slave dozing behind the stove to follow him. They crossed the fields and crawled through the sedge grass to the very edge of Goose Pond. The geese were there, all right. Mr. Moss lined up his sights and took a shot. With a great roar of wings and frantic honking they flew out over the bay, but nine fat geese floated on the surface of the lagoon.

Out into the icy water went the darky, and retrieved the game, but while bringing back the last one Mr. Moss noticed that he was groping around

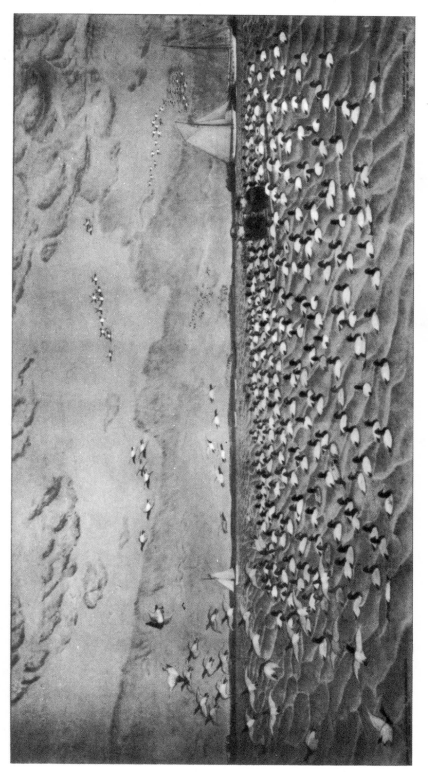

Canvasback on the Susquehanna. From an old print.

Single battery on Chesapeake Bay.

Double battery at sunrise on the Chesapeake.

in the water and mud with his hand as if hunting for some elusive object. Upon being asked what he was looking for he explained that he had put on the cook's wooden sandals when leaving the kitchen, and one had come off in the mud and could not be found.

"There," said Mr. Moss, "you have ruined the whole profit of the shot."

The early settlers seem, for the most part, to have accepted the Indian names—Susquehanna, Patuxent, Choptank, Potomac, Patapsco, or to have brought their names from England with them—Ringolds Point, Wickes Beach, Gray's Inn Creek, Chester River, Wye, Tred Avon. Then there are, of course, the familiar old American names—Beaver Dam, Elk River, Turkey Point, Cedar Point, Calf Pasture Creek, Still Pond, and so on.

All these names still identify blinds and points where Marylanders have for generations enjoyed wonderful duck shooting. New names come and go. Some places become well known for a while and then seem to die out, often because some storm covers the celery beds with sand or a freeze at extreme low tide kills the celery and widgeon grass roots. The city of Baltimore has encroached upon Back River, Spring Gardens and Reed Bird Island.

When a group of men purchase or lease a farm on the bay shore for a ducking club, they are often put to it to name the various blinds they intend to construct. It is remarkable to contemplate how difficult it is for several men to talk with their guides about the building of blinds on a shore three or four miles long when one cannot identify a particular spot with a name. A very successful blind in a rounded belly of the shore, where subsequently many limits of Pintail and Baldpate were shot, started out as "that clump of sedgegrass where we stood this morning between that long point in the third field and the north line of Mrs. Wood's farm." This name soon became shortened to "Mrs. Wood's belly."

A blind simply and unimaginatively named No. 7 has for years been a place where we have consistently shot our limit of Redheads. Then too, there is a blind which was built of driftwood that came ashore after a summer storm. Our guide showed it to us with pride, stating that all it cost to build was fifteen cents' worth of nails. Ever since it has been known as "The Fifteen-center."

To a Maryland duck shooter "The Flats" mean that wide expanse of water at the head of the bay, where for centuries the Susquehanna River has rolled down and deposited the sand and silt from its two great branches. The flats are a broad expanse of under-water delta extending from Perry Point and the North East River on the north to Swan Creek, Spesutic Island and Turkey Point on the south. The river channel divides them into east and west parts. To the north, reedy islands show above the surface of the water, which there has a depth of a few feet, increasing toward the south until the lower end is reached, at which point the water is more than nine feet deep and where the big, rollicking, long-necked, red-headed Canvasback congregate.

Interlaced all through the flats are ditches, which are natural channels about a hundred feet wide, deeper than the flats and softer. In these ditches the wild celery grows in greatest profusion. The Susquehanna Flats are roughly fifteen miles square. There for generations the duck shooting has been superb and the celery-fed Canvasback taken there have spread the fame and name of the Chesapeake and of the graciousness of Maryland living.

In my boyhood days the flats were heaven on earth to me. In partnership with three other gentlemen, my father owned a rig on the flats and at the age of eleven I was introduced to duck shooting from a sinkbox. There are various kinds of batteries and sinkboxes, but in Maryland they have always, as far as I know, been of one kind—a coffin-like box with a small oblong deck and hinged wings. The wings, for lightness, are made of slats and are covered with canvas. The whole is painted a dull, water-like gray.

When empty, the box floats about six inches above the water, but this is corrected with sections of cast-iron about an inch thick, which cover the floor of the box, and about ten iron decoys, which are placed on the deck. Then, when the gunner lies in the box, the whole is so flush with the water that small waves run over the deck and are only partially kept from running into the box by a double row of lead strips, three inches wide, nailed along one edge so that they can be bent up to break the waves. There is no doubt that a sinkbox is wet and cold. A bailer is a very necessary part of the equipment.

The sinkbox is moored with two anchors, a large one at the head and a smaller one at the foot, to keep it from swinging with the wind. Then the decoys, about three hundred of them, are set out, thick around the box, to help hide it, and thinner off to the sides and down wind from the foot. Often it was good practice to set a line of long-necked decoys off down wind to look like swimming ducks and act as tollers.

Besides the sinkbox and the decoys, the rig consisted of a large flat-bottom sailboat, upon which the gunners sailed out from Havre de Grace the afternoon before the shooting day, and which acted as the mother ship for the whole outfit. Usually, two large dory-like rowboats were towed. These rowboats were always painted white, had high bows and sides with a sloping, straight stern which was pierced with a three-inch hole through which the scull oar could be placed when bushwhacking.

Each rig had a captain, a cook and two or three men who acted as the crew. The old-time Susquehanna Flats' boats were large scows with leeboards and a schooner sail and jib. In later years, these were replaced with sharpies and "dead rises" with centerboard and leg-o'-mutton sails.

The wind, always important in duck shooting, was doubly so when one had to sail out to the shooting grounds, spend the night there, shoot the next day and then sail back to take the train for home. We often saw the last train for Baltimore cross the Pennsylvania Railroad bridge while we were yet miles away from the landing place. Mother never could tell when we would be home, once we started to go shooting. Also, no clients could ever reach father, even for the most important case. All of which made no difference to me in those days, as long as I was on the flats.

In case the wind gave out, as it frequently did, there were two twenty-foot poles aboard which we used to pole the boat back to port. A man would work on each side. Starting at the bow, he would place the pole over the side till it struck bottom. Then, pushing against it, walk back to the stern. Then he would carry the pole forward to the bow and start all over again. I once heard Uncle "Charley" Moore say, "I don't mind walking from Turkey Point to Havre de Grace [a distance of about fifteen miles] but I hate like hell to carry a pole."

In the early days the professionals, the market gunners, captains of rigs, would hold a meeting and decide upon the day for the start of the ducking season as well as the days for shooting each week—usually Mondays, Wednesdays and Fridays. Later these things were regulated by law and a State Police boat enforced them. But my observance has been that the rules that the captains made were lived up to better than those made by the legislature.

When the motor boats came, the sailboats disappeared. With them went much of the romance of sinkbox shooting, and a great deal of the hardship and uncertainty which to many of us added to the joy of the sport.

We would take the train from Union Station to Havre de Grace in the early afternoon. In those days all trains stopped at both Havre de Grace and Perryville, because of some old law that had to do with the license to build the railroad bridge and discontinue the ferry. At the station we were met by Jim and his one-horse hack, who would drive us to the landing, and give us, on the way, the local gossip about ducks and last week's shooting. At the landing there was a shop or two where the decoys were stored in the summer and painted each fall. Extra equipment and fishnets were stored there too.

Out in the stream was the *Jenny F. Moore,* a sharpie of about fifteen tons, that recently had been built to succeed the old scow *Susquehanna,* which was then rotting alongside in the marshes. A hail would bring Captain Harry O. Moore ashore for us. Captain Harry was my dearest friend. A contemporary of my father's, he was father, instructor and playmate to me. His father and grandfather had been gunners before him and he and his brothers, Captain Will Moore and "Uncle Charley," had come by their duck shooting naturally and with a pride and joy in their work that made

At the end of the day, Chesapeake Bay.

The author as a boy.

Captain Harry O. Moore.

Very old Buffle-head male, made of solid wood. From an old "rig" at Oxford, Md.

Canvasback drake of cast-iron, for the frame of a battery, to hold the same flush with the surface of the water. Made about 1890. From North East, Md.

Canvasback female of cast-iron. A so-called "battery wing duck," made to hold the frame of the battery flush with the surface of the water. Made in 1890. From Havre de Grace, Md.

the life of a professional gunner seem to me to be a thing most devoutly to be desired.

Captain and Mrs. Moore were good enough to come to my wedding in Philadelphia and, twenty-five years later, to my daughter's wedding in Baltimore. I had many, many happy days with him. His home in Havre de Grace was a second home to me. He taught me to sail and shoot. He showed me how to handle and care for a gun, but, greatest of all, he gave me comradeship. One of my cherished recollections is a call I made upon him in his home a few weeks before he died.

He was eighty years old and quite ill at the time, and yet, a few days before, he had sculled a bushwhacking boat all day on the flats. Mrs. Moore was taking him to task for having done that. He argued that it was necessary because "the younger men don't know how." He turned to me and said, "Kemp, she says I have to give up shooting, but I love it."

Aboard the *Jenny* there was warmth in the cabin thrown off by a small iron stove and several coal-oil lamps. A musty smell from the clothes (drying from the last trip), and from the carpet so close to the bilge, was not unpleasant because it was so closely associated with the shooting trip. Over the bunks, which were built in under the deck, hung the guns on brass racks, and such guns as they were! Big, heavy, ten-gauge doubles, with their thirty-two-inch full choke Damascus barrels and heavy locks, cleaned and polished so many times that they were the color of old, much-used silver, their walnut stocks black from weather and gun oil. Shells were often drying under the stove, for if there was any wind at all enough water would come into the sinkbox to drench everything there. We kept the shells in little cooking kettles, but even then they would get wet and swell so that a gadget to pull the empty case out of the barrels was often needed and was always kept with the shells in the kettle.

As supper was eaten, the crew put up the sail and hauled up the anchor and we were under way. The captain would watch the ducks the day before and frequently consult the barometer. If tomorrow promised to be calm and the ducks were ganging up on the "lower end," we would head for there. But if there was to be a north wind, we had better get in the lee of the islands and shallow water. Picking the right spot was a gamble, and the captain, who was most successful in doing so, could take just pride from the fact that the others watched him and followed him. Often, in the dead of night, Captain Moore had his crew silently take up the anchor and steal away from the fleet that had assembled around his boat, to the place he had intended to go all along.

As soon as we sailed on the flats all lights were extinguished and little curtains were drawn across the cabin windows. This was done for two reasons—first, no one could follow us and, second, it was thought that lights disturbed the ducks. Out over the water all was darkness. The red beam of the lighthouse at Havre de Grace was behind, and off to the starboard shone the white light on "The Battery." But what told us our position most accurately was the pole that showed the depth of the water and the hardness or softness of the bottom. Then, too, you could look along the pole and get a sight on a light on one shore and a hill on the other. When these two points were in line we sailed along that line until two other points lined up. Then the pole probed around for the center of the ditch and the anchor went down in the very spot where the ducks had been seen to be feeding the evening before. In fact, you could often hear them off in the darkness, making that roaring noise of many waterfowl feeding.

Long before daybreak we were awakened by the smell of bacon and coffee cooking in the galley forward where the crew were having their breakfast. Then the sinkbox was lifted from where it had been resting over the hatch and put overboard. The dories were brought alongside and filled with decoys, and soon all were taken off into the darkness while the gunners finished their breakfast. What a welcome sound it was to hear the dory bump alongside the boat and the captain call for the first two hunters to come! A short row brought us to the box out there where a lantern in it marked its location.

A quick light step on the deck of the box, then down to the foot so that your partner could follow without swamping the slippery, bobbing float.

Next, the guns and shells were passed in, sheepskins to lie on, and the lantern was handed out. Soon one could hear the sail going up and then the anchor, as the boat sailed off to a spot, about a mile away, from which the day's sport could be watched.

A few minutes sufficed to get settled, pull up or push down the leads as the waves demanded, move a few iron decoys for better vision, load the guns and lie down. From that position you looked directly up into the sky and the fading stars. Off to the east the day was breaking and along the water a few close decoys loomed large, while the others appeared as a thick dark line.

Usually, the first ducks came out of the dark—a rush of wings with a few blurred silhouettes. Sometimes a splash was the only announcement of the first arrival. In the days of black powder it was a wonderful sight to see the sharp, straight tongues of fire leap from the guns.

As it became lighter, the incoming flocks could be seen from a distance flying close to the water, a final rise and then a swing with set wings as they sailed over the decoys. It was very different from blind or point shooting. The ducks were usually much closer to you and they certainly seemed to be going faster. Lying flat on your back and watching them come in made them look large and slow. When you sat up and lifted your gun they looked smaller and faster.

"As long as their heads are pointed toward you, let them keep coming," was one of the first and best lessons Captain Harry taught me. The next was "Shoot in front of them, boy." What shots they used to make for us! How many points are there to a compass? Well, you had that many angles to figure out, plus the ups and downs and the circles, all the time allowing for the bobbing of the sinkbox.

Coming in from the left or crossing to the left gave you an opportunity to swing with them, but that same shot on the right-hand side was something else again. Captain Moore never missed that one. He showed me how to do it. "Pick up your gun with your left hand, put your right hand on the deck, throw out your feet and pivot on your tail." When I finally mastered that maneuver and could double-up a pair of Canvasbacks high-balling out of there over my right shoulder, I felt that I really had arrived.

You counted your dead ducks and watched the line of drift. It was pretty clear with the empty shells bobbing along, the wads and the white bellies floating. When you figured the first had drifted far enough, a signal was made to the boat, the dory put out and, working up the line of drift, they retrieved the ducks, brought out the relief and took you back to the boat. An hour or two was enough for most people, but Captain Harry and I have often spent the entire day at it.

Some days were good, very good, marvelous, with flights of from eight to twenty Canvasbacks all day long following each other in rapid succession. Other days were perfect duds. It would blow too hard to set out. A freeze would come on a calm night and a skim of ice would cover the flats with no ducks in sight. On some occasions the wind coming up with the dawn would "over blow" us in an hour or so and we would have to take up. On other days the ducks just didn't fly. But, for the most part, we got good shooting and modest bags. The good days were remembered and talked about, the poor days were soon forgotten. There were no limits in those days but, on the average, I think that we brought home about as many ducks as we do now—not many more, often less.

The old-timers, the market gunners, who loaded their muzzle-loaders by hand (no mean job in a sinkbox) wanted each shot to tell. They not only waited for the ducks to get close, they waited for them to cross and in that way frequently shot two with one barrel. A gang shot was seldom possible, but sometimes the Redheads would knot up as they swung over the decoys and then it was possible to cut a path through them with each barrel. The really good shots seldom missed getting a duck with each barrel and they developed the practice of taking two guns into the sinkbox with them. When bunches of ten or twelve came in they would let the first few alight, then, quickly going into action, they would cut down two ducks still in the air, put down the gun, pick up the other and get two more as they got out of the water. This was a difficult shot because it had to be done quickly and the

CANVASBACK

timing on each shot was so different. Then too, the guns were never matched pairs and were often different gauges.

Market gunners were respected citizens. They were men of affairs who knew their ducks as a Gloucester fisherman knew his cod. They were excellent shots and they never bragged about their shooting. They lived hard lives, but they thoroughly enjoyed their shooting. I have seen them make some remarkable shots, shots that still live in my memory. Once Captain Harry sculled me down on a drake Canvasback that had lit in the decoys and as our boat entered the stool the duck got up about fifty yards off. I fired twice and missed both times. Captain Harry stood up in the boat behind me. The duck was so far off that it seemed foolish to shoot but he folded him up as if the distance were not over twenty yards.

I watched a market gunner row down on the windward side of a sandbar. Ducks and geese were resting in the lee of the other side. As his boat touched the shore the wildfowl arose. He killed a Goose with his first barrel, a Blackduck with his second and then, reloading, shot two more Blackducks that looked to be on the extreme edge of effective range.

Bushwhacking was more or less of a sideline in the days of the sinkbox, but now that the latter has been banned bushwhacking is coming again into its own. A large stool of decoys is set out in the open water, then the boat, always painted white, is rowed up wind about a half mile. There it is anchored from the stern and the anchor is buoyed. White curtains about eight inches high are rigged around the bow. The gunners wear white coats and caps. When ducks are seen to light in the decoys the mooring is slipped, a long scull oar is placed through a round hole in the stern and with the gunners crouching in the bow the boat is rapidly sculled down wind to the decoys.

The live ducks usually swim to the far end of the decoys but for the most part they don't start to fly away until the boat starts bumping among the wooden blocks. Of course, they have to take off up wind, which brings them toward you for a few seconds. Usually they are a fair gunshot away when they start, so one has to shoot quickly and from a very uncomfortable kneeling position in a moving, bouncing boat. It is hard shooting and often very cold, but it is exciting and some good bags are made that way. Canvasbacks and Redheads "sit well" in the decoys. Sometimes Blackheads will too, but often they fly out before the boat gets into gunshot.

The flats are primarily a place for diving ducks—Canvasbacks, Redheads and Blackheads. "Good ducks," they are called there. Good they really are after a few weeks of feeding on the wild celery roots. That is why the Chesapeake Bay Canvasbacks have become nearly world famous. The Chinese Ambassador, many years ago, was fêted at the Maryland Club and the dinner menu included diamondback terrapin and Canvasback duck. When he was introduced he started his remarks with this statement: "Gentlemen, when you come to my country we cannot give you Canvasback duck nor Diamondback Turtles, but we can give you shark's fin and bird's-nest soup." I have never talked with anyone who has tried that combination, so can express no opinion as to the relative merits. But having been mentioned in the same breath with Canvasbacks, I would be willing to risk the bird's-nest soup.

The market gunners hung their ducks, pending sale, in their "shops" on the shore. They were always tied by the feet in pairs and hung from the ceiling in long rows. Captain Harry explained this to me: "It gives them a chance to drain and the insides fall away from the soft rears." There were buyers who had large storehouses and they were in touch with the city markets. Sometimes the market gunners sold their ducks direct to the clubs and hotels, shipping them in flour barrels. But for the most part they sold to the buyers who shipped them to market.

It was a familiar sight to see ducks hanging in the Baltimore markets and over the sidewalks on Camden Street in front of the stores of the commission merchants. The geese and swan were always picked except for the wings and neck. The ducks hung over the market stalls in Lexington and Richmond Markets and under them the terrapin would be displayed on their backs, slowly flapping their legs. It was a great treat to go to market with mother, and wander through the aisles and inspect the wildfowl, quail, rabbits and terrapin. Quail were $3.00 a dozen, Canvasbacks from $3.00 to $4.00 a pair, Redheads $2.00 and Blackheads $1.00. The old unshaven man with his gunning sack of terrapin and his string of Canvasbacks, standing on the corner of Calvert and Redwood Streets, was a familiar sight to Baltimoreans. A list of his customers would include the most prominent bankers and businessmen in Baltimore. At the Rennert Hotel:

Canvasback duck	$3.00
Redhead duck	2.50
Blackhead duck	1.50
Mallards	1.50

always appeared on the menu when they were in season. An order consisted of half a duck carved off the carcass, with the wing and leg attached, together with a large helping of hominy. If you asked for it the carcass would be put in a press and the juices and gravy poured over the hominy. Of course, oysters from Lynnhaven or Mobjack Bay would precede the meal, and a good heady claret or port wine would accompany it.

I don't believe the market gunners thrived financially. I knew a number of them. They lived in small houses and their valuable assets were their guns, boats and decoys. The boats and decoys were painted annually and constant repairs had to be made. I am very proud of a female Canvasback decoy that is part of my collection, which I know was used for eighty consecutive years by the Moore family on the flats. I often wonder how many coats of paint still remain on her and how many years she was painted as a drake and how often as a hen.

The business of shooting for the market was, of course, seasonable, and each season varied with the weather and the flight of ducks. Then, too, the market couldn't have been large, for most of the customers were also gunners, and the profits, if any, had to be divided between the buyer, the commission merchant and the market stall owner. The sight of ducks displayed in the market never tempted me to buy, but always tempted me to go shooting. Now that that temptation is removed each crisp fall morning takes its place and urges me to leave the city streets and head for the Shore.

Sinkboxes were at one time used on the Potomac, and as a boy I have seen one or two on the Eastern Shore. But they were outlawed there many years ago. Shore blinds and booby blinds are used almost exclusively for duck shooting on all parts of the Chesapeake Bay. In fact, now that the Federal law has prohibited the use of sinkboxes, booby blinds and floating blinds have appeared on the edges of the flats.

Blinds vary in construction from elaborate sunken ones, with nearly all the comforts of home, to a few bay bushes stuck in the edge of the marsh with a log behind them to sit on. Usually a blind is built on a point close to the edge of high tide. It is about nine or ten feet long and three feet wide. The front and sides are covered with sedge grass and bay bushes are stuck in front and at the corners to blend in with the shore. It should be as low and inconspicuous as possible and made to look like the rest of the shoreline. A bench for the gunners to sit on is essential and the rear wall should be higher than the occupants' heads so that they will be better hidden. A shelf on the inside of the front wall for shells and so forth is a great help.

If the water on the point is shallow, it is usually better to build the blind on stakes in about three feet of water and connect it to the shore with a run-way and a wall of bay bushes to tie it in with the point. A booby blind is simply one built on piles out in the open water. Behind such a blind it is necessary to have a hidden slip in which to hide the boat.

Blinds dot the shores of the Chesapeake Bay and its tributary rivers. Each fall they are repaired or renewed. Fresh sedge grass or wild-oat stalks are nailed on and new bay bushes are cut and stuck in around them. This work is usually done in late September before the first ducks come down. The best places for blinds are on the ends of long points or in small bays where the ducks feed. The boat for the decoys and for retrieving the ducks is hidden down the shore a piece. The decoys are placed in a string about ten yards wide and forty yards long in front of the blind.

There are many ways of setting out the stool of decoys. Almost every man has his pet theory about this. We like to have them strung out in an arc about a good gunshot from the blind. Often it is good practice to place two

Red-breasted Merganser, male, very old solid wood, from Hooper Island, Eastern Shore of Maryland.

Old Red-breasted Merganser ("Sawyer"), male, of solid wood from Hooper Island, Eastern Shore of Maryland. Date and maker unknown.

Canvasback drake. Made at North East, Md., about 1880 (probably by Captain Ben Dye).

Canvasback duck. Made by Captain Ben Dye, Havre de Grace, Md., in 1880. Specimen comes from a "rig" in North East, Md.

Canvasback female, made by Wm. Heverin at age 83; the oldest decoy maker on the Chesapeake. He lived at North East, Md.

Broadbill, female.

Broadbill.

Canvasback duck.

Canvasback drake.

Pintail duck.

Pintail drake.

CONTEMPORARY DECOYS MADE BY LEMUEL T. WARD, JR. OF CRISFIELD, MD.

or three goose decoys at each end of the string. They make the decoys show up better, and, who knows, sometimes a Goose will come too close. On some days it works well to set out about twelve Blackduck decoys in a bunch at one end of the string, on other days a few tollers way off down wind help.

That's all a part of the fun—trying out something new. They laugh at me when I wave a handkerchief or my hat at ducks flying past with no idea of coming close, but sometimes that makes them see the decoys and in they come. In a sinkbox we often would kick a foot up in the air and in that way attract ducks. Captain Moore said that the ducks thought it was other ducks lighting in the decoys. Maybe they did, for it really worked.

A great many of our gunners have developed into very good callers. We all try to make the same noises, but each sounds very different, and yet it brings the ducks. My theory is that a flock of ducks flying out over the water often don't see the decoys and any sound or movement that will not frighten them will attract their attention and cause them to see the stool.

A day in the blind is a delightful occasion. If there are ducks to be shot so much the better, but even a day in the open watching the bobbing decoys and the changing weather, with the good companionship of friends, is in itself a more than worth-while experience.

We are awakened in the black hour before dawn, dress before an open fire or red-hot iron stove throwing off the heat. We breakfast on hot coffee, eggs and buckwheat cakes; gather up guns, shells and dogs and trail off through the gray light and frosty air of breaking day, across the fields and over the marsh to the blinds. There, if we are members of a well-organized club, we find that the decoys have been set out by the guide and all is in readiness for us. If we are on our own and have merely rented the blind and are young and sturdy, we push the boat off from the shore, set out our decoys in the way that suits our individual fancy and retire to the blind, warm and exhilarated by our work.

As daylight comes the ducks move about, leave the big ricks in which they have spent the night and fly around in small bunches. The shooting is usually best in early morning and again late in the afternoon, though sometimes they seem to be on the move throughout the day. Of course, the weather and the wind have much to do with their flight. Only one thing is certain about duck shooting—you don't get it unless you go after it.

When I was a boy I used to believe that I got about one good day's shooting in five trips. The odds are better now, but that's because I know of better places to go and better times to choose for a trip to the shore. An experienced gunner will pay much attention to the weather reports and the barometer. The one I have in my living room is of more use to me than the one at the club. It helps to tell me when to go. When you are at the club, there you are, and you take the weather that comes, whether the barometer predicts it or not.

Don't get the idea that I believe that duck shooting can be reduced to a science. It can't. A day that is a good day for ducks often turns out to be an exceedingly poor one. As a rule, ducks don't fly much in falling weather, and yet there are exceptions. "Snap" and I shot our limit of Baldpates and Geese one day when the rain came down in torrents and you couldn't get one puff on a cigarette before it crumpled in your mouth. Dull days are sometimes good and at other times clear, sparkling, sunny days are the thing. I remember a cold, dull January day on the Potomac with Ralph Walter. There wasn't a breath of air and the river had a flat, glassy, gray sheen. The decoys were dark and still, only the tide made them seem to swim. All day long the Canvasbacks flew and decoyed, circling the decoys two or three times like express trains, but always coming close enough for a shot.

On another day—this one bright and sunny, with a fair west wind—my brother James and I struck the Canvasbacks at their prime on the Chester River. Flock after flock, each of about twenty, followed each other down the shore at regular spaced intervals. Each flock would decoy with a rush and a roar, one circle to the left showing their backs, the drakes flashing white in the sunshine and the hens showing brown and dark, a swing to the right when all the under parts were white as snow, then over the decoys with the red necks and heads gleaming like red-hot coals.

Ice can sometimes be good for the shooting and then again very bad. A sudden drop in the temperature on a still night will put a skim of ice on the water many yards from shore. On such a morning there will be many ducks in the air—great high strings of Canvasbacks and Redheads, good ducks from the upper bay where, because of the fresh water, the ice has frozen all over the flats and upper rivers. They are hungry and want to decoy. But ducks don't like to fly across ice and on most such occasions will not. We labor to cut long paths through the ice out to the open water and then push the ice fields out to make open water before the blind. Unless the tide helps often, the day is over before the ice is sufficiently cleared away. Sods cut from the marsh and placed on the edge of the ice will really bring the Black-ducks, but why this is so is one of the mysteries of duck shooting to me.

Some days that look the best for shooting turn out to be the worst and others that give no promise with the dawn bring the best shooting. After more than forty years of ducking, all the lore that I can really depend on is that for good shooting one needs wind, and that statement must be qualified by the fact that although it can on occasions blow too hard, much more often it doesn't blow hard enough.

As to decoys, when you remember that the cautious Blackduck will decoy readily to big square sods of marsh grass placed on the ice, it is easy to realize that almost any old wooden block decoy will often answer the purpose. Where we shoot we get a mixed bag and we use a mixed stool of decoys. We often mix Canvasbacks, Redheads and Blackhead decoys with a fair smattering of Baldpates, Sprigtails and Blackduck decoys, and they work to our satisfaction.

On the flats in the old days the saying was "A light stool in the winter and a dark stool in the spring." So in the first of the season drake Canvasback decoys predominated, and when March came these were picked out and replaced by Redheads and the stool really looked much darker. As a boy I gathered what decoys I could, made some with a hatchet and knife, painted them with what color paint was handy and did all right on Whiflers, Blackheads and such. I have shot over all kinds of decoys in all sorts of places and I can't recall that any worked remarkably better than others.

Of course, we all have our particular preferences. If you are going after a particular species of duck, use decoys of that kind and have them painted with a dull flat paint, not a glossy one. Most important of all, however, is to have them large enough and sturdily built. They get rough usage banging in and out of the boat, hauled to the shore and back again, stepped on, frozen in the ice and generally thrown around, so have them tough!

I have amused myself by making a collection of decoys, gathering them up in the various states that I have visited and they range from the crudest handmade things, through the commercial factory-produced ones, on to perfect masterpieces carved and painted by artists with every feather accurately painted in its proper iridescent color. The most surprising thing of all is that each will bring in the ducks.

X

Eastern Shore of Virginia

BY RICHARD L. PARKS

U. S. ROUTE 13 splits the Delmarva Peninsula like a broad, concrete cleaver. Through Delaware and a narrow corner of eastern Maryland it strikes the Eastern Shore of Virginia to bisect the fertile farming counties of Accomac and Northampton and run into the broad Chesapeake Bay at the little terminal town of Cape Charles, whence one takes a ferry to Norfolk, Old Point Comfort and all points south.

Rolling down the highway through the two counties, one sees flat, well-kept, heavily cultivated fields given mainly to corn, potatoes, tomatoes and beans. Fringing the fields are pine groves—alas, sadly depleted by the "emergency"—and thickets of honeysuckle, pine and oak. Every five miles or so there is a little town—usually with a quaint name like Accomac, Nassawadox, Machipongo or Cheriton—from the friendly Red Men who once hunted deer, turkey and "varmints" (including wolves) there.

It looks like good quail, rabbit and squirrel country—and is. But it is difficult to picture duck shooting, for there are no rivers, or even a glimpse of the beautiful Chesapeake Bay to the west—dancing, dazzling blue on white sand in summer; green, foam-flecked menace in winter gales—or of the vast expanse of salt marsh and its labyrinth of channels and islands to the east, flimsy barrier to the mighty Atlantic just beyond. Yet, at few points deep salt water is hardly a scant six miles from the main highway.

The "Shore" grew up long before the Pennsylvania (then the New York, Pennsylvania and Norfolk) Railroad and U.S. 13 drove their parallel wedges down its center. It was soon after Captain John Smith of Pocahontas fame sailed over from Jamestown on an exploring trip, stepped on a stingray, and fled post haste to England to recuperate, that the first settlers began to arrive here. They came in sailing ships, of course, and brought their families, household goods, and tools. Also they brought bonded servants to fell the virgin pine and oak and gum, build their homes, and work the thousand-acre land grant so generously bestowed by His Majesty the King—no doubt a pioneer in rehabilitation programs.

So it is along the water that the beautiful (sometimes decrepit) old colonial homes and remnants of once-proud plantations hide shyly from traffic behind their hedge and boxbush, content, genteelly, to rot and be eaten by termites or suffer the fate of renovation by Yankees with well-lined billfolds and a yen for a mild climate—the Gulf Stream is only forty miles east—fertile soil, deep anchorage, lovely view and really fine hunting and salt-water fishing.

It is a neighborly country and the pace of living is moderate. Big industry has not yet reared its ugly head and the folks take time to live. There is no real poverty and no case of starvation on record. The people take pride in their ancestry, paying their debts and keeping out of jail and there are few "foreigners." Even the Negroes are mostly descended from the slaves that tilled the old plantations and often bear the old family names.

Starting at Saxis Island, just south of the Maryland line, the Bayside runs some seventy-odd miles as the crow is supposed to fly (but seldom does) south to Kiptopeke—mere sandspit bravely struggling to hold its own between choppy—often decidedly rough—bay and the mighty, surging Atlantic—like a referee at a wrestling match. Within that airline seventy miles, along the bay, lie about eighteen large salt water creeks and many smaller ones. Time was—not long past—when these creeks furnished wonderful goose and duck shooting, though comparatively few spots on the Bayside have ever become widely known to outside sportsmen. Their main claim to fame has been the succulent seafood they produce in abundance—Cherrystone Creek clams and Old Plantation oysters, for instance. And then there are Messongo, Chescommessex, Onancock, Pungoteague, Occohannock, Hungars and Mattawomman, to name a few. Except in size and some variation in shape they are almost identical. Narrow mouths fringed by sandbars and small sandy islets—often bearing a few tall, lonely pines—emerging into broad, landlocked harbors running back into the peninsula two or three miles, often a mile or two wide.

The shores of the main creeks are sandy and there is little slope and seldom even a fringe of marsh grass. Farther inland they branch out into innumerable little "guts" and "dreans" where the bottom is muddy, the marsh grass dense, and little fresh water springs drain out of the "branches" —Midwesterners would call these "cricks." It is here that the wily Blackduck lurks in winter and often lingers to raise a brood the following spring. In the main creeks the ducks consist almost entirely of diving species. Once they fairly swarmed with Canvasback, Redhead, Scaup, Blackduck, Canada Geese, Brant and Swan. But with the eelgrass went the ducks and, though there is still fair shooting to be had, they no longer will stand the pressure of heavy, continuous attack.

The mouths of most of the creeks are quite narrow, and pass shooting at daylight and dusk, when the fowl fly in and out of the creeks and usually take a short cut overland, has served to discourage the more optimistic ones that do venture in. The seafood industry and its boats keep restless and wild even the comparatively few Geese, Scaup, Goldeneye and Mergansers that still come in.

Between the creeks—seldom more than two miles apart—lie necks of land, divided into farms of a hundred acres or so. Nestled in the pines, just inside the sandy shore of the bay, lie many shallow, small ponds of fresh water. When it is rough and the nor'westers howl, the Blackducks and even

Pintails pile into these ponds for refuge. On them at all times usually can be found a few Wood Duck, hooded Mergansers (hairy-heads) and an occasional "gray" Mallard. The ponds would be a duck paradise with the addition of some of the bountiful corn crops growing all around.

Even now fine shooting often is to be had out in the bay itself. About a half mile offshore run sandbars where the Geese and Brant are wont to raft. In the sloughs between bars feed the Goldeneye (Whistlers), Scaup (Broadbill, Bluebill or Flock Duck) and innumerable Scoters, Mergansers and Coots, to mention a few. There are always surprises, when almost any species may wander in and alight in the stool—Redheads, "Cans," Teal, Widgeon, and other varieties—obviously lost and off their range. But the sport has so declined with the passing of the eelgrass, about 1932 (praise Allah!—it shows some promise of coming back!), that one now seldom sees a blind stuck out in the bay or a pit for Geese on a high bar.

With the subsequent restrictions on baiting came a big reduction in the number of souls foolhardy enough to take the beating necessary to shoot ducks in the bay. With no way to localize the fowl, they now range far and wide to pick up their daily bread. Food habits of the ducks, especially the Geese (which now go inland to graze on rye fields), have changed alarmingly. Quite often the fowl you do bag are poor as Job's turkey, especially Brant—once a prized table delicacy, now scarcely edible.

While there used to be some market hunting on the Bayside, it was nothing compared to that on the Seaside, about which more anon. A few commercial duck clubs have flickered and died but shooting on the Seaside was so much better and easier than on the bay that only a few with some complex that made them love the wild, roaring, open water of the Chesapeake and the constant battle against nature, kept them at it. With the decline of market hunting and advent of duck trapping, the Blackducks in the creeks were sadly depleted, but these went to local markets under cover.

Fortunately, the farmers and other landowners hemming in the creeks frowned upon this practice and it soon died a natural death. At present there are a very few private clubs that shoot on the Bayside, and most of

A bayside frame blind made of cedars.

A "drean" or gut through the inner marsh.

A view of the author's ducking rig hauled out in wooded creek.

At low tide the mud is so soft a boat can be rowed on it.

Goose on nest with gander on guard.

Mallard drakes and ducks.

these consist of local men who merely get together for a week or so of their favorite sport each season, and, when the ducks don't stool, while away the hours playing poker and bending elbows—time-honored pastime of duck hunters.

Blinds on the Bayside always have been somewhat more elaborate and carefully built than on the Seaside and the boats were more seaworthy, for they had to stand up against rough water, high winds and strong tides. Before the laws became so stringent, floating blinds were highly favored. All summer long, duck hunters watched carefully for a telephone pole to blow down or become the victim of some careless motorist, then begged or "borrowed" it from the company. Split into halves, these cypress or white cedar poles made ideal pontoons for the blind. Holes were bored into the half logs about a foot apart and sharpened cedars or pines about three feet high stuck in. Slats were nailed crosswise on the under side, upon which the boat could be pulled inside the blind by merely stepping down on the sides. Then the affair was launched, towed to a favorite spot and anchored with an old auto engine.

They were highly efficient, for they remained at convenient shooting height regardless of tide and, with boat pulled up on the slats, furnished a pretty stable place from which to shoot, even in rough water. Besides which, they could be moved and had the further advantage of pointing ever into the wind.

Another type of blind formerly used extensively in the bay (now rarely seen) was the "house" type. In simple form, these blinds consist of six posts pumped into the bottom to a goodly depth, slats nailed around, and cedars jammed between the slats. There is a "cellar" for the boat and above, usually in front, an enclosed platform for the shooters.

Often this platform is partially roofed and protected against driving rain, snow and bitter cold by a swinging curtain. Some even have stoves, magazines and all the comforts of home. Naturally, the whole affair has to be built high enough for the boat to go under at high tide—so when the tide is low the thing resembles a skyscraper. Yet it is unbelievable how, in the old days, the ducks came in to these towers of Babel. When baited with corn, even the shrewd old Blackies would stool to them on most days. But then, as one old waterman once remarked, "Yer kin bait a Blackduck up a concrete road."

As for the Scaup, they came in droves and clouds to gobble hungrily by the bushel the corn dumped around the inevitable stake. All the old-timers believe no self-respecting Broadbill will come in to a blind without a stake stuck off about twenty yards—usually a small ash or gum sapling. Probably this belief has some justification, since the favorite feeding ground of the diving ducks is the oyster "rocks" and these are usually marked by stakes of this kind. There is no understanding the Scaup anyhow, for at times they can be the wariest of ducks—while at other times I have seen hunters stand up in the blind and shoot until their guns were hot and still the fool ducks came, wheeling again and again over the stool, two or three dropping out each time.

But the blind used most in the bay and creeks is a simple affair consisting of six poles sunk in the sand or mud, slats nailed around and bushes jammed between the slats. These, of course, have the disadvantage of being too high for good shooting at low tide and too low for suitable cover when the tide is full. With the wind whistling through the cedars without a break between Baltimore and the blind and the waves raising the boat three feet at a time and letting it drop with a sickening thud, one can form a good mental picture of the "comforts" enjoyed by one hunting these blinds and the enthusiasm it takes to venture forth into one.

Occasionally some optimistic soul has attempted to use a sinkbox or battery in the bay—with decidedly discouraging results. Outside of the help and equipment necessary, the bay is far too rough in good ducking weather to lie down in one of these contraptions and be doused by sheets of icy brine. Years ago a few stake blinds—three posts and a box built on top—were used with some success for goose hunting on sandbars, but they are practically never seen nowadays.

In some places point blinds placed in strategic spots on tips of sand or marsh have proved effective in very rough weather, when the wind drives the ducks in from the bay to seek shelter in the lee of any little point of land. These blinds are not too good for diving ducks and can be used so seldom during the now-short season that there is no pretense toward the elaborate sunken blinds in vogue on the Seaside even today. They usually consist of a few myrtle or bay bushes stuck around with a wooden box to sit on.

As for boats, almost any old tub can be used for ducking in calm weather in the sheltered creeks. But when the wind blows and for the open bay, a duck boat must really be able. The most popular type is locally known as the dead-rise bateau, built chiefly by Mr. Ira Hudson or the Wimbrow Brothers of Chincoteague out of choice Carolina white cedar—light, long-lasting and resistant to rot and worms. As the name implies, they have a dead-rise or "V" type bottom, quite sharp in front and tapering to almost flat from mid-section to stern. Thirteen or fourteen feet in length with ten- or twelve-inch sides, they are decked, save for an oval cockpit with low coaming to discourage breaking waves. More inclined to roll at anchor or in the blind than a flat-bottomed boat, they more than atone for this in ease of rowing and the way they ride the water like a duck without plopping into each trough of wave. To appreciate one you must try chasing a wing-tipped Brant, Goose or Whistler. However, those not fortunate enough to own one of these little craft make out very well with a flat-bottomed skiff of similar construction.

For some reason, most Bayside gunners have never taken particular pride in their decoys and figure that any old stool is good enough. For the creeks, a set usually consists of three or four Mergansers, two or three Goldeneye, half a dozen Geese, and a few miscellaneous blocks—Dippers (Bufflehead) and the like. Those who hunt the bay usually carry larger sets of stool—Blackduck, Geese, Brant, Scaup, Goldeneye and the like, totaling about thirty or more. They are strung out (upwind, of course) according to species, with Geese and Brant in a rough line just beyond the others. Blackies are bunched near the Geese, since Geese, Brant and Ducks are attracted by Blackduck decoys and vice versa.

However, Blackducks now seldom stool out in the open bay and use it more as a resting place preparatory to nightly excursions into the smaller creeks and fresh-water ponds in search of food. Strangely enough, Blackducks have never come into the fields of corn or rye as do their cousins, the "gray" Mallards. But for that matter, the "gray" Mallards (of which a few are killed each year) do not come into fields in this locality as they do in most places.

Few, if any, Baysiders make their own decoys and most are content to use a nondescript hodgepodge scrapped from barn lofts or picked up on the beach and patched up in some way at the last possible moment. It is laughable to see the combinations—mallard heads on scaup, goose heads on brant, and many others. To these they occasionally add a half dozen or so ordered from some mail-order house or else go up to Chincoteague and buy some of those made by Mr. Ira Hudson, Burch or others.

The former run highly to very slim, ultra-streamlined mallard stools that are repainted as scaup, blackducks, goldeneye, et al.—with ofttimes sorry results—to use a peculiarly southern expression. The latter are fairly good as commercial decoys run, but far and away too small—even smaller than life size. Anchors consist of assorted spark plugs, bearings and other scraps of iron. Balance weights run from railroad spikes to iron washers. There are, of course, exceptions to this rule and a few take pride in keeping very fair sets of stool.

Live decoys have never been extensively used on the Bayside save in fresh-water ponds along the shore. In rough water and small boats they are a nuisance to carry and fare badly from the pounding of the seas. Even in the creeks where they might have been used to some advantage they have not been popular, for most of the ducks killed are diving species.

Before we leave the Bayside for the Seaside, let us take one last, typical picture of it—of the first rosy dawn at our backs when the first Mergansers hurtle into the creek by twos and threes—long, vague shadows en route to little drains and guts away up the creek. Of thrilling whisper of Whistlers' wings growing ever shriller while eyes strain to catch a glimpse. Of flash of black and white and low swish as they hit the water beyond the stools and paddle swiftly in. Of eager hunters rising stiffly, off balance, to cut loose a salvo as they spring from the water. A brace floating, white belly up, webbed feet aimlessly paddling chilly air, little feathers scudding around. Another, hard-hit, swimming swiftly, instinctively toward the channel.

Shoot him again—quick—before he dives! Too late, he's under. No, there he is—a hundred yards away! Untie that boat! Fingers too numb? Here, let me try it. Now push her out. Row faster—faster! There he is. Bang! Bang! Ahhhh! Got him that time.

Back in the blind. Hurry, here come more—no, saw us, darn it! First rays of sun peeking over green pines to the back. Thunder of the bay on beach, dancing blue and white as the sun lights its choppy bosom. Honk of a thousand geese bestirring themselves from rye fields beyond the woods on both sides. Maybe a few will straggle over. Muffled boom of guns behind —away up the creek. Ah, here they come—air full of ducks! Shoot wildly. Desperately reload as they circle, swing, wheel, gain altitude. About over now, they tower high over a fringe of white sand and myrtle bushes in front, disappear over the bay. But they'll come back—maybe.

Let's pick up what we knocked down, swipe a few oysters off that "rock." Back in the blind—warmer now—too warm, not enough wind. Stools float almost motionless, so apparently wooden. Take a drink, relax and eat a few oysters.

Then laughing water disappears. Sun is blotted out. Wind shifts to nor'west—icy. Move the stools, button up jackets, huddle expectantly— they'll be coming back. Bay whipped suddenly into fury. Look out, there's a flock of Blackies! Too wise to stool but here they come over, long necks craned, a long chance.

Over the blind now. Shoot desperately! Hit him, by gosh! Towering, climbing, won't he ever stop? Then over, sliding down the face of the wind —ker-splash! Two hundred yards downwind and hard to get—but get him you will. Trough of the waves; freezing brine down your boots as boat swings round; fight back to the blind. For heaven's sake don't let that oar slip out!

Back in. Agonized relief, stinging, numb hands, welcome burn of fiery whisky, toast to the Blackie. Load up and bale out the slush. Ice forms on cedars, slippery boat pitches. Lord, it's cold!

Get down! Here they come! Rise and shoot! Fingers too cold to bend round triggers? Body too stiff to move? Too cold to care anyhow? Well, brother, this is IT—this is duck hunting! Untie that boat—let's get that cripple! Warm us up!

And now it's high time we left the Bayside and rounded the point of Cape Charles to take a look at the Seaside, so infinitely different from what we have seen. Let's make our mental trip by boat in dead of winter, while the ducks are there.

Even to a casual observer the change is immediately apparent as we make the channel between guardian, lonely Fisherman's Island—wandering vaguely off into the Atlantic—and the sandy tip of mainland known as Kiptopeke. Before us, into the northern horizon, opens a breath-taking panorama of marshland, winding channels, shallow bays or mud flats— according to the tide—narrow, sandy islands and rolling surf—ever- threatening—just beyond. For here as nowhere else one can take in at a glance a perfect cross section of the whole vast Seaside. It is like an aerial photograph of an extensive region taken at great height—reduced to a scale one can visualize. Even a mile farther north it spreads out until it is impos- sible to see more than a fraction of it at one time.

To the west is the mainland, here only half a mile wide. There is no sandy beach skirting dancing water. Instead, rich brown farmland slopes gently down to the sheltering pines that fringe the inner marsh. Farmhouses peep shyly through occasional breaks in the trees. Here and there twisted, gaunt skeletons of a once-noble pine stand, mute reminder of the fury of Sep- tember hurricanes (though they are rare).

Small creeks wind up into the woods every now and then. Known locally as guts, they go bare at low tide and carry only a couple of feet of water at high. At the head of some of these hide shallow, brackish ponds.

Over the trees along the marsh soar big red-tailed hawks, searching for rabbits or perchance a blacksnake out for a bit of winter sun. Above them wheel buzzards, waiting for death. Now a marsh hawk skims the sere, yellowed grass to hover, then pounce upon an unsuspecting sedge-hen (Clapper Rail), scattering the little marsh wrens like tufts of cattail in the wind.

The inner marsh is only a half mile wide here. Farther north it spreads for miles. Through it weave myriad little channels, winding their tortuous paths to the main channel. In these dreans, and the guts that drain into them, the Seasiders make their living, in constant conflict with slimy mud and swift, fickle tide.

In spring they "mud-flap" for "peelers" (shedder crabs). This little sport consists of wading the channels at low tide, knee-deep in mud, to pick up crabs buried to the eyes. In summer they rake the bars and flats for clams. In fall they tend trotlines redolent of "tripe" (defunct horse meat) and dip the crabs that fasten onto it. And now they are exercising their backs, tonging oysters from pitching little scows. Up the dreans, unnoticed by the watermen, Mergansers in pairs and trios wing swiftly by, emitting an occasional hoarse "awwrrk."

Far into the labyrinth of marshy channels putt-putts a boat, its sawed-in-half Model T Ford engine wheezing laboriously, while Blackducks spring up ahead of it in droves from some "open slash"—as little bare spots amidst the marsh grass are called—to wing swiftly over us toward the high marsh next the beach.

Ahead in the main channel bunches of Scaup, Whistlers and Dippers (Bufflehead) get up, only to settle back into the choppy water a few hundred yards ahead. A nice bunch of Brant give forth a guttural "addrrrmmmppp" as they feed over near a little tump of marsh. Canada Geese feed all over the flats between us and the inner marsh. A bald eagle flaps ponderously over and the air is full of fowl, hastening out of his path. The Geese rise amid many protesting "awonks" and head for the beach—probably more on account of the rising tide on the flats than fear of the national emblem.

On the east side of the main channel—a mere two hundred yards wide—lies Mockhorn—typical of the many inner islands—narrow fringe of sand and storm-killed pine stretching some five miles up the channel. In days gone by Mr. Larrimer Cushman of New York built a fine home here and made it a sanctuary for waterfowl. Since the Cushmans left and the '33 hurricane knocked the seawall galley-west, no more do the geese find fields of clover and rye planted for their benefit and the ducks are welcomed into the island's many shallow ponds with merciless lead instead of bushels of yellow corn. But even now the place is a refuge for waterfowl, especially on rough days and times of high tides. It is one of the typical spots where Teal, Widgeon, Pintails, Gadwall and other shallow-water ducks can be seen on the Seaside.

Beyond Mockhorn, across a narrow open channel that circles it to the east, stretch some three miles of high marsh, running clear to the sandy ocean beach. This territory compares favorably with Dismal Swamp and the famed Okeefenokee in loneliness, treachery and inaccessibility. Only a fool would venture into it without an experienced guide—and there are not too many such.

From a distance it looks like just more marsh. From the inside a tyro is lost in the first hundred yards. No buoys mark the maze of channels, many of them blind; most of them bare long before low water. No signs mark the mud pots where a false step may lead into bottomless ooze. The only signs of human life are one or two oyster shanties perched atop high poles miles apart, where come a handful of watermen willing to risk the loneliness and treachery of the high marsh in return for the abundance of prime seafood—there because of these very things. Sometimes they are marooned in these shacks for days, because of tide and weather. This particular stretch running between Mockhorn and Little Inlet they call "Down the River"—a fitting tribute!

But here is a real paradise for wildlife. The marsh is full of Blackducks,

Part of a raft of Broadbill.

Pintails and Mallards taking off.

Pintail drake feeding in shoal water.

Mallard duck with young.

few of which ever hear a gun fired at close range during their winter stay. All kinds of diving ducks seek refuge in its channels—seldom hunted. In early fall the place is alive with Clapper Rail but each year they meet the same fate—the first bad northeaster sweeps the tide completely over the marsh and they drift helplessly to the mainland to face a battery of hunters, intent on getting a potful. At other times their chief enemy is the prowling mink—all too plentiful.

Just beyond the high marsh, across a narrow channel, runs the most fascinating strip of land in the world—the outer beach. Rising out of a narrow stretch of marsh and shallow ponds into low sand dunes carpeted in places by clumps of myrtle and salt-water bushes, it slopes gradually down into the ocean, forming a broad, glistening white sand beach smooth enough to drive at any speed—provided you have an auto there!

Seldom more than a half mile wide, this desolate-looking paradise (for wildlife) runs from Fisherman's Island almost due north to Assateague near the Maryland line and on north into "Yankee Territory." Swift, deep inlets cut it into islands. Wrecks of sunken ships line its beach. Here and there a Coast Guard Station keeps lonely vigil. Only two or three years ago Coast Guard patrols picked up German souvenirs here—some of them alive—heard the blast of "ash-cans," saw things that even now they cannot tell.

On the gravelly sand flats come Snow Geese by the thousands to rest and get gravel to digest meals they either ate in some northern spot or are preparing to eat farther south, for they do not otherwise stop here and are shot only accidentally. Sometimes there are a few Blue Geese among them. Even the diving ducks come out of the water here on blustery, rough days to rest and pick gravel. And on the low flats just inside the beach plenty of Blackducks, Canada Geese, and many of the shallow-water ducks can almost always be found.

Even in spring and summer the beach is alive with wildlife. Countless thousands of shore birds stop here en route to South America or farther, and again on their way back north. Many species winter here. Terns and gulls and black skimmers (flood gulls) nest on the beach and, not too long ago, gull-egging was a favorite local sport. Before that, the beautiful little terns (known as strikers) were shot and their skins shipped north by the barrel to ornament millinery for thoughtless women who "wouldn't hurt a fly." And, since we have wandered from ducks, the channel bass still run heavy in the surf and it is easy in spring or fall to snag a couple of fifty-pounders off the beach anywhere up and down the coast.

But let us continue on up the Seaside, having seen a typical view. It is all alike—the mainland, marsh, channel, inner islands, high marsh and outer beach and inlets. But as you go north there is more of it.

First we pass Oyster, quaint little seafood capital, once a base for sportsmen, even now one of the best and most easily accessible. Passing Cobbs Island, another of the outer islands, about which more anon, we come to Hogg Island and the insular village of Broadwater, noted equally for good ducking and huge mosquitoes. Then by Little Machipongo Inlet and Parramore Island we wind up a seemingly endless deep water channel to Wachapreague, where there is a splendid hotel for sportsmen and good facilities for hunting and deepsea fishing.

Leaving here we come to Cedar Island and famous old Metomkin Inlet, replete with lore of bootleggers and rum runners and running battles with the Coast Guard. A few miles farther, at Assawaman Inlet, the Seaside narrows appreciably, to broaden again just beyond Wallops Island—where the government is building a huge proving ground to scare daylights out of the ducks—and enter Chincoteague Bay. Here we should stop and visit ashore for there is much of interest to see.

Chincoteague is one spot where one can get a fair picture of the main inner marsh from an automobile, for it is connected with the mainland by a hard-surface road leading over a causeway through the marsh. From it one can see cedar blinds stuck by shallow, salt-water ponds and the channels and sloughs that wind through the marsh, and get an idea of the vastness thereof. This is Blackduck territory at its best.

Though Chincoteague is just another of the inner islands, it is unique in that it is thickly populated and quite an up-and-coming place. Its people live almost entirely from the water and their talk and habits are vastly different from that of mainland folk. The annual pony penning is widely advertised—even though the ponies breed and range on neighboring Assateague Island—on the outer ocean beach.

Legend has it that a Spanish ship, laden with Arabian horses, went aground here and these ponies are their descendants. Each year about July Fourth the people get together and sally forth by boat to Assateague, round up the year's crop of ponies, drive them across the narrow channel, and have a sale—usually in conjunction with the annual Fireman's Carnival.

Then, too, a visitor should not fail to take in Pony Pines, rendezvous where the island people foregather almost religiously, come "Sadday" night, to imbibe liquid delights and dance as only they alone can dance. There is the decoy shop of Mr. Ira Hudson, a real old-timer, who manages to make a respectable living turning out decoys commercially, as well as boats. In years past there was also a "wild" duck farm that bred Mallards and English Call Ducks by the thousands for decoy purposes. But that has gone with the wind.

Get two duck hunters together and conversation swings invariably to tales of the old days, to times—not long gone—when half the fun was watching the pet quackers take little baths between flights of their wild brethren, when baiting was the proper way to localize ducks, when you naturally shot as long as you could see—sometimes when you couldn't—when you staggered home under weight of ducks enough to feed the neighborhood.

Yet, as we all know, these days we remember so fondly were as nothing to the years before—when flights of ducks, geese and shorebirds darkened the skies, daily bags counted by the barrels, and men made livings comparable to the speed with which they could shoot and reload.

It is pretty difficult to journey back there, even via the speedy medium of print. The old-timers were too busy just living to write for our edification. And so very few of them are left! It is my good fortune to know several who lived and loved those bygone days and they have attempted to recapture some of it for my benefit. Would I might portray it as they have told it to me! At least let me convey my gratitude to Messrs. Lucius and Arthur Cobb of Oyster for taking me briefly back into some of the days I would love to have lived. For they, and their fathers before them, came pretty close to living the history of duck hunting on the Eastern Shore.

The Cobbs come from a long line of seafaring folk. Nathan, senior, grandfather of Lucius and Arthur, hailed from Eastham, Cape Cod. Nathan's father owned a large whaling fleet and died about the same time as did that romantic, if odorous, business, when he was about twenty-eight years of age.

Nathan found himself saddled with responsibility. Business had slumped badly and he was forced to sell off the whaling ships for what he could get. Out of the wreckage he salvaged enough to buy a schooner, with which he engaged in coastwise freighting.

On his first trip down to the Eastern Shore to get a load of potatoes, he fell in love with the country. Yankee shrewdness told him this was the land of opportunity. For nowhere had he seen such fertile land, such swarms of wildfowl, such fishing, such untouched timber and fair islands. And about then his wife developed tuberculosis and doctors advised a milder climate.

So in 1833, the schooner put out from old Cape Cod for the last time and headed south. Aboard were Nathan and his frail, courageous wife and three sons—young Nathan, Warren and Albert. Albert, the youngest, was only four. With them they brought their furniture, tools, guns, clothes and sawn lumber for a home.

Just before reaching the Capes, a vicious storm forced them to put into the nearest inlet. Landing on what is now the Thomas farm, between Eastville and Oyster, friendly neighbors welcomed and helped them build their home. Later Nathan opened a little store just outside the fishing village of Oyster.

The store did quite well but the life was too tame—and there was the

Green-winged Teal female, solid wood, from the Eastern Shore of Virginia. Made about 1890-1900.

Green-winged Teal drake, solid wood, from the Eastern Shore of Virginia. Made about 1890-1900.

Feeding Brant, hollow wood, from Cobb's Island. Made by one of the Cobbs sixty years ago.

Very old solid wooden Blackduck, from Eastville, Virginia. Collected by Richard Parks.

Canada Goose, hollow wood, made at Cobb's Island. About 1880.

Male Broadbill of partially hollowed wood,
made by A. H. Cobb, Cobb's Island.
About 1880.

Female Broadbill of partially hollowed wood,
made by A. H. Cobb, Cobb's Island.
About 1880.

Male Lesser Scaup of solid wood, from an
old "rig" near Eastville, Va.

Canvasback drake, solid wood, made by one of
the Cobb family, Cobb's Island. About 1880.

Sleeping Canvasback drake, solid wood, found
on beach at Cobb's Island in 1885.

lovely schooner rotting in the mud. So Nathan got together a little band and went into the wrecking and salvage business. In those days there was no railroad and all transportation was by sailing vessel—so vulnerable to wind and tide and hungry ocean beach and bar. So the little "wracking" business prospered moderately, though it was hard, cruel, dangerous work.

Many were the lives they saved and many the ship they pulled to deep water. Some they inched off the jealous sand with huge rowboats like lifeboats, six oars and a coxswain. When the wind was favorable they hoisted sail to lend pressure. They became wizards at judging the proper stage of moon, tide and wind. The ships they couldn't get off they stripped of everything of value—masts, rigging, rare woods, lead, copper and even the copper nails. Even today one can pick up some of their old decoys made from the white pine masts and see in the very lead that they took from ships the copper nails they saved.

One of the most beautiful of the outer islands constantly haunted Nathan. Part of one of the original thousand-acre land grants, it was then owned by one "Hard-time" Fitchett. Nathan often went there to salvage ships and shoot among the teeming thousands of waterfowl and shorebirds that congregated in its marshes and on its sandy beach. One day he noticed a peculiar brown liquid seeping from the very beach, forming a wide, shallow pond. It was almost pure salt and resembled semi-liquid brown sugar. From somewhere he wangled three huge iron kettles, some ten feet in diameter, and set to work boiling this liquid. The upshot of it all was that he traded several hundred bags of salt (a precious commodity in those days) to "Hard-time" for the island—and his dreams began to come true.

Dismantling of the home on the mainland and the move to Cobbs Island are an epic in themselves—simple to relate, incredible to attempt under conditions then existing. Nathan's beloved wife did not long survive the move and was tenderly laid away in the little graveyard on the island that was then started. The Cobbs were an intensely religious family, and still are. But life went on. The sons grew up, courted on the mainland and married and Nathan himself remarried. The three sons married closely related girls eminently suited to their secluded, clannish, insular life.

The four Cobb families made a splendid living on their island. On it they grew vegetables and chickens and lived from the surrounding marsh and water. Clams, oysters and scallops were all around, begging to be taken. It was scarcely necessary to step outside the house to kill all the geese, ducks or shorebirds they could eat. Eight- and ten-pound weakfish could be caught in plenty off their little wharf on the lee side of the island.

In the spring they stepped over to the surf and heaved a heavy chalk line and hook baited with half a shedder crab and when the inevitable channel bass—that would average forty pounds—took hold, they would put the line over a shoulder and march up the bank with the "drum." These they would scale with a hoe, side and hang in the sun to dry. In fall when the bass returned they would salt more for winter. No, living was not a problem.

It was only natural that they should engage heavily in market hunting. In spring they shot shorebirds—big fat curlew, plover, red-breasted snipe, yellowlegs, and others. In fall and winter they shot ducks by the barrel for northern markets. It was not unusual for them to kill one hundred and fifty ducks to a man a day. They were on Nature's flyway and feeding ground and needed only the crudest of blinds and decoys. Many were the nights that all four families—they grew apace—sat up, hurriedly stripping feathers and dressing game. In the morning the men would load them in barrels on one of the sailing sloops they built and run them out the inlet to the sea. Here they would hail the first northbound ship beating up the coast and dicker with the captain as to freight rates. Most of their game went to the old New York firm of A. & M. Robbins.

Geese were a drug on the market and seldom shipped, for their flesh was too coarse for the epicures. But Blackduck, Brant, Canvasback, Redhead and Pintail often brought fifty cents apiece—real money in those times. Sea ducks were seldom shot for they brought only a quarter—and why take up time and space with them with plenty of the higher-priced kind for the shooting?

Powder was purchased by the twenty-five-pound keg. When breech loaders came into general use they loaded their own solid brass shells. They shot eight- and ten-gauge double guns with barrels ranging from thirty-two inches for "close" shooting to thirty-six and even thirty-eight inches for longer shots. I have been assured that a range of eighty yards was not considered long—and it must not have been, for they didn't waste powder or effort in reloading. Arthur still has a beautiful old eight-gauge double, made by Snyder, that his father, Warren, had converted from muzzle to breech loader.

Then came a change in the times. The country grew up rapidly, men made fortunes and worked too hard at it, there was a terrific demand for diversion. They cried for sport and relaxation—and in a young country that sport was hunting. The fame of shooting on Cobbs Island had spread wherever ducks were eaten or sold. The Cobbs were besieged by northern sportsmen, eager to pay any price to try some of the shooting.

Theirs must have been a grave decision, for it meant giving up a way of life they loved. At any rate, they began taking out a few paying guests—waiting on them as they called it. The railroad was still nonexistent but the Baltimore-Norfolk steamer came into Cherrystone Creek on the Bayside regularly. So they arranged to have the retainers of one Mr. Williams, a patrician plantation owner nearest them on the mainland, fetch and carry their guests from Cherrystone Landing to his place, where they transported them to Cobbs Island by sailing sloop.

Like Topsy, the thing "just grew"—grew beyond their wildest dreams. Their fame spread over the country and even across the sea. They were literally swamped with wealthy sportsmen who did not ask price—only a place to sleep and someone to take them out where they could shoot until their desire to relax and kill was satiated.

Something had to be done. The aging Nathan and his stalwart sons called a council of war. Plans were laid for a clubhouse. But whence would the money come? Building on an island is not only more difficult than on the mainland—it is many times as expensive.

Then the miracle happened. The coffee barque, the *Bar Cricket* out of Rio, was driven ashore almost in front of their house. They salvaged ship and cargo through almost superhuman efforts. First they put an eleven-thousand-pound anchor they had salvaged out in deep water. To it they rigged block and tackle. They brought powerful timbercart horses from the mainland for power. They watched the moon and caught a northeaster and high tide and used every rowboat and sailing vessel they could muster —and off she came, grudgingly, by inches. There followed a long legal dispute. The owners claimed the captain was under age and had no right to sign a contract awarding the Cobbs the $23,000 they had dreamed of for their clubhouse. But they came out with $18,000—and the clubhouse slowly became an accomplished fact.

And what a clubhouse! It was white and low and rambling, stretching some hundred and fifty feet. Around it they planted a green lawn and shrubbery. They built a little chapel and a ballroom. They deepened their channel and rebuilt the wharf that had served them so well. And, to top it off, they went across the bay to Norfolk and bought the first—and probably only—coal-burning steamer ever used on the Seaside. There were, of course, no gasoline boats in those days—the first of these remembered here was an old five-horse Lathrop about 1900.

They named their steamer the *NWA Cobb,* after the brothers Nathan, Warren and Albert. All this, of course, was not done in a day and they still salvaged ships and shot birds for market, but these days were already fading fast. Even then they could note a difference in the numbers of fowl and shorebirds and see the handwriting on the wall.

The place became known as Sportsman's Paradise. Wealthy "gents" and ladies came by the score, summer and winter. They wanted to establish a colony there and besieged the brothers with offers. Occasionally they would break down and sell a small lot, and the prices offered rose from $500 to $5000. They were palmy days!

In all, eight cottages were built. A preacher was imported. A noted taxidermist came down and stayed spring and summer and spent his time feverishly skinning thousands of the beautiful, diminutive Least Terns to ornament the bonnets of the women of the world. Even guests were not averse to going "striker" shooting, for they were absurdly easy to kill and the flats and beach teemed with them. They brought from fifteen to twenty-five cents each and powder was cheap. Besides, the guides would always sit up nights reloading shells.

The mainland also benefited. Arrogant old Mr. Williams, who owned the landing, became interested in his new financial bonanza and rebuilt his wharf and bought ornate new carriages and horses. He trained his Negroes as coachmen and even imported some coach dogs. Later his daughter married "Old Dr. Brockenborough," who went whole-heartedly into the stage business and built another wharf that extended out to deep water, thereby improving telegraph and mail facilities for the guests.

The island became almost as famous for surf bathing, fishing and gull-egging as it was for wildfowling, in addition to being an elite small social center. It has ever been one of the few places in this section where the Terns, Black Skimmers (flood gulls) and other gulls nest. It is fortunate that the "elect" who could be accommodated there were so few. Even so, it was inevitable that a pretty big hole should be made in the ranks of fowl and birds. For they shot the seemingly stupid shorebirds even more unmercifully than the ducks, simply because they traveled in larger flocks and could be shot in warm weather with so little effort.

Gradually, ever gradually, further changes occurred. A farm on the mainland had to be acquired to furnish vegetables, beef, pork and lamb for the guests. In order to furnish the kind of shooting to which the guests were accustomed, it became necessary to use more care in building and locating blinds. More attention had to be given to making, painting, rigging and setting out the decoys. Boats were improved so that some of the guests could row and handle them easily when all the local guides were in use.

So a new type of rowboat was born—the gunning "dink." Built of white cedar (in those days salvaged from ships), the dink is about thirteen feet overall. Her sides are only five or six inches high but her decks slope sharply up toward the center to make her seaworthy. She is decked and washboarded almost completely, save for a small cockpit surrounded by high coaming. Her bottom is flat and in the old days the boards were laid on lengthwise to insure easy skating on mud. She could actually be rowed on bare mud flats.

I doubt if there is anywhere a lighter or more practical duck boat. But, of course, the natives scorned—and still do—a rowboat, and relied on their trusty, utilitarian scows with a sculling oar at the stern. The tides cannot run too fast for them to buck, the waves cannot run too high in ordinary times. They can back a heavy scow off a mudbank with a single oar worked mysteriously over and around a solitary nail or wooden peg.

Meanwhile, a son came to each of the three brothers—Elkaneh (pronounced *Ell*-kenny) to Nathan, junior, Arthur to Warren and Lucius to Albert. These grew up, married and entered into the cycle. They listened to many new ideas on hunting broached by visitors and adapted them to their own peculiar needs. It was the younger generation who, some sixty-odd years ago, laboriously put in the first sunken blinds on points of marsh and rigged them with benches, floor covering, and even oil stoves—somewhat later. They also imported English Call Ducks and Mallards and saved crippled Blackducks, Geese and Brant for live decoys and raised them by the hundred in a three-acre lot. But there were still far too many ducks for them to bungalug around with live decoys and they were seldom used. For the first time, baiting was occasionally employed to localize the fowl, though this was because there was too much natural feed and not a dearth of it.

Expensive and fancy guns were brought in and sometimes the guests left their guns as a token of appreciation for marvelous shooting and real hospitality. One of the first four-gauges ever used locally was brought in by Dr. Henry Bigelow, a surgeon from Cohasset, Mass. It was a beautiful double breech loader with thirty-six-inch barrels and packed a tremendous wallop. Arthur still has some Winchester goose loads that are nearly six inches long. He assures me he has seen the gun—now owned by Warren Cobb at Cheriton—kill geese stone dead at one hundred and fifty yards.

Although the celebrities who shot at the island were legion, no records are left to list them (they went with the wind in '96) and they are only a hazy succession in the minds of those living today. In later days when Arthur, Lucius and Elkaneh were "waiting on" guests—fifty years and more ago—they recall a few names of those with whom they were on closest terms. There were Dr. Bigelow, Jeffries Wheelock and George Shattuck of Cohasset and George Walker of Scituate, Mass. Also, Thomas Dixon, author of the LEOPARD'S SPOTS, had one of the cottages there. They say he was really the finest gentleman ever to visit the island.

Lucius tells a couple of amusing anecdotes of the times some sixty-five years ago when his father was teaching him to take his place in the scheme of things. Albert was an outstanding shot among a family of superb marksmen and on this day particularly wanted to impress the boy. They were in a cedar-stuck blind with about thirty brant stools out in a strong tide and the decoy lines were soon matted with long streamers of eelgrass. A huge raft of Brant numbering almost a thousand pitched close by and swam right into the decoys and began eating the eelgrass off the lines.

Albert took careful aim, no doubt planning to kill ten or twelve on the water, and shot. Lucius says he will never forget his father's face when the entire flock jumped up and flew off, as he failed to shoot and his father didn't empty the other barrel. One lone Brant fell way out and drifted by. Albert said not a word but merely sculled out, wound up the stools and went home, disdaining even to pick up the dead Brant as they passed him by.

Both Lucius and Arthur tell of a pet goose decoy that grew attached to Albert and would follow him around and even became a nuisance. Every time he would go out ducking, the gander would manage to get aboard the sloop, go forward and stick his long neck out a little hole in the deck where there had been a mast. Arrived at the blind the gander would jump overboard and swim around, feeding among the wooden stools until he spied a wild flock. Then if they came in to his canny and loud honks of invitation, he would swim away off to the side until the shooting was over. If a flock failed to decoy he would swim straight to them, even up to a mile, and by some process toll them right to the blind, when he would again conveniently swim to one side.

The government established a lifeguard station—now the Coast Guard —on the island sometime not long before the birth of Arthur in 1866. There was little of discipline in those days and the captain and his crew of six oarsmen took active part in life and love on the island and participated in the hunting and other sports. In times of stress, when the mighty Atlantic swept ships on the sands like cockleshells, the Cobbs helped them wrest victims from the sea. Arthur joined the service as soon as he was old enough, served many years and is credited with an active part in rescuing a hundred and twenty-three persons.

Captain Crumb, taxidermist and naturalist of note, took over command of the station about 1869. He was a former member of the Union Army who fell in love and married a girl in Portsmouth, Virginia, and later joined the service. Nowhere except on the island could he have lived down the fact that he was a Yankee. On Cobbs he began a collection of rare birds that would do honor to a museum, for he mounted many ornithological records —birds and mammals that strayed here during unusual times—albinos, freaks of nature—brought to him from up and down the Seaside. But he has passed and his collection scattered to the four winds.

There is little more to tell. All good things must end. Old Nathan died in 1890 at a ripe old age. Lucius ran the club a year or two but somehow the spirit of the thing died with the old patriarch. So the brothers dissolved partnership and sold out to a syndicate from Lynchburg, Virginia, and it was organized into a business venture but still known as the Cobbs Island Club. They failed pretty miserably to maintain the standards of hospitality and sport furnished by the Cobb family and abandoned the project after one year. Captain Crumb of the Lifeguard Service ran it another year. Then Lucius and Captain Tom Spady, an old crony and former guide, took it over until the disastrous series of storms of 1896—the worst ever seen on the coast. Building by building, the beautiful island was beaten and stripped. The few that survived the first storm fell under the next—or the next.

And so ended an era. The island has never recovered. Where guests once played croquet on the green lawn large boats now chug noisily, for it is main channel. The Coast Guard put up another station, but no more have the Cobbs gone back—save in memory. Even the ducks, the geese and the shorebirds that visit there now seem but the ghosts of the millions that stopped, and lived, and died there!

It took nearly a century of unmerciful slaughter to make a noticeable dent in the countless thousands of waterfowl that once frequented the Eastern Shore, especially the Seaside marshes. But in the last half century their numbers have shrunken so fast that today it is scarcely worth while for even the most ardent wildfowler to maintain a boat, blinds and decoys, while the clubs have faded out of existence and it is difficult even to engage a local guide equipped to furnish a decent day's sport.

Shooting alone has not brought the sport to its present low ebb. Broadly, of course, the decline has come as a result of man's throwing to the four winds the balance of nature. Drainage, drought, waste of timber, futile farming of submarginal lands—all have done their share. Such predators as fox, mink, wildcat, lynx, snakes, hawks and owls have played a leading part. And man, the most voracious and bloodthirsty predator of them all, has not only killed the ducks, but so many other natural foods of the predators—the ones that seldom kill except to eat—that they have had to hunt still harder the small game he left. The while the "varmints" were left to increase by leaps and bounds.

Local trapping has also sadly reduced the wildfowl, especially the Geese and Blackducks. When the powers that be realized the waterfowl were heading toward that limbo where went the Passenger Pigeon, they feverishly began passing laws—laws that were well meant but difficult to enforce—laws that played into the hands of the unscrupulous. To a shorter hunting season! To less shooting! To fewer hunters on the marshes! These are the toasts of the duck trappers as they pluck our ducks and guzzle their rot-gut beside the roaring woodstove by night! For one duck trapper can bag more Blackducks in a season than a thousand license-paying sportsmen.

But the death knell of duck hunting on the Eastern Shore was sounded with the passing of the eelgrass sometime between 1932 and 1933. There never has been really decent shooting since. Some say a mysterious blight killed it off, others that the disastrous hurricane of August, 1933, smothered it with sand and mud. But it was definitely on the way out when that storm hit. We didn't call it eelgrass. It was "sea-oars"—usually mentioned in company with a string of choice cusswords. It clogged propellers, choked clam rakes, hid seafood, tore up fish nets by sheer weight, messed up fishing lines and anchor cables and littered bathing beaches.

How often we called down the wrath of heaven on this long, slimy green ribbon of hades! But with it went the wildfowl, the cream of salt-water fishing, most of the clams and crabs, and all of the scallops. Speed its return, for nature deserves it if we don't!

Despite the rapid decline of the sport in the past half century there had been, till the passing of the grass, plenty of shooting on the Seaside to satisfy anyone but a game hog. Quite a few commercial clubs have flourished and many local watermen "took out parties."

The Campbell Club at Little Inlet on upper Smith's Island operated for many years. But where the clubhouse once stood I caught a fifty-pound channel bass some six years ago. The Webb family on the island named for them off Machipongo took out parties for many years. And there was a club on Hog Island that flourished quite a few years during that period. Legend has it that, long ago, a man and a hog were washed ashore there; that the hog promptly died and the man lived—hence the name.

Boats, blinds and rigs used on the Seaside have changed little in the last fifty years, except in numbers. The standard boat is still the gunning dink described previously, still built of white cedar. Some of the natives call them sneak boats or sneak boxes.

The sunken point blind, built like a piano box and sunk to within six inches of the top of the marsh point, has been popular with the clubs and those able to take the time or spend the money to build and sink them. Cedar-stuck blinds, both framed and unframed, have been in still wider use. But perhaps fifty per cent of the ducks killed have been from grassed gunning dinks.

Sometimes these are grassed on the spot. More often they are grassed and wired in advance and towed to the spot, for they are difficult to row and maneuver in a wind. Occasionally some club has maintained a few open-water blinds (mainly for Scaup) built with a shooting platform— some made for the boat to go under; others tended by motorboat from long range.

Live decoys were formerly used extensively by the clubs, but local sportsmen and watermen taking out parties seldom bothered with them. Newfangled silhouette, canvas, rubber and plastic decoys have ever been frowned upon and are not generally practical for this section. The old standby has been the wooden block—hollow or solid, according to the whim of the maker. Few there are who now attempt the simple, pleasurable task of making their own.

The old-timers used to fell cotton-wood trees in winter and, in summer, chop and rasp out some pretty fair decoys. This wood is extremely light— not much heavier than cork—and easy to work, yet seldom splits under roughest handling. They were much larger than life size, and a far cry from the puny-looking commercial decoys now available. Few bothered to do a real job of painting, striving chiefly for effect.

As an old salt once told me, "When they get close 'nuff to tell they ain't real ducks, it's too danged late!" In fact, Blackduck stools were often wiped down with a rag dipped in chimney soot and kerosene, a little tan paint smeared on the head, and penciling done with a charred stick. And they brought results!

Yet the old days are done and it looks like the time has come to take stock of things and abandon some of the crude methods that used to suffice. Of late years, I have sometimes wondered—wondered as I knelt in two inches of slush in a boat pitching wildly in a crudely stuck blind wide open from the top, if a piece of netting stretched overhead would not have helped, if a little platform wouldn't have been worth a lot, if a few more nicely painted and carved decoys wouldn't have helped give me a shot at those few wide ones that would have made all the difference?

X I

James and Potomac Rivers

BY TRACY HAMMOND LEWIS

RICH man, poor man, beggarman, thief; doctor, lawyer, merchant, chief —they can all find a spot to fit their persuasion or their pocketbooks somewhere along the four hundred winding miles of the James River from away across the State of Virginia in the Blue Ridge to its wide, salty mouth where it empties into the broad Chesapeake Bay at Hampton Roads.

Perhaps, lest some of my shooting southern neighbors get wrong ideas in their heads, I should eliminate "beggarman" and "thief" from the old nursery rhyme. We ain't got no such animal down here in 'Ginny.

From Richmond west lies the poor man's game preserve—one upon which he can operate without expense if he has the necessary boat, shells and gun. No guides to pay at twenty or thirty dollars a day, no club dues, no donation to the club employees at Christmas time, no board bill, no tips. And if it were no birds as well, the Upper James and I wouldn't have seen as much of each other as we have.

But even in the years when Ducks Unlimited missed its guess pretty badly and ducks were few and far between, it was an odd day when one could paddle downstream without adding at least a bird or two to his bag. Or the explanation might lie in his shooting. The ducks, or lack of them, are not always to blame. The sportsman of the Upper James does not own free membership in a duck club alone. There is no telling what other kind of game he may come home with—perhaps a brace of Quail or "pa'tridge" or "birds" as they refer to them in Virginia; squirrels, rabbits, coons, 'possums or an occasional Goose (although the great rafts of them stay pretty well farther down the river). And probably there are few more likely places to find a wild turkey than on one of the many islands one coasts by in his descent of the river.

Deer, too, seem almost as plentiful on occasion as in the days when John Smith was fooling around with that Indian glamor girl, Pocahontas. I remember one trip when Ray Holland and I were sitting on the bank eating our lunch, on a brisk December day. We heard foxhounds baying some distance away.

"Sounds like they were running a deer," said Ray. Often I have to take what Ray says on faith, particularly when he reminisces of some distant place like the Saskatchewan where, through no lack of desire on my part, I have never been. But in this case evidence shortly presented itself to show how dependable he is in such matters. The sound of the hounds came nearer. Presently there was a crackling of the bushes. A buck with a nice rack of horns leaped to the edge of the river not twenty-five yards away and stood motionless as he stared at us. We didn't move, either. I didn't even swallow the last bite of the chicken sandwich I had in my mouth.

We didn't jump for our guns which were leaning against a nearby but too far off sycamore tree. They were unloaded, as guns should be when leaning against trees. Besides, we didn't have any buckshot loads. Besides, we didn't have a deer stamp posted on our licenses. Besides, after half a breath the deer plunged into the river. The river at that point was about half a mile wide and the river, high and red after two days of rain, was flowing oceanward at a rate of five or six miles an hour. The deer did a good sturdy job, however, and, by angling upstream, landed on the other side of the river not more than a couple of hundred yards below us.

His stunt, however, had pretty well tuckered him. He lay down on the bank, probably laughing to himself as the belated hounds milled around in our vicinity for awhile and then betook themselves off, telling whoever cared to listen what wonderful trailers they were. Rested and satisfied, the deer got to his feet and trotted out of sight with nothing in the world to worry him except scores of similar experiences that still lay ahead of him.

"Well," said Ray, breaking our silence at last, "that was more interesting than shooting him, wasn't it?"

"Yes," I replied; "like hell!"

But it's high time that I got back to the subject of wildfowl on the James.

When I was first introduced to James River shooting, it was by my friend and neighbor "Red." In my time I have been hunting with some excellent shots—I have just mentioned one of them—but with one or two exceptions Red tops them all. Part of his ability is due to experience, for there are few days in his life, as his wife will tell you, that he isn't either hunting or fishing. When duck hunting he is one of those fellows who either makes you sweat to hold your own or draw upon a futile imagination for alibis. The less experienced shot probably comes out of a trip with Red much happier than the lad who swings a shotgun fairly well himself.

When five Mallard jump up noisily from behind a point and four of them drop, the less experienced hunter is likely to experience a false thrill of accomplishment. Red, too, makes a gunner like myself feel a bit dubious when I explain some of my misses—I try to keep my explanations to myself, however—on the grounds that they are too far away. I have seen Red with his three-shot pump (Heaven knows what he would do in the days before we were compelled to plug the magazine) get his first two birds at forty or fifty yards and kill the third at an incredible distance that I refuse to name because I have been annoyed too many times by reading in print of ducks being killed at such distances. And when it comes to quail—but this is supposed to be about ducks and geese so I will have to skip that.

(It would be nice, though, to tell you about the two times when I "wiped his eye" on pa'tridge. But that would be neither pertinent nor modest.)

I met Red at a Scottsville shoot which could be called neither skeet nor straight down the line trap-shooting. We had an expert trap geared up to about a seventy-yard target with unknown angles, unknown elevation (except to the father of the boy who operated the trap) and varying distances for the firing line.

Red apparently thought my performance on the pigeons was good enough to be of some assistance to him on the river and he suggested that we try our collective hands at ducks.

I've done a lot of different kinds of duck hunting in the course of a moderately extended lifetime, but James River shooting was something new to me, even though it may be an old story to thousands of other duckers whom I haven't had the pleasure of meeting. For me it combined all the pleasures of Grouse hunting, without the irksome necessity of climbing mountainsides and pretending to the fellow who is with you that you aren't as wholeheartedly bushed as he is.

Both types of hunting scare the daylights out of you—or I should say, me—when the birds flush. I hope my blood never flows so sluggishly that my heart will fail to miss a beat or two when a Grouse explodes out of cover from almost under my feet. And the same goes for the moment when a bunch of from three to twenty Mallards or Blackducks fight their way through the brush overhanging the river bank as you round the bend. I prefer the ducks because I'm sitting down instead of Alpine climbing. It's surprising how much more excitement I can endure when reposing on my rear than on my feet.

Where did I leave Red? Oh, yes. He and I were about to go duck hunting on the James. The night before, we had loaded my plywood boat into the station wagon and I was to pick him up the following morning at 4:30. I was afraid he wouldn't be ready so I arrived at his house at 4:00 A.M., which was a good idea for I still don't know whether Red likes sleeping or hunting better. One thing you'll have to give him credit for, though: he had persuaded his very attractive, black-haired and black-eyed wife to

An unretouched photograph by LeRoy Anderson.

Mallards on the Potomac River.

Underwater mowing machine with which 10,000 acres have been cleared of water chestnut
in the Potomac.

drive us, at that early hour to Wingina, thirty miles upstream, and to meet us at sunset at Scottsville where we hoped to be at dusk if all went well.

Now a word about this James River shooting before we get started. It's a two-man proposition—one man in the stern seat, the other in the seat ahead of him. When the birds flush, the lad in front fires ad lib and the one in the rear gets to his feet and shoots as soon as he can be sure he isn't going to blow his friend's head off or blast his eardrum.

Don't think for a minute, either, that the man in front has all the best of the arrangements. When a bunch of ducks springs off the water he isn't thinking entirely of how many birds he is going to kill. In the back of a very important section of his mind he is wondering: "Is that so-and-so in back of me going to lose his balance and make a pattern on my head, or is he just going to blow off the end of my gun barrel when we both get lined up on a straight-away bird?" We are, of course, eliminating the possibilities that he may have any other concealed desire to shoot you unintentionally.

Nor is that all. Above Richmond—and that's my section—Old Man James is a tricky proposition. There are rocks and there are rapids. In fact, the best hangouts for the ducks are in the rapids. It doesn't make much difference whether the river is high or low, except that duck shooting conditions are better when it's high. If low, there are more rocks to hang up on and the current is still swift enough to fill your boat before you can say "Kilroy was here," if you and your partner don't do a lot of teamwork. If the river is high, you're just as badly off in case of trouble. It's deep then. And a lot of the larger rocks are below the surface. Try swimming with shooting clothes and rubber boots on!

So you've not only got to worry about keeping your head intact, but you are equally anxious to know that the man in the stern knows his river.

Red claimed that he knew all the rocks from Wingina to Scottsville by heart. That I didn't believe. Only a prodigy could know all the rocks in that stretch of the James. But the fact that he was still alive after many years on the river gave me some confidence, and I was sure this was because, like any good river man, he could tell where the rocks and the passages were by the appearance of the water. I could do it myself if I didn't like riding on the forward seat better.

While we were talking, Red and I and our charming chauffeuse had arrived at Wingina. There is a bridge there and an ornery steep bank beside it, down which we had to drag the boat. I'm glad we weren't landing at Wingina and reversing the procedure.

Dawn had broken a while back but, according to the law of the land, we were still early enough. A lot of ectoplasm from bygone ducks and fish was rising off the river—or perhaps it was only mist. The river was high, which was good; the current was swift, which was not so good, as far as embarking was concerned, but what the doctor ordered for getting ducks. When the river is low ducks can't hide along the banks under the willows and elders. They stay out in the middle of the river where they see you as soon as you see them. When a duck spots you, he knows the score just as well as you do.

Four creek Broadbills took wing after we had finally started down the river, which was encouraging—until we had paddled a couple of miles farther—helping out the river's current in our impatience, without seeing another sign of feathers.

Except to a hunter, that thirty-mile stretch of the James looks singularly forsaken. All its soft green beauty of summer had vanished with the touch of winter. Pale, ghost-like sycamores haunt its banks and numerous dead sentinels lean downstream in the direction in which they have been pushed by years of floods.

At frequent intervals cornfields stretch along its banks, offering a generous reward in good years to atone for the times when the floods take personal charge of the harvesting. They leave in their wake bunches of grass and driftwood like nests in the trees, fifteen or twenty feet above the low-water mark of the river.

Along the river banks unkempt willow trees and elder bushes offer deceptive hideouts for Mallards, Blackducks, Wood Ducks and creek Broadbills. Just how deceptive they can be I learned as we rounded a bend and saw an apparently deserted stretch of river ahead of us. Suddenly, with a bedlam that would have put a covey of Grouse to shame, three greenheads and a hen broke through the bushes about thirty yards ahead and climbed desperately into the air.

The sound of three shots bouncing off the top of my head brought me out of my daze and I sent one load futilely after three of them as they sped downstream. The other two had wilted in mid-air and fallen into the stream before I even got into action. Red had dropped his paddle, jumped to his feet and gone into efficient action before I had even pulled my thoughts out of another world into the realities of jump shooting on the James. I was too flabbergasted even to think of a fitting alibi.

"They don't tell you about it ahead of time, do they?" was Red's only comment.

As we drifted silently along, after picking up the birds, I resolved not to let that happen again and reflected upon what an important function the man in the stern fulfills, not only in bringing down birds when his partner is daydreaming but in many other ways even more vital. To you who contemplate this type of shooting, let me urge that you use even more care in choosing the man who is going to be behind you in the boat than you would in picking out a wife.

Radio crime programs to the contrary, the lives of most of us are comparatively safe, as far as our better halves are concerned. Even if you have guessed wrong the result is not necessarily fatal. But the man in the back seat can't make any mistakes. He has to get on his feet without losing his balance and be sure that there is no small object, such as a head, in the path of his gun before he fires. If he fails in this the divorce courts offer no aid.

Care in handling a gun is not the only requisite. Whether high or low, the James River and its rapids in its upper reaches are not the safest proposition for even a topnotch riverman. When the water is low, the number of rocks upon which you can hang up are multiplied. But there is a compensating feature in that you can wade in most places and dinner will be only that much later. However, when the rains come the river gets red and its hungry tongue licks at the floodbanks. You don't see so many rocks, but something happens when you do hang up on one. The stern swings around until the boat gets wedged and if the proper kind of teamwork fails to materialize, old man river rushes over the side—and that's that.

While Red can't hear me, let me add that even he, on one trip, when he was unfortunate enough not to have me for a companion, hung up on one such rock and his boat cracked in the middle. He and his friend lost their guns and everything else except the clothes they wore. They managed to get to an island where they had to spend the night, before their vocal efforts resulted in an early morning rescue and the mental relief of two wives who had begun to get wrong ideas.

There also were a couple of Scottsville preachers who had decided to repeat last year's sermons and go hunting in the time they saved. They, too, upset in the rapids below Scottsville, lost all their equipment and spent a cold, cheerless night on an island. Perhaps they would have perished but for years of proper living. In the same year, however, occurred a tragedy that had no such happy ending. Two boys upset. One managed to get ashore with the aid of an oar while the other one was drowned.

Well, let's not get morbid but return instead to our trip down the James. We had reached the end of a narrow island. As an aid to preparedness I had laid my paddle on the seat ahead and peered expectantly around the point. Never have my anticipations been more satisfactorily fulfilled. At the instant I caught sight of them, eight Blackducks shot into the air, as if jet-propelled. My loads caught two of them full amidships and they somersaulted to the river with a splash, as two others that Red had taken care of followed suit. I needed that good fortune to save face. Red apparently had a face that seldom needed saving.

The four unharmed birds wheeled down the river, leaving us with the comfortable feeling that we might meet again.

Not many minutes later I picked up with my binoculars a bunch of one of the most beautiful ducks that swims—Wood Duck. Summer Ducks or "Squealers" (because of their peculiar whistle when in flight) are the names by which they are better known down here. Forewarned, by spotting them first, we devoted our attention to hugging the shore cautiously and seeing how close we could approach before flushing them. Ironically they offered us the best shot of the day, as a dozen of them sprang off the water. We had to restrain itchy trigger fingers, for Wood Duck were protected that season, though in this section they are about as numerous as other varieties.

Even now the hazard they offer to one's peace of mind on a river trip has not been eased much by changing the law to permit one Wood Duck in the bag. Their white head markings and their whistling as they take wing help to distinguish them from Teal, Ruddies or several other of the smaller species one might easily imagine them to be. But the surprise element in jump shooting doesn't encourage the niceties of bird differentiation. Some birds must even be shot with a prayer, through a protecting screen of foliage, much as one would bag a Grouse. So the limit of one Wood Duck just postpones the hot seat a bit. After you have killed your legal limit you are just as likely to commit a violation, intentionally or otherwise, as you were in previous years.

Soon afterward we heard the rush of the first rapids ahead and Red whispered an encouraging prediction. Rapids are a favorite hangout for the river ducks—food being more easily available and the roar preventing the birds from hearing the occasional scraping of the boat on rocks. Also, the rounded boulders and small islands with which the rapids are dotted offer greater opportunity for concealment.

From the moment that our boat felt the lift of the white water, Red had his hands full and the most he could offer, when two Mallards took off from behind a large rock, was to yell: "Give it to them!"

I was getting acclimated. With a minimum of delay I shoved my heart back into my mouth, threw my gun up and pulled ahead of the shining greenhead and saw him crumple. I fired at the second one, a hen, and my heart threatened to return to its forward position again as the bird continued on for a brief interval before it, too, fell to the water. The first one had lodged between two rocks and it was necessary to fight our way back a few yards upstream to reach it. Try that, sometime, in a sixteen-foot row-boat in rapids if you feel that your waist line is getting the upper hand. Probably no one would work as hard as we did under any other incentive except that of sport. We finally lifted the dripping bird into the boat and retrieving the other one upon which we kept one eye as it swept downstream was not such a difficult proposition.

Success, apparently, goes easily to my head. I had now attained the mood where I felt like turning to Red and saying: "Bring on your ducks! I'll handle 'em!"

They came sooner than I anticipated. Red had just told me we wouldn't reach a good stretch until a mile or so ahead of us, when an ungodly commotion took place along the bank about thirty yards away. Blackducks! They seemed as numerous and as noisy as thirty or more had any right to be, yet twelve to twenty would probably have completed their census. My ears were confused with the crack of Red's gun, which again seemed to bounce off the top of my head, a churning of water and an impressive rush of desperate wings.

The transition from the Nimrod who was mowing them down as they came to the dazed person who sighted first on one duck and then changed to others, as they seemed to offer better shots, was too rapid for me to give you an entirely accurate account of what happened. I'm quite sure I fired twice. To my amazement, the birds I fired at seemed to find new vigor in life. Out of the corner of my eye I was vaguely conscious of birds tumbling toward the swirling river.

When all the excitement was over two birds and a very sick cripple, which we later got, were in the water. By no stretch of my imagination, unless I was crosseyed, were any of the ducks my victims. My mind cleared sufficiently to compliment Red and to keep a reflective silence for some-time afterwards.

We stopped for lunch on the banks of an island, but Red never did finish his. As he lingered over the last sandwich, keeping watch up the river as he did so, he suddenly threw his sandwich to the ground, grabbed his gun and rammed three shells into it. Pretty fast going, but I could see it was wasted effort.

"Too far," I said, as the birds whisked by opposite us, well out in the river.

Red fired twice and the lead bird, a Green-wing Teal, plunked into the river. Wrong again, but at least my sandwich was intact. That ended our lunch period and soon afterward I had my first glimpse of one of the many ferries that one finds on the James. These flat scows can accommodate two automobiles and are fastened by a combination of steel ropes and wheels to an overhead cable that stretches across the river. The boat crosses at an angle with the current, working against it much as a sailboat tacks unto the wind.

Some distance below this we passed along the shore of a big island—big, that is, for the James, as it was perhaps a half mile in length.

On a later trip Red disembarked at the upper end and beat down the length of it, while I waited at the far end in the boat. A pair of Turkeys had flown over for a little rest after feeding on corn on the mainland. After what seemed an age-long wait, I heard a big commotion as they flushed ahead of Red. Another wait followed—so long that it seemed a certainty they had taken some other course. Then they sailed out, just below treetop level, the nearest one about sixty yards away from me.

I shot, and the No. 2s seemed to go to the right place, for the huge bird turned over in a tangle of wings and legs. I was so intent on making sure of at least one that I let him have the second barrel, too, which was probably a good idea, as Turkeys have an amazing amount of vitality and the second bird was undoubtedly too far away for results. It was a fifteen-pound hen—a big bird for either sex—and I am forced to admit, duck and goose lover that I am, that my heart has never pounded with more excited satisfaction.

After leaving the ferry we paddled a few broad stretches where the current swirled lazily along and the banks were grown with full-sized trees, instead of willows and brush. Few birds ever were killed in such places and this day was no exception. But the occasional rapids nearer Howardsville, with the scattering of islands and rocks among them, added more ducks to our bag and ate into the afternoon with surprising speed.

"We've got to get busy and paddle," said Red, looking a bit worried. "We won't hit the rapids above Scottsville before dusk and they're tough."

I didn't know what a gem of understatement that was until we reached the spot. It was dusk in spite of the energy with which we had been helping the current. To me it looked as if Red picked the whitest part of the white water and then headed for the two largest rocks he could find. The river seemed to snatch our boat to its bosom as we were whisked along in boiling foam. Water began to come over the bow, both sides and, as I learned later, over the stern as well. I was too transfixed by our situation to think of looking back. I can't figure out now why we weren't swamped. Probably the alarming speed with which we were swept along helped—together with the fact that the narrowest and most turbulent part of the pass was not very long. We were soon through and in quieter surroundings before we were more than a third full of water. Twenty minutes of bailing and we were ready to complete the brief remainder of our journey.

I've made many trips down the James since then, but none quite so hair-raising as that particular part of my initiation. And I'll even confess that a few times we planned to disembark at Howardsville, with the sole idea of avoiding that particular bit of water. Sometimes sport assumes a bit too rugged an aspect for even an ardent duck hunter—especially if he is middle-aged.

As far down as the falls of Richmond the jump shooting continues dependable. As in most other localities, rough weather helps matters, as the birds are then looking for a softer berth on the river. A high river and an overcast sky help still more. Then more refuge along the banks is afforded. The birds don't swim out to the middle and stretch their necks to attenuated attention as you approach and take wing five gunshots away. But even under the worst conditions, it is seldom that you'll come home skunked, unless you are sadly off form.

I even have heard a hunter, in whom I have considerable confidence,

AMERICAN WIDGEON

boast that last season, which was a poor one here, he got the limit on each of several trips he made in the stretch above Richmond. Occasionally, too, a goose or two is added to the bag. But that doesn't happen often. The goose is a much warier proposition and, too, he prefers the wide stretches to the east of Richmond, where an increasingly large concentration is found each year.

But at Richmond the poor man can say good-by to his private game preserve. From there on the river widens into a majestically impressive body of water that is navigable all the way to the Chesapeake.

Along the banks are large estates oozing with history, and high-powered hunting clubs that have as fine duck and goose shooting as can be found on the Atlantic Coast—which, if I can judge safely from the complaints I have heard recently from various sections, still leaves something to be desired. You can choose between a shore blind on some point, or a platform blind, mounted on posts and concealed by brush, some by law, five hundred yards at least from the nearest blind of a similar type and in water not eight feet deep at high tide. Then comparative values are largely dependent upon how frequently they have been used.

Large clubs are able to set aside a portion of their property each year for feeding and rest purposes. Even the blinds in use allow days of idleness to elapse between gunning parties. Where commercial blinds predominate, and when a fusilade greets a bird when he approaches within one hundred yards of it, it doesn't take the birds in the vicinity long to become educated.

But the lower James is famous for its goose shooting, rather than for its ducks. I believe some of the finest goose shooting in the East is enjoyed by the Curles Neck Club, Turkey Island, and other favored organizations.

Geese like territory where they can maraud the wheat and corn fields. The law against feeding or "baiting" wildfowl applies only to artificial feeding. Are you surprised, then, that much of the grain goes unharvested on the lands of the larger clubs? The club member can shoot from a pit, if he insists on being fancy, but with the limit restricted to two birds a man such frills are hardly necessary.

A corn shock in a field makes as good a hide-out as any. A few decoys further simplify his job, together with an ability to imitate a goose call either with his own voice or with an artificial gadget. It is best to consult with someone who knows his stuff, however, before you get too promiscuous with your calling. There is no better way to frighten the daylights out of a bird than to emit one of these sounds that are supposed to be duck or goose calls.

And far too large a percentage of hunters are like bathroom singers. It's pretty hard to convince them that they could not make a living singing for the radio even if they spent more time at it.

In many cases the members don't even bother about corn shocks for a hide-out, or a pit, in the case of a wheat field. They find some natural place of concealment along the flyway that the geese are using to reach the food and then indulge in a form of what could be called pass shooting. Either the morning shooting alone, when great clouds of them go out to raft up in the river, to loll around all day, or the late afternoon flight, when they return again to fill their crops, should be sufficient for the average shot to fill his meager limit.

Until the mouth of the Appomattox is reached, the river twists mightily and the hard-worked boatman must sweat sixteen miles to make six. In places it almost resembles a series of lakes more than a river.

Here the stream broadens. After Jamestown is reached, only twice, and then only briefly, is it less than two miles wide. For the greater part of its length it is as much as four miles in width. Near its mouth the banks are low, giving the impression of a still wider expanse of water etched on the horizon by bush and trees.

But even a confirmed duck and goose hunter scarcely can fail to be impressed by the fact that the river and its banks are as rich a source of history as are any in the country.

When Captain John Smith settled at Jamestown, in 1607, he beat the Pilgrim Fathers to it by thirteen years. It was on the banks of the Chickahominy River, which meanders into the James near Green Point, that John

Smith really broke into the headlines when Pocahontas, daughter of the Great Chief Powhatan, rescued him from certain death. John had been captured by Openchanough, brother of Chief Powhatan, and had been led all over Tidewater Virginia as a prisoner. Then, tired of this amusement, they decided to make a field day of it and lop Captain Smith's head off on the banks of the York River. As the tomahawk was about to descend, Pocahontas made a dive for the chopping block and got her own copper-hued neck between John's and the ax, whereupon Powhatan decided to let the Englishman live. Even those early Indians realized the might of a determined woman. My history book fails to explain how John Smith and Pocahontas had become so chummy that she was willing to risk her all for him. It likewise neglects to explain how it subsequently remained for John Rolfe instead of John Smith to provide the conventional ending of matrimony for such a dramatic romance.

Less heart interest, but possibly more historical significance, is contributed by the fact that the Harrison family who lived in Brandon, one of the most famous houses on the James, furnished two presidents to the United States, William Henry Harrison and his grandson, Benjamin Harrison. A third president, John Tyler, owned two houses on the banks.

Three capitals, too, were the James' quota—Jamestown, which is now pretty much gone; Williamsburg, which John D. Rockefeller, Jr., has restored to its original charm; and Richmond.

All along the James, too, some of the bitterest battles of the Civil War were fought. The closer one gets to Richmond the more difficult it is to find a spot that does not bear historical significance.

But as for me, though the ducks may be somewhat diminished in numbers and the geese at least considerably wilder than they were then in the "good old days," I would prefer to take pot luck with the game under modern conditions than I would to be making history in the swamps of the Chickahominy or lining my sights on a uniform at Malvern Hill, instead of letting both barrels go today when a covey of Quail explodes out of the cover. I might add that I likewise prefer the palpitations born of a flock of Mallards springing from cover around the bend or the thrill that strikes to my marrow when a goose opens up with his wild yodel.

When I moved to Virginia, some years ago, the paradise it offered to one, who is as wildfowl minded as myself, did not take me entirely by surprise. But the pleasures of the Potomac, to which Virginia can claim nearly a half interest, had not entered my mind.

When it comes to Canvasbacks, the James cannot be mentioned in the same breath as the Potomac. And, as a side dish, the latter offers more Bluebills, Mallards, Redheads, Pintails and Blackducks than the James, for primarily the Potomac is a duck river, while the James appeals more to the goose population. This is because there are more marshes along the Potomac and more wheat and corn fields along the James.

Like the James, however, the Potomac is divided into two sections, each of a different type. The division comes at the Big Rapids above Washington, while in the James it comes at Richmond.

Above the falls the Potomac is a thing of beauty and a joy to anyone who loves fishing. Below, it is a tidal stream, with brackish water, but ideally adapted to the growth of duck food, chief of which is wild celery, which, as any duck hunter knows, a Canvasback regards as highly as a small boy does a plate of ice cream.

With nature providing bountifully, from a duck standpoint, as she was in the Potomac, it is a little puzzling to understand how any so-called conservationist could go as far astray as was the case in the waters near Arlington.

Not content with seeing rafts of Canvasback come in every year to feed upon their favorite food, someone felt that he must start something. He did —with a vengeance.

The introduction of the caltrop, or water chestnut, as it is called, was his mental baby. In case you don't know, a water chestnut is a floating plant growing on a long slender stem from six inches to sixteen feet in length. It forms a rosette from ten to sixteen inches in diameter, with leaves that unfold like a cabbage, and a small white flower. The mature seed is about the size of, and as hard as, a hickory nut and it is covered with tough, sharp spikes that will penetrate shoe leather. They start sproutings in April. The rosettes appear in May and keep coming as fast as you can say "game conservationist," until late in August. Dandy duck food!

In 1923, a two-acre patch was planted in the Oxon River, which empties into the Potomac, although prior opportunity had been afforded for anyone, who wished to study the qualifications of the caltrop, by plantings made in Soetra, N. Y., in 1884.

In one way the experiment was a success. It grew. Great gods and little fishes, how it grew! The Oxon and the upper reaches of the Potomac became choked with the plants, stopping not only navigation but—naturally this is of far greater importance—stopping the wild celery and Canvasback, too.

The usual fiery letters were written to the papers, signed "Indignant Nimrod," "Outraged Hunter," etc. But that would probably have been the limit to any concrete action had not the late Franklin D. Roosevelt been annoyed one day at the obstacles which this obnoxious marine growth presented to the presidential yacht reaching Arlington, for which he was bound.

"Something ought to be done about it," he said.

Royalty had spoken. But even so, the mills of the gods grind slowly. The Bureau of Biological Survey (now the U. S. Wildlife Service) worked ten years with Francis M. Uhler. It had the co-operation of the Hallowing Point Club and the Sweeden Point picnic area.

Fire was tried. No go.

In 1938 a mass meeting of the Izaak Walton League was held, attended by more than two hundred and fifty persons, including Lansdale G. Sasscer and Howard W. Smith—both representatives in Congress—besides a great many other persons you don't know.

The Potomac River Water Chestnut Eradication Commission was formed, with Judge William S. Snow of Alexandria, president, and J. S. Hamill of Washington, D. C., secretary-treasurer.

These men got things started. In 1940, gasoline-driven scows with a new type of water mower (developed in Michigan) went to work. In 1941 two more mowers were sent to help out the good work. These mowers were attached to the bow of the scows and cut a twelve-foot swath two to three feet below the surface of the water. Each of the machines accounted for eight acres a day, which is pretty good going.

In 1942, Engineer William H. Dvorachek was put in charge of the work. Lighter machines followed the heavier trail blazers and things continued to hum. The commanding officer of the airport at Indian Head contributed two more machines and things hummed ever more.

In all, forty miles of river were cleared. The tide obligingly carried the cut caltrops to sea and solved what might otherwise have been something of a problem.

Now the wild celery is reappearing where it formerly grew in such quantities, and it is safe to assume that the Canvasback will follow suit, although, at the time of this writing, it is too early and the weather too mild for the Canvasback to leave northern food and waters. He likes to wait until the weather is such that our non-duck-hunting friends are convinced we are crazy when we don our shooting togs in the dark hours of the morning.

Sometimes it seems that, if it isn't one thing for us duck shooters, it's another. The water chestnut menace to our serenity on the Potomac has been removed. Well, what's next? Probably they'll reduce the limit to two birds a day as they have for geese.

However, let's cast aside such dyspeptic thoughts. Far from Arlington to the famous Chesapeake Bay, the winding river unfolds an area that is a paradise, not only for the ducks but for duck hunters. The abundance of marshes with creeks twisting through them are, perhaps, even better adapted to jump shooting than the upper part of the James.

Its extent is lined with great estates which justify the name of "manor," a term which has long been lightly used. Thomas Cornwallis, for instance, owned 8,000 acres. *St. Clements,* owned by Thomas Gerrard, comprised 11,400 acres. In 1649, the whole of Northern Neck was granted to Lord

Baltimore and I won't even try to guess how many acres. In 1663, Richard Lee owned 20,000 acres on both sides of the Potomac.

The boys didn't believe in being cramped in those days and, of course, some of the joy of owning so much property was dulled by the danger of getting an arrow in the seat of the pants if one got too far away from home.

Such large holdings naturally couldn't continue indefinitely in a world that has slowly but surely been drifting toward a thirty-hour week with fifty-four hours' pay. The manors have been broken up into smaller pieces, but even these seem rather enormous to our modern eyes.

In both beauty and historical significance the Potomac rivals its near neighbor, the James. It, too, furnished its quota of presidents. Up Pope's Creek, which flows into the Potomac, once stood the house in which was born the man who was "first in war, first in peace, first in the hearts of his countrymen." Two other presidents, James Monroe and James Madison, were born near Colonial Beach, now a summer resort.

But before the country started drawing upon the James and the Potomac for its presidents, history was being made along the banks of the Potomac as well. It is believed that the Spanish were the first to discover it, 'way back in 1565, and enjoyed five years of interesting exploration until a whole party of missionaries was wiped out in 1570. The English didn't come until about 1585.

A few years later our friend John Smith who, like Kilroy, seemed to have been everywhere, popped up. He found the river "navigable one hundred and fortie" miles, and made a surprisingly accurate map. He was particularly interested in the fine fishing it offered. Fish were so thick that the seamen on his boat tried to dip them out with frying pans. As this scheme succeeded rather slowly, Captain John waded in the shallow water along the shore and tried nailing them to the bottom with his sword. Paul Wiestach tells us in his book POTOMAC LANDINGS that John Smith wrote of this:

"We tooke more in one houre than we could eate in a day."

In the country near the Potomac were fought some of the bloody battles of the Civil War and, to a historian, some of the most interesting ones.

But it's hard to let one's thoughts dwell much on this when one is out in a Potomac duck blind or paddling up one of its countless marshy creeks jumping wildfowl.

So let's throw that history book overboard! A flock of fifteen Blackducks has just wheeled in our direction. Hold down, now!

Cap'n Billy's Rig, from an etching by Roland Clark.

1904

Dec. 4th   Van Rensselaer arrived & rowed
to the Bay, baiting the blinds East
& West. Many geese & duck in the
meadows & bay

Dec. 5th   Took the wooden geese &
white duck decoys to Mill Creek
Point, in Sandy Bend — Killed, geese   22
duck, Canvass & Red head 2
Mallard, Sprig, widgeon Etc.   36
wind ↗ to N. moderate & clear
Van Rensselaer Killed in   122
in Sands broad pond mostly mallard,
black, Sprig. widgeon

Dec. 7th   Rest day — J. H Dixon arrived
Made a new gate for the East
Dam & put it in place — Painted
the blinds and saw many ducks —
Fished with net in Sands Broad
& caught the finest lot of white
Perch ever seen —

Dec. 8th
wind
W. Cold   Dixon in Little Point Cove Killed   98
Van Rensselaer in Mill Creek "   161
4 Red Head — Mallard, Black
Sprig. Etc. 11 gadwell

244

To kill a Mallard in the Sand Bridge Marsh is a rather uncommon occurrence. Yet, at
the turn of the century, this fine species constituted a large majority of the birds killed.

X I I

Back Bay

BY FREDERICK K. BARBOUR

BACK BAY wildfowling area is in Princess Anne County, Virginia, and is situated approximately twenty-five miles, as the duck flies, southeast of Norfolk. It is in the northernmost section, below Chesapeake Bay, on the inland waterway which lies between the strip of ocean beach and the mainland along the Atlantic Coast. The area is comprised of five bays—North Bay, Redhead Bay, Ship's Bay, Sand Bay, and Back Bay respectively. The surface area of Back Bay constitutes at least half of the total area.

The water just misses being fresh. The degree of salinity is about six per cent of that of sea water. If, as happens from time to time, because of storms and high tides, sea water invades the area, the salt content will, of course, be intensified. When the degree of salinity exceeds nine per cent, a growth of barnacles appears, which symptom is viewed with alarm, because it means that the widgeon grass and wild celery are in jeopardy.

Back Bay, as this whole area is known, has been a wildfowler's paradise for nearly a century. However, in the nature of things, sport generally is subject to the processes of attrition. It should be here recorded that the immediate present and the prospects for the future suffer very much by comparison with the conditions that obtained in days gone by.

Old gunners can recall, as recently as the early 1930's, when they came to their blinds or batteries at dawn, a veritable cloud of ducks and geese over the waters of Back Bay. From about 1933 to 1943, the number of birds diminished and then increased so that, in the early 1940's, there seemed to be present only a large fraction of the bird population that used to be there. The last several years have witnessed a noticeable diminution in the wildfowl in the bay, and the shooting has fallen off badly.

Probably the best single shooting property is, or I should say was, Ragged Island. Yet, on occasions, the shooting to be had in the Long Island Marsh and the adjoining Seelinger Marsh would make Ragged Island look to its laurels.

In referring to some of the islands, mention should be made of Little Stinger, if only to illustrate the point that often best things come in small packages. In about three hops, an able-bodied frog could span Little Stinger lengthwise. This tiny island, however, changed hands on one occasion for a very fancy price indeed. What a place it was to kill diving ducks when the stage was properly set! Today but a few spiles remain as tombstones to commemorate the glories of Little Stinger.

The practice in Back Bay, for sportsmen who were landowners either in their capacity as individuals or as members of clubs, was to shoot almost entirely from permanent blinds, which were used year after year. Being permanent, these blinds were usually countersunk into the marsh, concrete-lined, and camouflaged with reeds. They were uncovered, which fact prompted many an exciting moment when incoming birds circled behind the blind when coming in to stool. A rabbit in his form is no more motionless than is an experienced gunner at this tense moment.

Guides—they were good ones—bore surnames that are a delight to the ear. I will mention a few to make this point clear: Whitehurst, Lovett, Hill, Carroll, Dozier, Roe, Bassnight, Lee, Land and Waterfield. In nearly every instance their English grass roots were apparent from the curious transposition in their pronunciation of "w" for "v." Thus "very" becomes "wery," "warnish" for "varnish," and the like.

Based on my experience, the guides in these environs were not versatile duck callers, as compared with the guides, for example, in the Missouri River bottoms. This is particularly true in the case of Blackducks and Mallards. In fact, I have never seen a guide who owned a duck call. I think the reason for this is because of the live callers that we were permitted to use before they became subject to the frown of the law. In support of this theory, these men were good in mocking the wheezy sibilance of the Widgeon and the flutelike double note of the Pintail, which varieties, of course, are not used as decoy ducks. When it came to honking in geese, most of these guides were past masters. They may have had their peers elsewhere, but I am sure they never were surpassed.

Back Bay gunning accounted for a rather wide variety of species, which included both marsh ducks and diving ducks. Points that fronted on deep water afforded superb shooting for Canvasbacks, Redheads and Lesser Scaup, as well as the Greater. Sportsmen did not do much with the Ruddies. They would not decoy well to the point blinds and, as a consequence, were largely garnered by the market gunners. In the marshes, the bulk of the bag would be Widgeon, Pintail, Blackduck, Broadbill, Ringnecks, and Mallards. In the early part of the season, there would be a few Blue-wing Teal, with the Green-wings coming along later. An occasional Gadwall and Spoonbill would leaven the loaf.

The present-day gunner would be simply appalled at what was taken as a matter of course in the way of a day's bag in, say, the 1880's. I believe, on certain of the South Sea Islands, there is no concept of the word "weather," because one day is much like another. In the same way, the thought or idea of a bag limit never entered one's mind. I am sure it would be of interest to the reader to see some photostatic copies of the entries which appear in some of the old game books of the Princess Anne Club, Seelinger's Marsh, and at Sand Bridge.

I recall an instance where sixty-eight Canvasbacks were gathered on the first pick-up when shooting from Shell Point on Long Island. The birds came in so fast that there was no lull in the shooting to make an earlier pick-up possible. No imputations of guilt were attached to such scores and such an episode was merely regarded as a grand day when conditions were right. I can recall my father killing sixty-three geese, when in the Teal Island blind situated on a property called Barbour's Hill.

Numbers in possession were unlimited and it should be noted that all these birds, of course, were shipped to various and sundry friends and so were not wasted. In retrospect, it hardly seems conceivable that a pair of Canada Geese should constitute a limit. In times past, the gunning season extended through February. During the winter months, the bays would freeze tight, with the exception of an airhole here and there. I recall a wild-fowling confrere of mine considering himself quite fortunate in knocking off one hundred and six Ruddies in such an airhole.

Today, of course, such slaughter seems absolutely indefensible. But as I have said before, at the time these performances were chalked up they were regarded merely as outstanding days with thousands of birds available. The Raised Eyebrow Department was conspicuous by its absence.

For some reason or other, Mallards were very much more abundant at the turn of the century than they are today. It would appear they have rather abandoned this flyway.

A remarkable instance of survival under adverse circumstances is the flock of White Brant, or Snow Geese, which has, for as long as I can remember, used the beach strip between the bay and the ocean within a limit of five miles from the old Princess Anne Club property down toward Barbour's Hill. What a sight it was when this flock got up! There were well over five thousand in number and they flew around a few miles before lighting again, their white backs and wings gleaming in the sunlight as they wheeled. As far as I know, there is not another flock of Snow Geese of any size on the Atlantic Coast.

In discussing this abundance of birds, it now becomes pertinent to refer briefly to the legislation which first undertook to control the untrammeled

To get in on a good canvasback "fly" requires more than a little luck. The birds must be present and using in the vicinity of the blind.

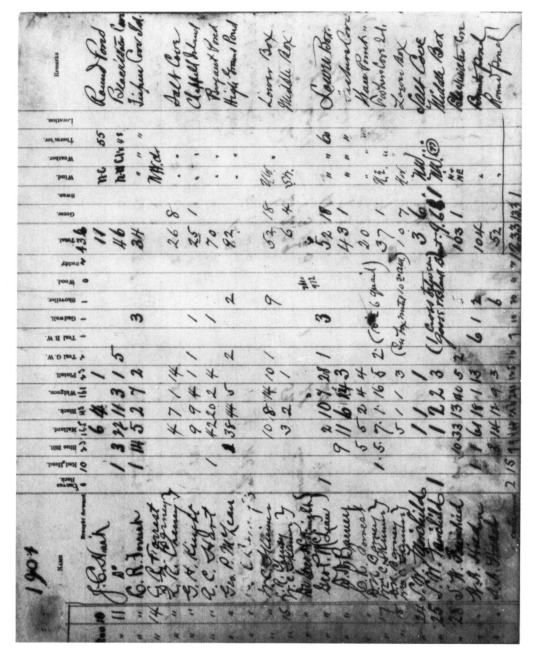

1904 appears to have been an outstanding year. Sand Bridge "doings" reflect December performance, and certainly the Princess Anne gunners were not idle in November.

burning of powder. The first Federal duck law was passed on March 4, 1913, but was promptly declared unconstitutional. In the fall of 1916, we entered into a treaty with Canada and on July 3, 1918, an enabling act was passed putting teeth in this treaty. This was the first Federal law that referred to the sale of wildfowl. Little attempt was made to enforce the regulation against sale until after April 19, 1920, when the United States Supreme Court gave its blessing to this stipulation.

With regard to bag limits, as distinguished from the matter of the sale of game, the limitation of twenty-five ducks a day was first established in July, 1918, and, as my readers know, such a daily limit has been modified from time to time as circumstances seemed to necessitate.

Let me now acquaint you with an old-timer's daily routine. You would be awakened about three-quarters of an hour before sunrise and sit down to a breakfast that left nothing to be desired. After stowing away, let us say, hot cereal, ham and eggs, some pancakes and several cups of coffee, you would go down to the dock and impatiently await the first showing of the sun, which, to mix a metaphor, constituted the green light to start you on your way for whatever the day might hold in store. Other gunners, too, of course, would be getting under way. In a few minutes the sunrise sky would be laced with ducks and geese flying hither and yon because of the disturbance.

In this mind's-eye project of ours, let us say we are going to tie out in the northwest head of Fisher's Cove. The two gunners would install themselves in the blind and the guide would get busy with the greatest possible dispatch in staking out the decoys. Twelve to fourteen live birds would soon start to dabble and preen themselves. Their number would be supplemented by a varying number of block decoys, and soon all would be in readiness. If a goodly number of birds had been using the cove, business would start to pick up at once and, in a great majority of cases, at least three-quarters of the birds to be killed on that day would be in hand by ten o'clock.

Our shooting tapers off, and we toy with the idea of lunch. It is pretty hard to resist the impulse to gnaw on a cold roast Teal or to have a cup of hot soup long before the noon hour has struck. Even though our sport has begun to taper off, it is always a pleasure to watch the antics of the live decoys and observe the ruthless routine of the marsh, where an eagle soars on high, watching for a crippled duck, and perhaps a marsh hawk or two are engaged in their never-ending search for prey.

By this time, a goodly number of wildfowl have been garnered. The live decoys, with their wheezy "crate calls," are serving notice that the time is at hand to consider returning to the clubhouse.

On our return to our spacious living room, the day's doings are reviewed with our confreres. Such discussion is enlivened by a toddy or two, designed, presumably, to dispose of the day's chill.

Dinner was indeed a gastronomic hurly-burly. Lynnhaven Bay oysters were forthcoming as a matter of course. Perhaps some side bets would be made on the number of oyster crabs that might be found ensconced in their hosts. Before their virtual disappearance, a dish of terrapin might brighten the occasion. With the terrapin now about gone, perhaps a six- or eight-pound rockfish, taken offshore the same day with a drag seine, would put in an appearance. This, together with a roast duck apiece, with a side dish of collards and sweet potatoes, would almost forestall any keen inquiry in the matter of dessert. If some member were to be so kindly as to furnish a bottle or two of Burgundy, so much the better.

Again we repair to the living room. After a somewhat labored bit of chit-chat on the day's sport, we are off to bed.

Few sportsmen shot from a sinkbox. This rig was pretty much monopolized by the market gunners. The sinkbox was a heavy, cumbersome device accommodating one or two persons. It was countersunk flush with the surface of the water by the weight of the incumbent, which was supplemented by iron decoys placed around the edge of the rig's framework. Extending out in all directions were wooden outriders, to which burlap bagging was attached. These shutterlike devices, riding on the surface, would break up the wavelets which otherwise would flood the occupant. There were also little lead foil flaps extending around the edge of the cockpit that could be turned up on edge, affording further protection in this respect. Even with this protection, they could not keep afloat in rough weather.

About two hundred decoys were used. After they were in position, the tender would go downwind to await developments. As the gunner could sit down, he was not subject to the stresses and strains which characterized shooting from a battery box. By leaning over, he could keep his head and shoulders pretty much flush with the water and straighten up when the split second arrived to start operations. These market gunners were amazing shots, but I do not suppose they were better than their counterparts elsewhere. Expenditure of shells, of course, was the principal expense involved.

Old-timers tell me that on Redheads a good man should average about one hundred per cent. This outstanding performance is because of this bird's characteristic of "balling up" at the head end of the squadron as they come in to stool. Canvasbacks are not characterized by such behavior, and it was considered good performance to account for two birds with an expenditure of three cartridges. In passing, I might mention that Canvasbacks had to weigh six pounds to the pair to rate as No. 1 birds.

The little Ruddies were duck soup, as they flew on an even keel and came for the decoys very close to the surface. I well can remember, as a boy, watching these men shoot Ruddies. Their automatics would bark five times and, more often than not, there would be four or five splashes, representing the final resting place of a like number of cleanly killed ducks.

The number of licenses given to operate these sinkboxes was far greater than the area could support. In the larger waters south of the North Carolina line no such mistake was made. I think at one time there were something like one hundred and ten sinkboxes licensed to operate in the Back Bay area.

I am of the opinion that more birds would have been killed had this number been restricted to, say, twenty-five. The birds were being constantly chevied by the battery tenders and, unless it was a pretty rough day on the ocean, the birds, when first disturbed, would fly out to sea and there sit the day out.

Today these wildfowl do not go to sea as of yore. When disturbed, they find refuge in the Federal sanctuary, which consists of the very sizeable area that formerly constituted the property of the Princess Anne Club, the Ragged Island Club and Seelinger's Marsh.

If a casual wildfowler wants a day's shooting today in this area, he is not confronted with a very alluring prospect. The native baymen can no longer shoot for market. Hence, they cannot be blamed for trying otherwise to make an honest dollar from wildfowling. The stake blind affords the only answer, which blind must be located at least five hundred yards from any other stake blind and a like distance from any licensed point.

These permanent installations, which are of such a size as to engulf skiff and gunners, stand up like sore thumbs and greatly detract from the general appearance of this area. How a self-respecting duck can toll into such a monstrosity is beyond me, but in rough weather, the occupants can get some birds. Win, lose or draw, the duck hunter is charged up to twenty-five dollars a day and the odds against his having good sport, I should say, roughly compare with what is paid off on the general run of daily doubles.

The Back Bay area undoubtedly will provide sport for wildfowlers for many years to come, unless conditions become more severe and the regulations affecting duck shooting are increased. While the abolition of baiting and the discontinuance of live decoys was unquestionably necessary because of the reduction in the number of birds, it is to be hoped that the stock will increase in due course of time and once more the wildfowler's heart will be gladdened by the sight of thousands of ducks over Back Bay, as he wends his way toward his blind in the glory of the dawn.

XIII

Currituck Sound

BY FREDERICK C. HAVEMEYER, 2ND

CURRITUCK SOUND boasts one of the oldest shooting clubs in America. Being a favorite place for migrating waterfowl, it is naturally a choice rendezvous for sportsmen. The sound, about thirty miles long and two to three miles wide, is located in a region highly interesting historically. Its northern tip reaches into Virginia, where it forms Back Bay. The main portion lies along the North Carolina Coast, joining Albemarle Sound and Roanoke Island at the southern end. The name "Currituck" came from the Currituck Indians who inhabited that part of the country.

There once was a large Indian settlement here, as proved by the many Indian mounds, oyster shell heaps and the numerous Indian-named towns and rivers. The first expedition sent by Sir Walter Raleigh in 1584 explored as far as Albemarle Sound, adjacent to Currituck. And the first settlers, sent again by Raleigh in 1585, landed on Roanoke Island. The Chickahominy River, where Pocahontas met Captain John Smith in 1607, is only sixty miles from Currituck. And the James River, site of much early exploration, is but twenty miles distant.

Currituck Sound first attracted explorers and adventurers, then outlaws, desperadoes and even pirates. One of the most notorious characters in this area was Black Beard, the pirate. In OLD VIRGINIA AND HER NEIGHBORS, by John Fiske, you can read how Black Beard, circa 1718, ranged up and down Chesapeake Bay and Pamlico Sound, robbing, plundering and killing. Doubtless he made forays into Currituck for it was in the immediate vicinity.

Governor Spotswood of Virginia finally dispatched two cruisers to track the pirate down and Black Beard's ship was discovered near Ocracoke Inlet, only some seventy miles from Currituck. The cruisers engaged the pirate ship, Black Beard was killed, the crew taken prisoner and hung. Black Beard's head was cut off and placed on the bowsprit of one of the cruisers, which sailed in triumph up the coast, around Currituck Sound, to the James River.

Anyone interested in the history of this part of the country could spend years of research, and write tome after tome. Kittyhawk, where the Wright Brothers first flew their plane, is at the southern end of Currituck. You can see the monument there, and inspect the high dunes where the plane took off.

There have been many contour changes in Currituck Sound. Indications are that it was first a bay, its shoreline broken into sand islands, estuaries and inlets. Then gradually, because of severe ocean storms, the sand was pushed up till it formed one continuous, broad sand barrier. This turned the one-time salt water bay, where oysters and shellfish grew, into a stretch of quasi-fresh water abounding with waterplants and grasses—an ideal feeding-ground for waterfowl.

Currituck would never be a huntsman's mecca if this had not taken place. The coastal line is still changing, changing all the time. The sand barrier, of dunes often reaching heights of a hundred and fifty feet, is ever on the move southward. Day and night these dunes creep on. At a snail's pace, yes—only covering a mile in thirty years, but still engulfing everything in their path. You find the houses there protected by great sand fences and barricades. Even the Currituck Club house has its system of sand barriers. Sand beating on the windowpanes frosts the glass, and panes often must be replaced. Sand, too, carves and polishes the driftwood into magic shapes.

Wind, sand and water notwithstanding, Currituck became definitely established as an inland sound. If the sea did manage to force an opening through the coastal barrier, the break was immediately filled in by sand, wind-blown. There wasn't even a sea tide to menace the shores from within, because the nearest ocean inlet opened into Albemarle Sound, and not into Currituck. What tide there was was a tide blown by the wind. Then came the Albemarle and Chesapeake Canal to destroy nearly all of nature's work and make an end to Currituck shooting. In 1865, the canal was dug from Norfolk to Munden, the northern, or Virginia end, of Currituck Sound. The canal resumed again above Coinjock, in the central portion of the sound, and continued south, then west to Elizabeth City, creating a continuous waterway from Norfolk to Elizabeth City. A fine idea for navigation, and all very well for Currituck Sound—until the locks were removed.

This allowed the salt waters of Chesapeake Bay to pour down from Norfolk, to Munden and into the sound. Much of the waterfowl feed was destroyed—duck plants, wild celery, widgeon grass, and duck potatoes. It meant the end of Canvasback and Redhead shooting at Currituck. For that matter all the shooting was seriously affected. A few years ago Mr. Corey and Mr. Knapp, two local sportsmen, arranged to have the locks replaced. Now the precious duck plants can grow again and the birds are coming back to feed as usual. With the locks in, Currituck Sound will always be the perfect feeding place for migrating waterfowl. Rafts of birds will fill the sound from shore to shore and gunners may try their luck to their hearts' content.

The earliest shooting at Currituck was undoubtedly done by the Indians. Then by the first English settlers. There followed a long period when birds were hunted for market and shipped in great quantities to Baltimore, Washington, Philadelphia and New York. This was the era of systematic slaughter. Mallards and Blackduck suffered the most, not because they were better table birds but because they fed near shore and were easiest to kill. Redheads, Canvasbacks and Geese escaped, the two former because they rafted away out on the water, the latter because they were exceptionally wary birds and not as popular for eating purposes. But later, means were devised to shoot these birds too.

It is interesting to note how these market hunters got their game. They used a single barrel flint-lock gun, a heavy six-gauge affair, rammed full of powder. They shot the birds on the sit, feeding, and only when they were properly bunched. You can imagine the massacre which ensued. When the sale of wildfowl became prohibited, market hunting died a natural death.

The first recorded sporting gunners at Currituck were a group of northerners who stayed at Poplar Branch in 1854. In this party were Valentine Hicks, E. Wade, Colonel Edwin Post, E. C. Lindsey, J. H. Dimon, Messrs. Carrington, Lily and Beckwith. Possibly having tasted market Currituck duck, they hastened to see the birds at first hand. These gentlemen drove down from Norfolk by buggy and carryall and put up with Mr. Poyner, father of T. J. Poyner, second superintendent of Currituck Club. They came back three years in succession, and in 1857 they founded Currituck Club, the first shooting club in these parts.

The club lands consisted of 3,100 acres, bought at a dollar an acre. The property included four miles of ocean beach and another four miles along the sound, with marshlands intersected by leads, ponds and creeks, and covered by a dense growth of reeds and rushes. The gentlemen themselves were among the first club members. Their guides were Lewis Rowe and his son Eben Rowe, two Long Islanders, who introduced the then unknown art of wing shooting over decoys. It was a long trip down from New York, so these sportsmen stayed for long visits. Guns were a great matter for discussion. Those were the days of the Purdys, Westly Richards, Greeners, and Mullins. They were muzzle-loading guns which used central fire percussion caps and pink-edged felt wads. Powder flasks were employed, shot flasks, cans of black powder and bags of shot. All these were brought and stored in great quantity.

These first members of Currituck built a clubhouse with eight rooms, and accommodations at one time for some dozen members, plus space for the

Fish & Wildlife Service

Canada Goose standing in rough water.

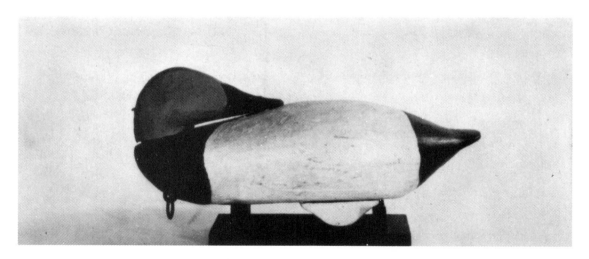

Sleeping Canvasback drake. Made about 1900 by one of the Saunders family, Poplar Branch, on Currituck Sound, N. C.

A typical goose box along the shore.

Typical duck marsh at Currituck.

Shoal draft boats tied up to the Club Dock.

guides. A new clubhouse was built later, in 1879, and stood about seventy-five yards from the old one. There are twenty-one bedrooms, one for each of the members, in the new building. Since the founding of the club the number of members has never changed—never more nor less than twenty-one.

In ten years Currituck Club will celebrate its hundredth anniversary. In the early days of its founding the club had to contend not only with pot-hunters, and the removal of the canal locks, but also with the Civil War. Because the property belonged to a group of northerners, the southern patriots raided the place, took everything off, including guns, ammunition and decoys, and sold all to the highest bidder. Feeling ran high even after the cessation of hostilities, and local southerners kept on damaging the club, scuttling the club launches. Though some of our good friends in the south are still fighting the War Between the States, at least they only fight it now in words, and Currituck Club hasn't suffered any physical damage of late.

Currituck is not by any means the only club on the sound. There are quite a few others (Monkey Island, Swan Island, and Pine Island clubs and so on), but, of course, they all shoot under pretty much the same conditions. Too, there is considerable gunning done by independent sportsmen who belong to no club or group. They hire guides who have blinds licensed for the season. These are usually bush blinds along the edge of the marsh, by the channels and open water, because the clubs own the best pond shooting. These blinds are one right next to the other, are shot day after day throughout the season, and the birds are soon scared away.

The public guides' fees are prohibitive, the sport they offer very poor in comparison. At least they are usually amusing local characters, with a fund of anecdotes to keep up your spirits. The independent gunner has many places to stay in the neighborhood. Van Slack's Tavern at Poplar Branch, founded in 1865, is one of the most popular stopovers. Rumor has it that a Russian Grand Duke once put up here for the night.

The shooting customs at Currituck Club have varied through the years. In the old days duck-shooting stands were a matter of first come, first served.

Breakfast was bolted down, equipment grabbed on the run, and there followed a general scramble for the boat landing. Then the real race was on. With much sweating and swearing the boatmen vied one with the other in this mad race to the shooting grounds, until at last the first wooden decoy flung overboard secured the vantage spot. The southeast point of Indian Gap was then considered best for Canvasback shooting. Until a member understood this custom, he never had a chance at the choice stand.

A story is told about a novice at Currituck who found himself left behind at the first day's shooting. He was a fellow of resource, so that night he hid all the other members' shooting caps. The other men lost precious minutes of time searching unsuccessfully for their headgear next morning, while our young friend was happily out on Indian Gap. They never did find their shooting caps, and were forced to don the only headgear they had available —the stovepipes they had worn down on the train. Imagine a string of irate, top-hatted men tumbling aboard their skiffs and foaming away for stands!

Nowadays the club members draw duck stands by lot before going out to shoot. The ponds have colorful names such as "Blackduck Hole," "Nigger Creek," "Brant Marsh," "Canvasback Lead," and so on. These ponds are well protected and cared for by club funds. There are dykes to maintain the proper water level, and assure the growth and supply of natural feed for the ducks. Until two years ago, when it was prohibited by law, the rig was the deadly battery rig. This type of rig is so widely known there is no use going into it here. A double battery, out in open water, surrounded by several hundred decoys, was nothing short of murder. On stormy days, when ducks poured into these rigs, and there was no legal limit to the number of birds shot, it was only a question of how many you wanted to kill, or how much pounding your shoulder could take.

But these battery rigs had their definite physical drawbacks. They were usually flush with the water, and you had to lie down in them, so as not to be seen by the ducks overhead. On a windy winter's day the cold waves splashed right in on you, you got wet all over, water even ran down the back of your neck. It was anything but pleasant.

I took a friend out in one of these rigs on a bitter December day. He endured it silently and I admired him for his Spartan qualities. But once home, sitting with his feet in a tub of hot water, his teeth still chattering as he tried to drink a hot grog, he said: "Just imagine doing that for fun! *Fun!* If it wasn't for the ducks, you couldn't pay me a million dollars to go out there."

Now that the new shooting laws proscribe the battery rig and its exquisite form of torture, Currituck duck shooting is usually pond shooting. You go out at sunrise, crossing the sound and riding up the channels by powerboat, then poling up to the pond in your skiff. Once there, you choose from two or three blinds, trying to find one with the wind at your back, or nearly from the back, because ducks come in against wind. If there is no blind with a favorable wind, you improvise one. You put out your stool, then settle down to wait.

The sun rises, ducks appear overhead, and shooting is on. You must never count on perfect weather conditions at Currituck. You get sunny days and stormy days, hot days and biting cold days. Some days are good for shooting ducks, others for dreaming duck. It is all chance and all part of the game. In the last few years Widgeon, Pintail, Mallard and Blacks comprised the bulk of the shooting. But almost any kind of duck may come by. You are often disappointed by undesirable birds such as Broadbill, "hairy crowns" (or Hooded Mergansers), Spoonbills and Goldeneyes. But then you get Ruddies, Gadwalls and sometimes a Ringneck. If there is a no'theaster blowing, you will come across a number of Redheads and Canvasbacks. There are records of all kinds and types of birds killed at Currituck: Eider Duck, European Widgeon, Bean Geese, Blue Geese and White-Fronted Geese. You will see flocks of snow-white Swans. There is even a snipe bog near the clubhouse, and on off days I have gone there and knocked down a snipe or two.

The usual shooting custom here is ducks at sunrise and during the day, geese in the afternoon, when they are more likely to be on the move.

The goose boxes, or blinds, are usually sunk in the ground near the shore of the sound. They are most frequently made of cement, with four sides and a bottom, so surrounded by brush they become one with the landscape. A few years ago, when live decoys were used, a flock of tame geese was brought to the blind and staked out around it. Sometimes as many as thirty or forty geese were used, and it was quite a labor to set them out. In the days of no limit, it was worth the time expended. But when the limit decreased to three geese a day, live geese decoys were pretty much discontinued. Later, all live decoys were prohibited by law.

The first shooting trip I ever made was to Currituck. It was obvious I should go there first, because both my father and grandfather had done most of their shooting at Currituck. I went down by train to Cape Charles, and in the cold, early dawn boarded the steamer for Norfolk. My fellow travelers were all sportsmen. Duffel bags and guns were piled high in the cabin, everyone was talking ducks and geese. From the deck I saw Scoters and Old Squaws rise off the water, the first birds to whet my appetite for what was to come.

From Norfolk I went by car to Virginia Beach and then along the dunes to Currituck. As we bowled along on the sand, I wished I had been able to go down with a Currituck huntsman before the turn of the century. In those days you went by train to Munden's Point, then sailed down the sound. What an experience to pass all the rafts of birds on the way! But even so, there was plenty to see on the ocean beach. The pounding surf and high dunes alone were enough to hold your interest. Then there were the many wrecks along the sand, some recent, others old, with only a few twisted timbers remaining.

This is a dangerous piece of coastline, with many shoals and sandbars. Ships often strand too far out to be reached by breeches buoy or bombline, and the surf is too heavy to launch a lifeboat. There is a story that ships were once lured onto the shoals by the light of a lantern, swinging around a horse's neck, which the mariners mistook for another boat, bobbing on quiet bay waters.

As we drove farther down the beach I saw eagles soaring high over the marsh. Flocks of ducks, geese and even flocks of swans were trading back

The Currituck Club House and its sandy surroundings.

A fine lot of Canada Geese.

Wading ashore from the goose box.

A two-man blind at one of the ponds.

Breaking up skim ice by rocking the boat.

Skiffs moored near the Club Dock.

and forth. By evening I was in the actual land of waterfowl. Marshes stretched out as far as I could see. Pale tints of rosy pink, blue, and green streaked the sky—the sun was setting, casting its iridescent lights on the darkening scene. Then was when the birds rose, honking and quacking for the evening flight to feeding grounds along the sound.

More and more birds came in from the ocean. When it became too dark to see, you could still hear—distinctly hear—the swish of wings as flock after flock passed overhead. I walked into the gray-shingled clubhouse with the muffled sound of passing wings still throbbing in my ears, birds still flying before my mind's eye, and the tang of the ocean air, the sharp, brackish odor of the marshes, still filling my nostrils.

Dinner at Currituck Club is always a feast. The table groans with Hunger Creek oysters, roasted Teal and red wine. You eat until you cannot swallow another morsel, then you stand with your back to the fire and take part in the talk of shooting, past and present. Talk of bluebird weather, no'theasters, driving snowstorms. Talk of blinds, rigs, record bags, guns, ammunition and decoys. And most of all—talk of birds.

You hear that certain sportsmen have spied the "Great White Wavies," or Snow Geese, at Currituck. You hear they come down from the Arctic Circle, stop in the Gulf of St. Lawrence, and aren't seen again till they reach this region. You are told Snow Geese are wary and extremely difficult to decoy. They move only in a heavy blow or a sudden change of weather. Then you hunt them along the sand dunes where they rest. You listen to how to make your decoys—with newspaper over a heap of sand to simulate the body, and another piece of paper, wrapped around a stick and put into the sand-heap, to look like a head.

You are told how to dig down in the sand and hide yourself the best you can, until the flight comes over. You hear how hard these birds are to bag—when they fly, they never bunch. You only can hope that one or two will waver in the ranks and give you a stray shot. Yes, they tell you, you can be proud indeed if you get a Snow Goose. Should you ever down two with a double, you will go down in shooting annals. Few shots have ever done it, and few ever will.

As to the Lesser Snow Goose, you won't see any at Currituck, they say, because these birds are never found on the Atlantic Coast.

Then you are told tales of Canada Geese, always popular in these parts. You hear they come down in great hordes each winter, to spend the fair weather sitting on the dunes. You are told to be sure to look across at the faraway sand dunes, when you are in a pond waiting for ducks to decoy. You will see an amazing sight—dark patches on the yellow sand, which are nothing but hordes of geese, preening and dozing in the sun. And they tell you that geese aren't easy to decoy either. On a bluebird day they won't move till evening. Then it's too late to shoot.

The best time to hunt geese, they say, is in heavy weather. And they tell you the way to get a really close look at these birds is after a big blow. Then they huddle on shore, tired and disheveled, their feathers loaded with wet sand. They wait there till the sand dries out enough for them to shake off their load of it and rise from the ground. Ah, but then, they tell you, just wait till you see your first flock coming in over the decoys. You'll see how big they are, how powerful. You'll hear the rhythmic beat of their wings, their loud, piercing honk. Yes, the gunners will all agree as they stand about the fire, no sight and no sound can so gladden your heart as a flight of Canada Geese dropping into the blind.

In a few days I had my own tales of geese to recount, though some were more wonderful memories than shooting exploits. There was the time I crouched under some bushes on the shoreline, before sunset, and saw a flock of geese rise about a mile away. Rise desultorily, in small bunches, into the air. Then move slowly into formation, honking all the while, and start toward me.

By the time they were overhead they were in perfect V formation, the leader well out in front. A light breeze was quartering them, so they flew on a diagonal. Their wings beat very slowly, the outer half seeming hardly to fan the air, while the inner, or more muscular half, remained quite still. The sun fell below the horizon, darkness set in and still they came on, bunch after bunch. As I walked back in the encircling darkness, I could hear them on the move, honking as they went. This was indeed "wild chorus."

Another day I had an experience not so felicitous. It was a heavy blow, the kind of weather which makes geese look for protection in the ponds and marshes. Though we were shooting duck, we set out a few goose decoys on the side of the stool, just in case. I downed a Teal, which fell into the neck-high marsh, so I got out of the blind to look for my bird. Just as I found him in the reeds, there was the sound of geese overhead. They came over our blind and decoyed. My shooting companion downed two beauties, and there I was—tramping back from the marsh, carrying a tiny Teal. Shooting geese is a matter of luck. You have to know your place and your weather, and you have to be right on the spot when they come over.

But, as the saying goes, every dog has his day and I had mine. This same fellow-huntsman and I were in a goose-box on the dunes, and we'd been sitting there for hours without seeing a single bird of any sort. He decided to go in and pack, for it happened to be the last day of our trip. I, fortunately, elected to sit it out for another half hour. I settled myself back to wait, and then—the geese rose off the dunes. My guide opened up with his goose call, and the birds poured by overhead. I got my limit in no time, could easily have downed many more.

There was also the day I sat in that same box and saw five thousand geese in the air at one time. The sky was simply filled with them. I took colored photographs of this amazing sight and mailed the film to be developed. The film came back with a letter telling me to clean my camera lens. The dirty lens was responsible for those spots in the sky.

Spots! They weren't spots—they were those myriad geese. When the film was projected on a screen you could see the geese very distinctly.

Once I happened to shoot one of Jack Miner's geese. Miner has a preserve in Ontario, Canada, near the shores of Lake Erie. He calls his place "The Mission" and his birds "The Missionaries." They are banded each one with a quotation from the Bible. You get quite a start when you shoot a goose, pick it up, and see "Repent, Ye Sinner" around the creature's leg! And sinner you feel to have murdered a "Missionary."

Yes, taken all in all, the Currituck shooting is pretty darn good sport. I happen to prefer shooting geese, but ducks have their thrill, too; and I have many fond memories of ducking at Currituck.

I'll remember leaving the dock in the cold gray dawn. I'll remember the sound of the powerboat sputtering in the quiet morning air. The skiff, full of decoys, bobbing along astern. I'll remember poling up the lead to our pond, slowly rounding the bend. I'll always remember the ducks springing into the air in all directions. And the birds as they decoy. I'll remember the slim, graceful Pintail. The large, thick Blackduck who circles carefully before he comes in. I'll remember the fast-flying Widgeon, with his whistling call. The tiny Teal who swoops and stunts, and necessitates a quick, accurate shot. I'll remember the aristocratic Mallard, with his shiny green head. And the sleek Gadwall.

But to have these shooting memories, and be able to go out and garner more of them, we must protect our wildfowl. Only by protecting the wildfowl can we preserve this greatest and most thrilling of American sports. I, for one, am glad limits have been put on the number of birds to be shot.

When first I went to Currituck we had a bag limit of twenty-five ducks and three geese, though Wednesday, Saturday and Sunday were rest days. The bag was gradually reduced, year by year, until the limit was only ten ducks and two geese. In 1943 and 1944 the ducks were coming back in such quantities there were hopes the limit could be raised. But in 1946 we again found a reduced season and a smaller bag. The limit now is seven ducks and two geese. That isn't many birds for a day's shooting, but I am happy to see the limit low if the waterfowl are decreasing in number. I want to be sure that our sons and our sons' sons can go to Currituck and witness the hordes of whistling wings. I want them to see a flock of Pintail hovering overhead at sunset. I want them to be out in the driving snow while Canvasbacks are flying. I want them to feel the cold on their bare hands, and fingers numbing to cold steel. I want them to see a flock of Brant tumbling into the decoys.

I want them to trudge home in the dark, in a driving no'theaster, carrying some big "honkers" slung over their shoulders. I want them to stalk the Snow Geese along the dunes, to see the Swan all rosy-pink at dawn. As I have said, I want to preserve the birds for them, I want them to be able to enjoy Currituck as I have. Currituck, the land of waterfowl, which is, and always will be, I hope, hard to beat as a huntsman's paradise.

X I V

Pamlico Sound

BY DR. EDGAR BURKE

PAMLICO SOUND, which begins at Manteo and ends just south of Atlantic, both in North Carolina, is approximately one hundred miles long. Its width varies, but averages about thirty miles. The waters of this huge salt sound are mostly shallow. It abounds in great sand flats, exposed at low tide and stretching in all directions for miles. The winters are mild in this section of the coast, which makes it an ideal resort for the vast flocks of all kinds of wildfowl which spend the cold months on its waters. More Brant and Canada Geese winter here than at any other spot on the whole length of the Atlantic Coast. Flocks of Broadbill and Redhead containing ten thousand individuals are a commonplace here. It is, of course, one of the most classic shooting grounds of the eastern littoral.

The first thing that a stranger visiting Pamlico Sound notices when looking over its broad expanse are the stake-blinds that stud the reefs in which this section is so rich. "What are those things sticking up out of the water?" is the inevitable question when the uninitiated first see them from afar. Built, usually, about three-quarters to a mile apart, they extend for long distances off shore, until the farthest appear as mere dots on the horizon.

Many, indeed, are a good five miles from the nearest land. Erected during the late summer months, they are standing when the first fowl arrive from the north. These soon regard them as a natural and inoffensive part of the landscape, unhesitatingly feeding in immediate proximity to them. In the days when baiting was legal, one could often see both geese and ducks gleaning stray grains under the floors of the boxes.

The dimensions of these blinds, designed for occupancy by two gunners, are usually about three and one-half feet wide by four feet deep. Seats run along both sides. A sort of well affords room for the feet. Situated around the sides are peepholes, or slits, conveniently arranged so that, when seated, a man of average stature will find them at exact eye level. Through these apertures decoying fowl can be comfortably watched without exposing oneself to their sight. Most men rise to their feet when about to shoot, the top of the walls or sides of the box then coming up to about breast level. The whole structure is supported, at the four corners, by stout stakes, usually unpeeled tree trunks, which are sunk deep into the sand of the bar or reef on which the blind is set. A number of cross-slats, nailed to the corner supports, serve as a ladder by which one enters or leaves.

While flimsy and crude in outward appearance, stake-blinds afford a surprising degree of shelter when cold and piercing winds are blowing. A cushion or two will add materially to one's comfort.

Stake-blinds are almost always erected on sandbars covered by water not too deep for wading. On Pamlico the tides depend upon the direction and force of the wind and not on the almanac. It is customary for the sportsman to climb out and gather in his own game. Only in the case of birds which fall far out in deep water do the boatmen do the retrieving. In some cases a mile or more of wadable water surrounds the individual blinds on all sides. From a distance it is a curious sight to see a man apparently walking on the surface of the deep!

The shooting is very varied—Geese, Brant and several species of ducks make up an average day's bag. The bulk of these last will be either Pintail or Broadbill. Blackduck, while regular, are relatively few in number and are seldom shot out of the stake-blinds. They prefer the salt marshes on the sound side of the banks and do not often go out on the reefs. Redhead occasionally give a good day's sport, especially at the northern extremity of the sound. Canvasback are few and far between.

Pamlico is a trifle too far south for them and it is only after a spell of exceptional cold, severe enough to freeze up Currituck solid, that they seek open water in this area. Widgeon vary from season to season. They are likely to consort with the great flocks of Pintail inhabiting these waters. In some years they figure in the bag almost daily; in others but few are seen. "Ducks," on Pamlico, means Pintail, unless otherwise specified! Swans are seen now and then,—sometimes a Greater Snow Goose strays down from the Pea Island Reserve, some sixty miles to the northward.

During the last few seasons one or two small gaggles of Blue Geese have appeared. In 1945 three were shot, two adults and one specimen in the juvenile plumage. Virtually every species of waterfowl known to inhabit the eastern North American continent, has been brought to bag on Pamlico at some time. Last year two Northern Eiders were killed there, which probably constitutes a new southern record for the species. Mallard, curiously enough, are among the rarities, as are Wood Duck.

The winters are mild on the banks, punctuated by occasional short periods of really cold weather, severe enough to make heaviest shooting clothes indispensable. Even more frequently "spells" of summer-like warmth may be expected—so-called bluebird days, when shooting enthusiasm temporarily wanes. Low tides are likely to accompany these periods of unseasonable warmth, which still further depress the quality and the quantity of the sport. However, this is not always true. I have known days so bright and calm and warm that the most experienced of wildfowlers would have pronounced them hopeless, which have produced the finest of shooting and limit bags to every gun. Northwest winds bring clear, cold, high water and optimum shooting, as a general rule.

Low tides expose the flats and leave the stake-blinds high and dry. During the fortnight immediately preceding Christmas, this state of affairs is par-

Typical stake blind showing entrance door.

The Green Island Club at Ocracoke, N. C.

Wild geese picked up starving. Will be liberated when strong.

Lynn Bogue Hunt in a Pamlico Sound stake blind.

A Currituck sit-down battery, about 1900.

This picture with one opposite shows whole rig set out.

Canada Goose, solid wood, made by Charlie McWilliams, at the Green Island Club, Ocracoke.

Brant, solid wood, made in Hatteras Village, N. C., in 1900. From the Green Island Club.

Philip H. Babcock

Setting out the battery rig at Pea Island. 1913.

Philip H. Babcock

Setting out for geese at Pea Island in 1913.

Philip H. Babcock

Battery rigged out at Pea Island in 1913.

Philip H. Babcock

Bound for Pea Island on the *Hattie Creef*. 1913

ticularly likely to obtain. This period is, consequently, not a good selection for a shooting trip to this sector, which is, at all times, a poor area to select for a short "on the spur of the moment" shooting trip. The quality of the sport to be expected depends too much upon unpredictable conditions. With luck, several days of superb shooting might be one's lot. Without it, the reward may well be a series of virtually blank days.

Nowhere on the eastern coast will the sportsman see more game than here—which is by no means synonymous with *shoot!* The writer has, many times, sat in a blind and watched ten thousand Redheads and as many Geese and Brant from sun-up until sunset without firing a shot all day. This is a common experience. The shooting grounds are so vast in their extent that conditions must be well-nigh perfect really to insure sport of a high order. The game is there, however, and there need never be an idle or a dull moment. Flocks of Geese are more or less constantly passing, as are bunches of Pintail. As the tide falls, exposing the flats more and more, the flight increases.

While rubber hip boots are better than nothing, the heavy rubber waders worn by commercial deep-sea fishermen are almost an essential item of the gunner's wardrobe when shooting from stake-blinds on the Pamlico flats. Water inevitably will enter the first-named through splashing when the sportsman is pursuing a crippled fowl in shallow water, bringing immediate misery and, later, possibly a disabling cold. Equipped with the heavier, higher waders, deep spots can be crossed without danger of getting wet, since these garments reach well above the waistline.

Duck calls have no place in this shooting. Neither Pintail nor Broadbill pay attention to them. Mallards and Blackduck are really the only species regularly responsive to calling and they rarely occur on the flats. A goose call, used with judicious restraint, will occasionally turn a passing flock of Canadas and bring them into gun-range, but one cannot count upon it.

The decoy sets are necessarily large. From one hundred to one hundred and fifty stool are not too many Geese are essential, since they are the best lure for Pintail as well as for the species which they counterfeit. Next in importance are good pintail decoys. Commercial examples are almost always much too small. The natives appreciate this and all locally made stool are ample in size, whatever other qualities they may lack. A good stand of mixed broadbill and redhead completes the really important part of the rig. Most men throw out three or four blackduck, "just in case," but they are seldom productive of any tangible results. If used, they are best placed

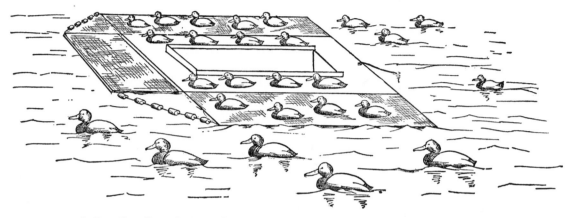

A Pamlico Sound single battery, drawn from a sketch by Capt. Gary Bragg of Ocracoke, N. C. Iron decoys placed on edges of box, and wooden decoys on floating wings. Battery was anchored at both ends to prevent swinging with wind or tide.

well off by themselves, away from the body of the set. The use of brant stool is optional, depending upon whether their killing is legal. Brant do not often come to decoys other than their own. On Pamlico reefs, Geese, Pintail and Brant feed together as though they were of one kind.

The best possible companion for a day in a stake-blind is a good pair of field glasses! Even though the shooting be indifferent, there is nothing that will while away the hours half as entertainingly or as profitably. Aside from this, the advantage of being able to identify game from afar is obvious. I have spent a lifetime in observing and hunting waterfowl of every description and it is safe to say that half of what I have seen I owe to a good glass.

Always a center of battery shooting during the years when this form of gunning was legal, Ocracoke and other villages on the banks are strewn with the weathered remains of these engines of destruction. The coffin-like boxes, which held their one-time occupants, have been largely resurrected and now do efficient duty as what one might term "dry-land blinds" for marsh shooting. The boxes, when detached from the rest of the battery,

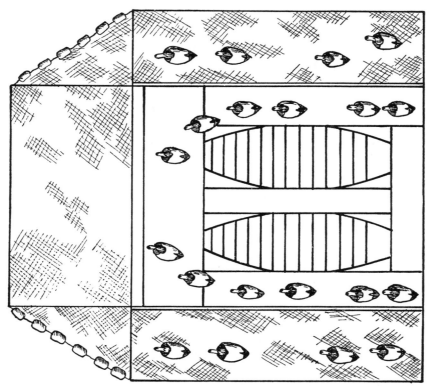

Top view of a Pamlico Sound double lie-down battery, from a sketch by Capt. Gary Bragg. Burlap wings hinged to decks with three-inch double strips of leather. Net corks float the burlap extensions at bow.

resemble small, very narrow, flat-bottomed skiffs. With a rope attached to one end, it is almost as easy to drag one across marshland as though it were a birchbark canoe of lightest weight.

With rushes or marshgrass nailed all around their four sides, they make the most perfect hide imaginable for a man lying on his back. The whole contraption is easily lifted up and carried on a truck, riding crossways upon the body. Dropped into the center of a natural clump of reeds or weeds on the open salt meadow, its presence cannot be detected five paces away. The gunner reclining in such a box is as completely hidden as though he were buried far below the level of the ground. If the bottom is water-tight, as it should be, a folded blanket, an old sheepskin or even a bundle of hay will make him comfortable.

Short of the battery itself, no deadlier way of killing geese has ever been devised. Stick-up goose decoys are, of course, used with this device. If a small meadow puddle is adjacent, duck decoys, preferably pintails, with a very few blackducks, may be advantageously employed with the profile geese. Superb shooting is the rule from such a rig, provided the gunner "has brains enough to keep his head down," as my somewhat pungent old captain usually expresses it. Northwesterly blows are the days for this type of shooting on the banks. The heavier the wind the more certain it is that, at dawn, the salt meadows will be teeming with geese and Pintail, driven to shelter and feed there by the force of the gale and the consequent rising water.

On such a day suitable marsh areas are a sight long to be remembered. The countless flocks of geese appear to be hanging suspended in the air, their slowly flapping wings seemingly impotent to carry them against the force of the blow. Not so the ducks! Like bullets they speed from place to place, obviously unhampered by the gale that so impedes the progress of the larger fowl. Under such conditions it is the simplest matter for even an indifferent shot to kill his limit in the space of minutes. I have seen many days of this type when it would have been as easy to kill a hundred geese as three! Decoys appear, then, to have a magical attraction for the birds, and these are the conditions under which, in the bad old days, wagonloads of fowl were slaughtered.

Brant keep to the flats, rarely approaching the marshlands of the banks proper. Stake-blind shooting on the open sound is the surest way of getting sport out of them. The old birds are uncertain in their response to decoys, particularly during the fall and winter months, and the best that can be expected from them is shots at flocks passing in range but making no pretense of coming into the stool. The young birds are much more susceptible to the lure of a good rig. Often their simplicity and trustfulness challenge belief. I have had them come in when I was standing among the decoys, picking up a dead bird or rearranging the set. I have had them swimming within easy gun range while so engaged. Sometimes years pass without a dozen young Brant being killed on Pamlico. It was so during the five years following 1939. During the winters of 1944-45, as well as 1945-46, they were, happily, again abundant. Because of their trustfulness, the heaviest shooting toll falls upon the birds of the year. By their second winter they are, to all intents and purposes, adult and indistinguishable from the parent birds in appearance as well as in mentality.

The disappearance of the eelgrass, which began about 1932, and is due to a fungous disease allegedly originating on the coast of France, has had an extremely serious effect upon the shooting in this area, as elsewhere. The Brant depended upon this marine growth almost to the exclusion of all other feed. It formed a major portion of the winter ration of the Canada Geese and these, more than any other species of fowl, appear to have been most adversely affected by its extinction. Owing to their inability to dive, they are compelled to feed in water no deeper than the reach of their necks, so that today their staple is the roots of the widgeon grass that cover portions of the Pamlico flats. Everywhere these are pitted by the funnel-shaped holes left by the geese in their quest for this food. In the Ocracoke sector, and in others as well, the available supply is inadequate to tide the birds over the whole of the winter. Often enough the grass is practically all consumed as early as January. The bleak salt meadows of the adjacent banks furnish but scant forage at this season, with the result that in some years geese perish by hundreds from sheer starvation.

I have known times when two men walking the marshlands could fill a truck in an afternoon's search with these birds. I have run down dozens of them too weak to fly and have in my possession, at this writing, live geese that I nursed back to life and strength after they had been so reduced by hunger that I picked them up on the open marsh as though I were retrieving dead birds. The lice, normally present as parasites upon all geese, gain an ascendancy when the birds are reduced beyond a certain point by hunger that in itself spells the doom of the host. Such birds are, then, literally eaten alive by these vermin.

The great body of the geese which have wintered on Pamlico leave for the north on the full moon of March. Some hundreds remain all summer and I am convinced that the bulk of these are individuals so depleted by a prolonged period of starvation that they were incapable of responding to the migratory urge during the normally circumscribed period when it comes upon them. This conviction is strengthened by the observation that greater numbers of birds summer in these waters in years when the preceding winter's death toll has been most heavy. As, when observed in the warm months, these non-migrating flocks are perfectly strong on the wing, the theory that they represent fowl crippled during the previous hunting season is scarcely tenable. The gulls and the eagles attend to these!

Those emaciated pairs which manage to reach the northern nesting grounds must do so in the most unfavorable physical condition for successful breeding, with a resultant much reduced crop of goslings. Repeated efforts, aimed at stirring the Fish and Wildlife Department of the Federal government into some type of effective activity in connection with this matter, have resulted in absolute failure.

Shooting from so-called "rolling blinds" has always been popular on the Carolina banks, particularly among the native gunners. Rolling blinds are exactly what the name implies—blinds which can be rolled up to resting fowl. They consist of four walls, like those of a square box from which lid and bottom have been removed. The construction is simple, consisting, as it does, of a light framework over which burlap, Japanese matting or some other similar material is tacked. Free-running, small wheels are attached at the four corners. It is usual to have a small, hinged door at the back, although many lack this convenience, the gunner then simply clambering into the machine as best he can, over the sides. These are usually about three feet high. Peepholes in the front wall enable the shooter to watch the game.

The entire structure must be built so light that a gentle push from the man kneeling inside will propel it forward. It will be understood that reasonably smooth and level ground is necessary for its operation and, consequently, it is almost exclusively employed on the open salt meadows or on low-lying sandbars or flats, not usually completely covered at highest tide. It is left unoccupied on a suitable and much frequented feeding ground for at least a few days—a week being better—before attempting to use it. During that period the fowl, usually geese, have become accustomed to its not very conspicuous presence. In the old days the ground was invariably first heavily baited with corn.

The successful manipulation of this machine requires a combination of experience and patience. In the hands of one accustomed to its use it is deadly in its effectiveness. The gunner takes his station in the blind and waits until a flock has alighted some distance away—it may be as far as a half a mile. After giving the birds time to become settled, the blind is slowly set in motion, the reaction of the birds being carefully watched every moment. At the slightest sign of suspicion in any of the fowl, usually indicated by raised and peering heads, all motion must cease, not to be resumed until every member of the flock is either again feeding or at rest. This slow approach is continued, punctuated by the necessary pauses, until easy shooting range has been attained. One shot is usually discharged into the resting flock, the other, if a double gun is being used, into the dense mass of rising birds. While geese, as I have said, are the usual victims, I have known large bags of Pintail, and even Blackduck, to be made from a rolling blind. One shot usually ends the performance but one shot is generally all that is required to achieve a limit bag.

I have described this form of shooting with distaste and only because it is so characteristic of these grounds. A single experience with it usually suffices for the novice, since it is physically exhausting to remain so long in a crouching position, besides being extremely hard on the knees. One hesitates to list it under the name of sport, undeniably effective as it often is.

In market gunning days Ocracoke Village was the center of this activity and it produced some very remarkable shots. Probably the outstanding examples living today are the O'Neal twins, Ike and Walter. These men are now approaching their seventh decade but tales of their prowess are still related with gusto by their contemporaries who witnessed them. It is unlikely that their feats of consistent marksmanship will be equaled today— to say nothing of excelled—for in their heyday the abundance of game, and the fact that they shot from dawn to dark throughout the long seasons customary at the time, afforded them a degree of practice which could not possibly be duplicated under existing conditions.

Among the older men of the banks this virtuosity was general and aroused no particular interest or comment—unless, as in the case of the O'Neals, it reached very unusual heights. Always a region favored by sportsmen, a good proportion of the men acted as guides season after season. Outstanding among them is the widely and favorably known Captain Gary Bragg, a man of the richest experience who, despite advancing years, is still actively engaged in the business.

Captain Tom Bragg, a distant kinsman, from nearby Portsmouth, is also widely known to a host of sportsmen, as is Charlie McWilliams, custodian of the Green Island Club. Expert boatmen all, these men have spent a lifetime on and by salt water and their versatility and resourcefulness are limitless and respect-compelling. No better companions exist. Being themselves keen sportsmen, the store of their anecdotes and reminiscences is inexhaustible. By no means the least enjoyable feature of a shooting trip to the Pamlico Sound country are the evenings spent in storytelling around the driftwood stove in the living room.

Ocracoke Village lies on the southern end of the eighteen-mile-long island of the same name. It is the only permanent settlement on the island, if one excepts the Coast Guard station on Hatteras Inlet, at the opposite or northern extremity. Its population is approximately six hundred. The history of this community is but imperfectly known, at least so far as the more remote past is concerned. That whites were in residence there previous to

CANADA GEESE AND BRANT

the American Revolution is established but who they were and how they got there is conjectural.

Vague legends and beliefs connected with this era of the community's history are so contradictory and jumbled that little is to be made of them. It has been said that the present inhabitants are the descendants of ship-wrecked sailors and of buccaneers, who are known to have infested these waters in the early decades of the eighteenth century, but proof is completely lacking. There is a singular absence of tradition in the individual families, whose forefathers certainly lived there long before the tardy establishment of written records. The writer has been at some pains to unearth dependable, or even plausible, data in connection with what one might term "Ocracoke's dark ages," but questioning of the older men and women has resulted in little or nothing. It is not that they are reluctant to tell but that they simply don't know.

The island has not always been a part of Hyde County, having originally belonged to Carteret County. The transfer is the result of a gerrymander, some seventy- or eighty-odd years ago. This has made an understandable muddle of some of the older land titles, many of which were lost or mislaid during their transportation from one county seat to the other. A great deal of the land is held more on the basis of tradition than on that of valid deeds and it is doubtful whether many of the titles would stand the test of search. Boundaries are vague and often in dispute.

Howard, O'Neal, Williams, Styron, Garrish and Gaskill are the ever-recurrent family names. Intermarriage between these clans has been going on for several centuries, with few outwardly discernible stigmata of degeneration. Many of the men exceed six feet in stature and are physically well adapted to the strenuous life which the isolation of their island and a livelihood largely derived from the adjacent waters, both ocean and sound, demand.

Fishing and oystering form the chief industry. The soil is practically pure sand and no agriculture, other than the cultivation of small truck patches, is possible. Originally heavily forested, the island is now almost denuded of trees. Ruthless lumbering in past decades, the inroads of the salt water and the occasional devastating West Indian hurricanes to which this section is subject, accounting for its present barrenness. Here and there in the heart of the village one comes upon the storm-mutilated remnants of what were once magnificent live oaks, struggling to prolong a patently doomed existence. Only a single small grove of these has survived intact. It is situated at the extreme southerly tip of the island.

Ocracoke saw its heyday in the decades just preceding the War between the States, when it was a not unimportant port of entry. Even before that period large storage warehouses were located there. Of all this activity no trace remains. Various writers have periodically attempted to weave a mantle of mystery and more or less fictitious romance about the settlement but with little success and less justification. Much has been made of its "quaintness," the villagers allegedly speaking the Devonshire dialect of Shakespeare's day. Were one to take these highly imaginary accounts at their face value one would logically expect a visit to the island to be tantamount to setting the calendar back several centuries and finding oneself suddenly in the heart of a small channel port of Elizabethan England.

Whatever slender basis for these poetic flights of fancy may once have existed has, long since, been erased by the gas engine, the mail-order catalogue, the aeroplane and the ubiquitous radio. The Ocracoke of 1946 differs in no essentials from other villages of the same size on the mainland. The natives are a kindly, friendly and hospitable people, completely modern in every respect.

In the days when the use of live decoys was legal and universal, Ocracoke, Portsmouth and the other villages of the banks had a large domesticated Canada Goose population. Almost every family had its flock. Each owner web-marked his birds for easy identification when, after the close of the winter shooting season, the birds were turned out to grass in one large community herd. It was the local custom that ownership of the goose determined ownership of the brood, regardless of whose the gander might be. Good honkers were highly prized. It not infrequently happened that some amateur Nimrod, excited by the sudden appearance of a flock over the live decoys, inadvertently killed one of the latter. The penalty for this solecism was uniform and inflexible—five dollars.

Captain Bragg, at the height of his long career as a sportsmen's guide, was accustomed to peg out no less than thirty-six birds to a stake blind. This entailed a herculean amount of labor—as anyone who has ever handled live geese will understand—but it insured success.

All that is changed today. The introduction of dogs—mortal enemies of the geese—has made keeping honkers a precarious business. Few are left. There is no economic incentive to keeping them, and grain for winter feeding has been both scarce and dear during the last few years. It is a pity, for the stately birds lent a touch of interest to the community that nothing else can quite replace. They were the true and natural hallmark of Ocracoke and the other banks settlements. Brant, too, were sometimes domesticated. They became gentle and tame but never bred, nor did they thrive for long in captivity, being subject to sudden and inexplicable death.

There is nothing particularly characteristic about the decoys of this region, as there is about those of the Connecticut and the New Jersey shores. All stool from this part of the southern coastline are of solid wood, the dugouts of the Barnegat Bay district being unknown. From Hatteras village on down the coast the species most often counterfeited are, first of all, Canada Geese and Brant, then Broadbill and Redhead. Pintail are the only freshwater species regularly imitated, with here and there a few Blackduck. I have never seen canvasback decoys south of Currituck Sound and I have yet to see mallard or goldeneye stool anywhere in the Pamlico Sound country.

I know of no local decoy maker of note today, although a decade or so ago there were a few of purely regional fame. Such examples of their work as have survived have no great claim to distinction. Most of the men who regularly gun these waters made their own decoys. All are heavy and massive. Among the goose and brant stool one often finds thoroughly adequate examples. The duck decoys are regularly of lesser quality. Most of the local makers use branched cedar trunks for heads. As the branch stubs from which the bills are carved seldom grow out at precisely the correct angle, many of these decoys have a ludicrously Semitic look. Painting is conventional and less stress seems to be placed upon it than upon form and size. Large numbers of decoys are included in the individual rigs and they are, necessarily, often subjected to rough handling, so that sturdiness of construction is a primary consideration never neglected.

The abolition of battery shooting and the apparently permanent ban on the use of live decoys has wrought an appreciable change in the shooting customs of the Pamlico section. Today there remains only stake-blind shooting and, in heavy weather, shooting on the salt marshes from bush or box blinds. Under favorable conditions of wind, tide and weather, both Geese and Pintail resort to these low-lying salt meadows in large numbers. Transporting the heavy, solid wooden goose stool peculiar to the banks in a towed dory behind a motorboat is *one* thing, while carrying them across pathless salt marshes by sheer man power is quite another!

A change in the decoy customs of this entire sector of the coast was unintentionally set in motion by the writer. To overcome the burdensome, time-consuming labor of toting the heavy floating geese, he made a set of silhouette decoys during the first winter that he shot at Ocracoke Island. One man can carry a dozen or more of these with little effort. They were, furthermore, so extremely effective that they caught on among the native gunners at once and now they seem largely to have displaced the full-bodied decoys for all marsh shooting. Extensive use is being made of them, even on the flats, where, at low water, their employment is entirely practical.

A day's stake-blind shooting out of Ocracoke requires a degree of preparation and an outfit reminiscent of old battery shooting days. Long before dawn comes a rap at the bedroom door.

"It looks like a good day. You'd best lose no time!" is the captain's morning greeting. While dressing I can hear the rumble of the guides' voices in the living room downstairs. Breakfast is eaten by artificial light. The truck is waiting at the door. The old captain and I pile into the driver's cab, the guides finding room as best they can amid a motley assortment of gun cases, lunchboxes, water bottles and shell boxes in the back.

It is a rough but, happily, a short ride. If the tide is low, we drive over hard-packed sand to the boat landing on the lake, as the small landlocked harbor is locally known, via the beach in front of the house. If the tide be high, we take the back road—a euphemism for a puddle-studded series of ruts that eventually lands us at the same destination.

The first glimmer of dawn is visible over the picturesque harbor as we board the cabined motorboat. It tows a large skiff, stacked with stool, as well as a small, flat-bottomed dinghy for use on the shallow flats. We chug through the narrow channel which connects the lake with the sound, to the accompaniment of the staccato barking of the motors of a half dozen oyster-ing skiffs, which trail behind us. Their destination lies in the direction opposite to ours.

It is getting lighter by the moment now. We have the open sound before us, with a deep-water channel all the way, and we head for Howard's Reef. A run of twenty-five minutes, shortened by the fascinating spectacle of the play of colors in the eastern sky, heralding sun-up over the banks a mile away, brings us within reach of the long, stake-blind dotted reef. We train our glasses upon it. Geese and Brant by the thousands are feeding there. Flocks of Broadbill and Redhead have been continuously crossing our bows or circling high above us. It is an enthralling sight and one well cal-culated to drive the newcomer to these grounds frantic with unrestrain-able impatience.

At the edge of the channel we drop anchor. I step into the decoy boat with the guides. They pole over the shallows, a good half mile to the blind. Fowl are about us everywhere, rising from the water in singles and in small bunches, only to settle again a few gunshots off.

Arrived at the blind, I clamber out. My equipment, gun case, shells, field glass, water bottle and lunchbox are handed in to me. The guides begin setting out the stool. There are twenty geese, twenty-four brant, fifty broad-bill and redheads, the rest pintail, with three or four blackducks—these last dropped off to one side, away from the main set. When they have done, I am surrounded by a horseshoe-shaped mass of decoys. The geese are out in front, followed by brant and pintail. Off to the other side are the sea ducks. The now empty decoy boat pushes off to where the motorboat is anchored. Through my binoculars I can see them starting the motor to move to a new location, three-quarters of a mile down wind from me.

I have scarcely set down the glasses when a Pintail drake, flying high, gives me my first opportunity. At the shot he crashes. I clamber down and gather him in. For a quarter hour nothing happens. In all directions I can see fowl moving, but nothing comes near me. I can hear both Geese and Brant honking. The sound of their mingled notes has a curious ventriloquial quality as it comes across the water, making it hard to locate the exact location of the flocks. I train the glass upon the motorboat. One of the guides is just pushing away from it in the dinghy. He is setting out to stir up bedded fowl which I cannot see.

While watching him, a pair of Broadbill catch me off guard. They came in without my having seen them and they leave as quickly as they came. I send a futile shot after them. Almost immediately thereafter I spot three Pintail coming over. They are high but not too high. The rig has caught their attention but they make no pretense of decoying, only passing over in full flight. At the shot, the duck of the trio wavers, then comes spinning crazily down. She is wing broken. I climb down and begin the weary pursuit. She leads me a merry chase across the flats, diving and swimming under water as I reach for her. As I turn, panting, back to the blind, the duck in my hand, I see a pair of Brant flutter across the rig! This never fails. I am accustomed to it and am not unduly disturbed by the lost chance.

I have scarcely scrambled back into the box when things begin to happen. Owen, the guide, has put up a huge raft of miscellaneous fowl. I can see them milling about, out over the far edge of the reef, like puffs of smoke against the clear sky. Some are settling again but I can see a large flock working toward me. They are Redheads and they have seen my set. A few moments of suspense follow. They are working back toward their original feeding ground. But no—they're not! Not *all* of them, at any rate. Some twenty birds have broken off from their companions. They are circling—once, twice. What has made them suspicious? They are just out of range and they are giving me the once over with a vengeance. Then, their misgivings apparently lulled, they set wings and paddles and come in. There is a considerable gap between the Broadbill and the Redhead stool and for this open water they head. At the shot three birds drop. Out of the corner of my eye I can see that one is only crippled. The second shot cuts down the tailender—a fine drake.

I reload quickly on the off chance that they may return once more. A single bird swings back and hovers, with disastrous results. By the time I have climbed down from the blind the cripple has swum off, far out of gun-range. I signal to the motorboat and leave him to Owen. Four prime Redhead lie on the wooden seat before me. A glance through the glasses shows the guide just reaching out to pick up my now dead cripple, making the score five.

Follows a long pause. The sun is climbing higher and the tide is falling. A bunch of Pintail is sitting three hundred yards off. They came in without my seeing them. Perhaps they will swim in to me. (Perhaps *not*, too!) As I watch them they are joined by another flock and I reflect upon how fine it would be if they would drop into my set as confidently as they join feeding birds of their own kind.

When next I look at them they have drifted still farther off. Several Brant are now swimming among them. This is bad. Incoming birds will stool to this group instead of to my rig. If I want any more shooting I can't escape the drudgery of wading over the flats to drive them off. Better get at it and have done with it. While still far out of range, the Pintail jump from the water and head north. The Brant, young of the year, are swimming off. It takes two hundred more yards of wading and much arm waving and shouting to get them on the wing. My labor is not wasted. I have hardly more than got settled again, shedding my now far-too-warm shooting coat the while, when a dozen Pintail pass high over the blind—a perfect opportunity.

Two drakes drop at the double report. They are dead when they hit the water with a satisfying smack. Before I can retrieve them a single Broadbill passes over the decoys. Both shots pass harmlessly behind him. He never even hesitates and is soon lost to sight. Another pause. Then more Pintail. A miss here and a kill there have brought the pile of birds in the blind very close to the limit. But as yet no Geese have come near me. I can hear thousands of them honking and gabbling and through my binoculars I can see that the outer reef edge is packed with them. Pintail and Brant are there too.

I hear the putt-putt of an outboard motor. It is an oysterman, heading into Ocracoke after the morning's tonging. If he keeps to his course he will stir up a bunch of about a dozen Geese that are sitting on a bar just off the low-lying sector of the distant banks known as "the plains." I keep the glasses glued on the Geese. They are raising their heads. One or two of them are beginning to walk to the edge of the bar. Now they have taken off. Unquestionably they will head for the host on the outer reef edge and they may give me a passing shot. Over the water comes an inquiring honk. I answer at once. The temptation to keep on calling at them is great but I lay down the call and reach for the gun. They are close at hand now. Surely they will stool! Through the peepholes in the wall of the blind I can see them plainly. One or two of the leaders are setting their wings. In a moment they will be in range. As I rise to shoot, they flare with frightened honks. The first shot drops one. The second is a clean miss. As I watch them pass out of range I see a bird sag and waver. The next moment he hits the water with a thud that sends the spray flying high.

In the meantime, more Pintail have dropped into that seemingly favored spot over the shallows where I drove off the bunch earlier in the forenoon. More are joining them all the time. There must be several hundred in all. From the north I see what looks like a flight of bombing planes heading for the Pintails. They are Geese and I watch their slow and graceful descent to the water. The tide must have fallen rapidly for I can see that some of the Geese are on their feet. From this distance they look black and big.

Brant are drifting in in pairs and in singles to join what is rapidly beginning to assume the proportions of a raft of fowl. One or two of my goose decoys are already aground and I realize, ruefully, that there will be but little more shooting for me today. The sun has become almost hot and I am conscious of an increasing drowsiness. With my shooting coat rolled up in lieu of a pillow I compose myself for a nap. The chances are that I'll miss little or nothing by so doing.

When I awake, cramped and uncomfortable, I am conscious at once of a subtle change. The sun has dropped low on the horizon. It has become much cooler. A glance through the peepholes discloses the sound as still and rippleless as the surface of a mirror. Brant, Geese and Pintail are on the water all around me—all just out of range. My watch shows that it will soon be four. I have slept two hours! I see the motorboat begin to move in my direction. It comes to anchor at the edge of the channel. The skiff pushes off. At that moment two Brant head in over the stool and one falls on an exposed bit of the bar at the shot. As the skiff approaches nearer and nearer I pack up my paraphernalia and clamber down. The water now is not much more than up to my ankles. In the course of the years, the captain, Owen and I have taken up so many rigs together that we have developed a regular routine. In fifteen minutes the one hundred and twenty-odd decoys are neatly wound and stacked and we push off.

"Well! You didn't do so bad!" is the captain's comment as he fingers the bag. "With this bright day and the wind dropping off like it did, I never thought you'd get much." The westering sun is on our starboard during all of the long run home and the beauty of the sunset increases with every moment.

"Look at 'em! Just look at 'em!" cries Owen, pointing to where a huge bunch of Pintail is dropping in not ten yards away from where the rig had ridden at anchor. The evening flight is on and the long miles of exposed reef present much the same picture that we gazed upon at sunrise.

"I told George Simpson to bring in a bushel of oysters this morning," says the captain, "and Pinta left a couple of bottles of beer for you."

Not all of shooting to shoot!

No description of the Pamlico Sound country, however sketchy or cursory, would be complete without at least a reference to the Green Island Club. Consisting of approximately fourteen hundred acres of marsh and beach land, this sporting Eden lies at the northern end of eighteen-mile-long Ocracoke Island. The Hatteras Coast Guard Station is built upon a part of the property, the bulk of which lies on the sound side of the inlet of the same name. Most of it is salt marsh, traversed by winding creeks and dotted with little pondholes of brackish water. Points jut out here and there. Outlying, grassy islands, strategically situated, add immensely to its value from the standpoint of the wildfowler. No better shooting ground exists along the whole length of the Atlantic coastline. Waterfowl teem here. Years ago it belonged to a long since defunct gunning club. Hence the name. It has passed through various hands, finally to become the property of Samuel Jones, Esquire, of Norfolk, Virginia.

A roomy and comfortable clubhouse stands facing the outer beach and the eternal battering of the Atlantic. Behind it stretches the marsh. Behind that, the sound. The present owner has greatly improved the property which, despite its exposed situation, miraculously escaped serious damage in the disastrous hurricane of 1944.

Every suitable point is equipped with a well-built sinkbox. Stake-blinds, portable as well as stationary, dot the flats. No matter what the wind or the weather, Green Island can always provide good shooting. To the sportsman fortunate enough to have been numbered among its many guests, names like "The Tar Hole," "Outer Green Island" and "The Cockerel Creek Blind" will always awaken the pleasantest among his sporting memories. It has been my privilege to enjoy Green Island's overflowing hospitality many times. Every day spent there has provided me with rich additions to my store of cherished sporting memorabilia. I never think of it without being suffused by a glow of appreciative gratitude.

X V

Florida

BY LOU S. CAINE

HOW will you have your duck hunting? Bright, clear, sunny weather? Mid-summer heat? Cold, raw, blustery days? Rain, fog and a "norther" blowing? Gentlemen, Florida has them all.

Do you like pass shooting? Pothole shooting? Jump shooting? Decoy shooting? Pit shooting? Gentlemen, Florida has them all.

There are no statistics to prove it, but the coldest place in the United States—outside of Harve, wherever that is—is a duck blind in Florida, one hour before sunrise. Six hours after sunrise this same blind will generate heat and hot air like several widely known southern senators.

When you go hunting in Florida, you start the day with all the clothes you own on your back—and still you're cold. By noon you are stripped to your underwear—and still you're hot.

Florida really does offer many different types of duck hunting, duplicating the famous duck hunting grounds in various parts of the country. There are the typical fresh-water duck marshes covered with the cattails of the north. There are off-shore islands in the gulf where the hunters use pits. There are channels used as flyways where the Bluebills and Pintails whistle by. There are potholes into which the Mallards drop. There are cypress swamps that furnish the "timber shooting" of the Mississippi valley and— there are also ducks.

The great majority of the ducks in the North American continent visit Florida in winter. Two species, the Wood Duck and Florida Duck, are native to it. Some species appear in large numbers, others in goodly amounts, while still others are rarely seen. So that the sportsman going to Florida for the first time may know who his fellow tourists are, the following list is given, subdivided according to the abundance of the ducks. Under the proper common name of each duck are given various local names by which it is also known.

PLENTIFUL

BALDPATE—*Mareca americana* (Gmelin)
   Widgeon
FLORIDA DUCK—*Anas fulvigula fulvigula* (Ridgway)
   Florida Mallard, Native Mallard, Mallard
PINTAIL—*Dafila acuta tzitzihoa* (Vieillot)
   Sprig
RINGNECKED DUCK—*Nyroca collaris* (Donovan)
   Bullneck
SCAUP, LESSER—*Nyroca affinis* (Eyton)
   Bluebill, Broadbill
TEAL, BLUE-WINGED—*Querquedula discors* (Linnaeus)
   Blue-wing
TEAL, GREEN-WINGED—*Nettion carolinense* (Gmelin)
   Green-wing
WOOD DUCK—*Aix sponsa* (Linnaeus)
   Summer Duck

MODERATE

BLACKDUCK—*Anas rubripes tristis* (Brewster)
   Black Mallard
MALLARD—*Anas platyrhynchos platyrhynchos* (Linnaeus)
   Greenhead, Greenhead Mallard

SCAUP, GREATER—*Nyroca marila* (Linnaeus)
  Bluebill, Greater Bluebill
SHOVELER—*Spatula clypeata* (Linnaeus)
  Spoonbill, Spoon-billed Teal, Spoon-billed Widgeon

SCARCE

BUFFLEHEAD—*Charitonetta albeola* (Linnaeus)
  Butterball
CANVASBACK—*Nyroca valisineria* (Wilson)
GADWALL—*Chaulelasmus streperus* (Linnaeus)
GOLDENEYE—*Glaucionetta clangula americana* (Bonaparte)
  Whistler
REDHEAD—*Nyroca americana* (Eyton)
RUDDY DUCK—*Erismatura jamaicensis rubida* (Wilson)
  Butterball, Brown Coot
TEAL, CINNAMON—*Querquedula cyanoptera* (Vieillot)
  Coot-teal, Brown Coot

Years ago the famous Canaveral Club, located on the headwaters of the Banana River, was in its prime. Founded about the time the East Coast Railroad went only as far as Titusville, it consisted of a spacious clubhouse at the head of a lagoon only a stone's throw from the ocean. Today, the club is a forlorn wreck of its former glory.

There are now no worth while duck clubs in Florida. In fact, duck hunting, as far as the natives of the state are concerned, plays a very definite second fiddle to deer, turkey and quail, and it is the northern sportsmen who really appreciate it.

There are no good duck guides in Florida—at least in a quarter century's hunting I have never seen one. Most of them are commercial fishermen who "take out" hunters once in a while and they know as much about ducks as some Washington officials know about sane government. They know where the ducks "have been a-usin' " and know where they "see'd some a-flyin' " and know where there "orter be a good place to hide," and that's about all.

The real duck hunter will find that his own knowledge will really pay off, for when the places the ducks are "a-usin' " are pointed out to him, he can use his previous experience in locating the blind and setting out the decoys.

Use the guide to show you the territory, handle the boat and help in putting out decoys, but use your own judgment in other matters, and you'll have better shooting.

Among the most famous duck-hunting waters of Florida is the Indian River district of the East Coast, which lies south of New Smyrna and north of Melbourne. This area embraces thousands of acres of salt-water marsh, shallow tidal lagoons and creeks and bays. Mosquito Lagoon, the Banana River and the Ten Thousand Islands opposite Cocoa offer some of the choicest shooting.

Along these bodies of water are hundreds of mangrove-surrounded ponds which offer excellent early morning and late evening shooting. During the morning the ducks move back and forth between these ponds and then go to the larger open waters to spend the day in comparative safety. In the evening they return.

Excellent blinds may be made in the mangroves. Just take along a camp-stool and hide yourself well, with the wind at your back, and *sit still*. The ducks will come in if not scared out. Decoys should be used and a duck caller, *if you know how to use one.*

No special type of decoys are peculiar to Florida—the ducks do not seem to pay too much attention to what species they represent. Mallard, pintail, widgeon and bluebill are all equally effective. Not many are needed, never more than a dozen, and usually half that number is sufficient for pond shooting. For open water, a larger spread is desirable.

In addition to the ponds bordering the large lagoons and rivers, there are many points extending out into these rivers which afford fine shooting. This type of shooting is a modified type of pass-shooting. Decoys are used to "pull" the ducks in range and they are shot as they go whizzing by, for rarely do they ever circle the decoys.

The St. Johns River offers splendid fresh-water duck shooting and its many marshes and ponds resemble the duck grounds of the north to a large extent. Mallard and Pintail predominate here, with Teal thrown in for good measure.

While hunting from blinds over decoys is the favored method, it is also an excellent place for jump shooting. Numerous sloughs run into the river and by quietly poling or paddling up these, it is possible to jump Mallard from tiny potholes along the sides.

The West Coast presents an entirely different type of gunning. In the area around the Homosassa and Chassahowitzka Rivers, the Gulf Coast is a maze of thousands of mangrove islands, bays and creeks. Here a guide is really needed, for if one were not born in this country, he is hopelessly lost before he starts.

At high tide these islands are covered by a foot or so of water but, of course, the protective foliage of the mangroves extends five to eight feet above the normal high tide mark. At low tide the entire islands are a foot or so out of water.

It is necessary to enter blinds in this area at high tide—and also to wait until the next high tide before leaving. As the tide drops, feeding grounds, which are covered by high water at high tide, become accessible. The ducks, aware of this, come in to feed as the tide lowers the water level. Here the location of the proper blind is essential, for if one is only a hundred yards away from where he should be, "dere he is" and there is nothing to be done about it. The mud is usually too deep to wade and it is necessary for the tide to fill before a boat can approach.

The Gulf Coast in northwestern Florida, especially the stretch from south of Tallahassee to Pensacola, offers some excellent shooting with the possibility of picking up a goose or two. While most of the clear-water, sand-bottomed lakes, so generously sprinkled throughout the state, do not have sufficient ducks to make hunting worth while, still there are several outstanding exceptions to this.

Such lakes as Okeechobee, Apopka, Trafford, Orange, Tohopekaliga, Miccosukee and Tamonia at times offer splendid sport and provide the hunter a chance to turn angler by giving the Florida largemouth bass a whirl, if the ducks are not flying.

As previously mentioned, duck hunting in Florida is a mixture of the various types of hunting found in the north. I well remember one morning at our camp on the East Coast. We were awakened by the wind, and Florida really does have wind—*real* wind, with force behind it. It shook the camp, it bowed the palm trees and—it dampened our spirits. The latter were quickly rectified by a quick dose of the doctor's favorite prescription, and then Frank voiced what we all knew: "Boys, our boats won't hold together crossing the lagoon, and if they did, we couldn't stay in them. What'll we do?"

"Let's hit the river," suggested Bill.

It was a good thought, for the winding, twisting St. Johns River offered ideal protection from the howling "norther." A quick drive of twenty-five miles and we were loading guns, decoys, gas cans and motors into the skiffs moored on the river. Day began to break just as we reached the northern end of Lake Cane. In the switchgrass bordering a likely looking overflow, Bill and I made a hasty blind while Frank and Tom went farther up the river to jump shoot some narrow sloughs.

Just after daybreak we heard their shots and in a minute or so a flock of seven Mallards appeared, headed our way. They saw the decoys, so no calling was necessary. Slowly they circled and—four flew away.

A flock of Teal streaked by, and caught us both napping. Two Bluebills skimming the water tried to get past—and were successful. A quiet spell. Then about twenty Pintails endeavored to light in our decoys. We repulsed the invasion. Two Blackducks came down the river, high overhead. A soft call and they turned, circled and swung into range. Both decided to stay. The main flight was over. Occasionally a single breezed upriver—and then we heard Frank and Tom's motor.

As they cut the motor and drifted toward us, Frank held up four Mallards and two Blacks, all jumped from potholes along the slough, and yelled: "Lou, I've got an idea." We congratulated him and paused for him to ex-

Duck blind on a mango island which will be covered at high tide.

In a duck camp on the Homosassa River in Florida.

Snow Geese and Blue Geese concentrated at a gravel pit.

Fish & Wildlife Service

pound. "With this wind blowing, let's go to Baldpate Pond this evening. You won't be able to keep the Widgeon out."

It sounded good. Baldpate Pond lies a stone's throw from the ocean and a mile or two, airline, from Indian River and would be ideal for "roosting" in weather like this. It is possible to drive through the sand to within a quarter mile of it and then necessary to "bust through" a jungle of palmettos, sawgrass and switchgrass. About four o'clock that afternoon we "busted through."

Frank and Tom made a blind at the north end of the pond with the wind at their backs, while Bill and I took second choice in a small cove at the lower end. When we arrived, there were hundreds of ducks on the pond, but none of us made the mistake of firing at them as they took off, knowing that in due time the majority would return. As a matter of fact, they started coming back while we were placing our last decoys.

Just as we were settled in the blind, a small flock of Baldpates whistled their shrill notes overhead. I couldn't resist whistling back, they answered and swung in. Another small flock circled and set their wings. And then, as darkness approached, they came from all directions. We just sat and watched them—we had all we wanted and if there is a more glorious sight than watching circling, wheeling, tumbling waterfowl, I do not know what it is.

We returned to camp. The next day was fair, the sun shone, the mosquitoes buzzed, and the ducks—just where in the devil do ducks go in ideal weather? We did not care—a fellow cannot break par all the time, and all of us had just experienced one of those rare days when the red gods really smile.

X V I

Louisiana Marshes

BY LYNN BOGUE HUNT

THE Louisiana marshes are a huge area of mudlands laced with bayous, canals and narrow waterways and dotted with ponds and little lakes. The vegetation of the mud flats is a jungle of profusion of hog cane, phragmites and many other of the reed family. The open water is lined and choked with alligator grass and water plants of all sorts. Water lilies grow in profusion. In many places it is impossible to push a boat through the reeds, narrow as the pirogues are. This almost sub-tropical region is from fifteen to thirty miles wide and stretches all along the Gulf of Mexico to eastern Texas from New Orleans, so vast it is. The drive to the marshes in Vermilion Parish, where we were to shoot, is along the mainland edge of this wilderness. This is a hundred and eighty miles of sheer beauty and romance. Old plantation houses, tremendous live oaks bearded with eight- and ten-foot streamers of Spanish moss, fields of sugar cane standing and being harvested, streams, ponds, lakes and picturesque little towns all the way. Fine, upstanding and courteous people, too. At the end of the run the road led to a muddy bank where a couple of unpretentious buildings stood. In spite of appearances, this place bore the imposing name of Gulf City. Here the fast

DUCK SHOOTING ON THE VERMILION MARSHES, LOUISIANA

boats were waiting to take us to the club, a journey which seemed endless after the long drag from New York and the long drive from New Orleans.

It was dark when we pulled up at the club docks. Restoring drinks were waiting and introductions all around, for it was a big party as gunning parties go. This was an annual affair for the members who have their yearly business meeting with four days' shooting on the side. After an excellent dinner, all seated at one long table, lots were drawn for blinds and guides for the start at four o'clock the next morning. By start I mean getting out of bed. Breakfast was at four-forty-five and the start for the blinds was scheduled for five-thirty. This start in the pitch dark of middle-of-November mornings is not without reason, for some of the blinds on this vast marsh are twenty or more miles away and since, in this latitude, the witching hour for duck shooting at sunrise is six-thirty, we needed the fast V-bottom cabin boats and all their speed.

On the dock I met my guide for the first time. His name was George. He was a stocky, good-looking man of about forty. I said, "Bon jour." He said, "Good morning." Well, I had been told or had assumed that all the people in this region were Cajuns from away back and spoke only French. So I said, like a dope, "Do you speak English?" "Oh, yes," said George. "I was born in England." He was a good guide and I enjoyed his conversation and his company for the four days I had him. I did notice that all the other guides spoke French among themselves, though they had English for the gunners and mostly without accent, too.

Each of the club boats carried three gunners and their guides and a man at the wheel, and dropped them off in turn as we reached the entrances to the ponds to which we were assigned. We tore along in the growing light and as we got well away from our start we began to hear, and later to see, great swarms of ducks take the air from the bayou we were running and from the ponds we were passing. About every hundred yards or more we heard great thumps on the bottom of the boat. Each time the helmsman would look back at our wake with a grin on his face. I asked George what that could be. Said George, "That's big alligator gars. There's lots of them in here. All these bayous are full of them. They're awful destructive to any-thing that lives in the water. Muskrats, ducks, frogs, 'gators—anything they can handle. Any of the big ones could handle a man, but I never heard of that happening. It could, though, and we let 'em alone. They get more 'rats than we trappers do."

George and I were the second pair to be dropped and right where we were to step out lay a big cotton-mouth moccasin, his ugly head drawn back and his tongue flicking. The custom of the country is to give a shell to an ugly like this. I gave mine two but he was still writhing when the boatman flapped him out of there with a push pole.

We got ashore. George untied the small, narrow, shallow craft that lay in the entrance. It was a pirogue, clinker built but exactly of a pattern with those dug out from cypress that I had seen from the car on the way down. I got aboard in a gingerly, hair-parted-in-the-middle fashion and parked the shells, lunch and raincoat in front of the small box I was sitting on. Then George stepped in the stern, upright and steady as a tree, and we began our journey to the blind. As soon as we pushed past a wall of phragmites, the ducks began to pile out of the pond. The air was full of them, all kinds— Teal, Mallards, Pintails, Widgeon, Gadwall and Wood Ducks.

The Coots stayed on the water. There were hundreds of them. Never before had I seen such a conglomeration of species in one spot. Our pond was about two acres in extent, as pretty as could be. It was completely en-closed in cane and reed walls with alligator grass, bright green, growing all around the edges. The still water was broken only by the paddling Coots, the lily pads and muskrat houses, and the numbers of fish of mysterious sorts that swam beneath. Clear sky and not a breath of wind. No day for duck shooting, I thought.

We poled across this peaceful scene to the blind. This blind was a one-man affair erected on a wooden platform with a wooden frame thatched with phragmites and standing, scarcely visible, against a tall wall of reeds. George pushed the pirogue into an alley behind, and I, after looking it over well for moccasins, climbed in. It had a seat in one corner and in the other was a shelf for shells. The top was just below eye-level when seated. George pushed out and tossed a half dozen mallard decoys about twenty yards off, got back into his alley with the boat and we were ready.

It was not long until the ducks began to come back. First two Pintail drakes and a hen. Then a Mallard hen, a pair of Gadwalls, a single Ruddie and, of all things, a Fulvous Tree Duck. I got my limit in about twenty minutes—ten ducks, in 1945. In the bag were two Pintails, one Mallard hen, one Redhead, one Canvasback, one Gadwall, one Green-wing Teal, one Blue-wing Teal, one Shoveler drake—a prime one for the skin collection— and the Tree Duck. Where else in the world could you mix them up like that?

It would be two hours before the boat called at our entrance to pick us up. So George and I poked about to see what we could see beside ducks. There were, of course, Coots by the hundred. They had been made a little panicky by the shooting but not many had left the pond. George likes them on the table so I shot a few. Every little while, beside the small fish rippling, there would be a terrific rushing disturbance in the calm water.

"What's making all that uproar?" I asked. Said George, "That's an alligator gar." "Must be a big one," said I, "to make all that foamy mess." "That one would be, maybe, a hundred pounds, I reckon," said George.

I had a fish book to illustrate when I got back to New York and among the eighty-eight species to be painted was the alligator gar and I had never seen one in the flesh; so I asked George if it would be possible to get one. "Oh, yes," said he; "I'll pole up to one and you poke your gun over the side, close to the water, and shoot. That will stun him and we can drag him in the boat. But it won't be any hundred-pounder. He would come to, aboard, and we would have to go overside among the moccasins. I'll find you about a ten-pounder. He'll be trouble enough."

I got one to George's specifications and got my sketches for the book. Other fish of all sizes were gadding about and among these were some that made familiar breaks and humped wakes. According to George, these were green trout. Now trout all through the southeastern and south middle states are black bass, so it was not strange that their maneuverings looked so home-like to me. They were big-mouth black bass and many of them.

As we continued our nature explorations around our pond we saw thousands of red-wing blackbirds and bobolinks in winter plumage. Gigantic grackles, iridescent and with "white eyes," as the natives call them. Marsh wrens, gallinules, herons, ibis and rails abounded. Among the mammals we saw numbers of muskrats, a couple of 'coons, a mink and one rather large thing that lifted its head and immediately went under. This, George said, must be an otter, since nothing else could answer to its brief appearance. So we named it "otter by elimination."

I was told there are abundant whitetail deer in the marshes and an occasional black bear. As to reptiles, there are alligators, of which we saw none, and plenty of cotton-mouth moccasins, of which we saw too many, and many turtles, including the great alligator snapper, as tough a killer as the alligator gar. Living, in this area of abundant life, must be a matter of eternal vigilance and agility for the weak and small.

During all our projecting around, Blue and Snow Geese were going over high. Above all these, away up in the blue and bright in the sun, was a big flock of White Pelicans, soaring in a great circle and drifting north on the gentle breeze. Louisiana is well named the Pelican State.

Warm weather and bright sun do not seem to make much difference in the shooting on the Louisiana marshes. The myriad ducks and geese are there for the winter and they trade around. Every day was a bluebird day —clear skies and gentle winds with a temperature of about forty-five degrees each morning, getting rather hot by ten o'clock. The ducks moved freely up to that hour, after which they all settled down until evening when, as George put it, "they must be serving champagne."

It didn't take long to get the limit any of the three days I gunned for ducks, and the variety was astounding. My bag for the shoot consisted of fourteen species—Pintail, Green-wing Teal, Blue-wing Teal, Mallard, Widgeon, Gadwall, Shoveler, Wood Duck, Redhead, Canvasback, lesser

BLUE AND SNOW GOOSE SHOOTING IN THE VERMILION MARSHES,

Scaup, Ring-neck, Ruddie and the one Tree Duck. All this in such balmy weather as would not produce a single duck in the windy, frozen north.

So much for the duck shooting in this paradise. The story about the Blue and Snow Geese follows the same pattern as to weather and abundance. There are several million Blue and Snow Geese living on these marshes, the winter home of practically all the Blue Geese in North America. The Snow Geese are about one in forty of the Blues where I gunned. But they increase in proportion as you go west toward Texas, until the Blues disappear almost completely. There are Canadas at times but when I was there the honkers were all far to the east, many miles away and I saw none. But the swarms of Blues and Snows were a sight to behold.

Getting to the feeding grounds of the hordes of the lesser geese is rare adventure. It calls for all the fortitude an avid gunner may possess and he gets his Blue and Snow Geese only because he wants to with all his might and main. The marshes are so vast and so muddy and the millions of fowl are so minute in proportion to the area, that going afoot is utterly out of the question. The gunner could be mired and he could be lost hopelessly in the tall cane. The strongest man could not walk the great distances even on dry land. In the difficulties of getting to where the geese may be at the moment, lies a large element of their safety from man, making for their continued abundance.

At the time I was there the Blues were all south of headquarters, along the shore of the Gulf of Mexico and seventeen miles away—seventeen miles of impossible going. Here the cane had been burned off early by the trappers and by the few people who pasture cattle on the slightly higher land that borders the marsh along the Gulf, and fresh new cane sprouts were coming up in lush abundance—just the thing for goose pasture. Centuries of wind and waves have built up a slight rise of land between the Gulf and the marsh along all the hundreds of miles from the mouth of the Mississippi west to the coast of Texas. This higher land is fairly well grown with small trees and bushes which merge abruptly into marsh.

To get to where the geese are known to be, there has been invented a fearsome thing called a marsh buggy. This consists of a car chassis on which is mounted a wagon-box affair with wooden seats across. The wheels are of iron and resemble those of the old-time threshing engine. These wheels are shod with heavy oak slats, five feet long on the rear and about three feet long on the front. This furnishes wide traction for the soft going. The motor has no hood and above it is a big water tank to supplement the radiator, for the going is laborious, first gear for the really soft places and second for the mud which is not full of water.

This marsh buggy can do from four to five miles an hour in most places and down to two or three over the bad spots. Even in cool weather the motor heats at times and has to be given a rest.

Of the seventeen miles from headquarters, about ten are run in the fast boats through the canals and bayous. At the end of the boat ride, stand the mighty conquerors of the Louisiana mud—two marsh buggies. The crew was there when we arrived and everything was steamed up to go. Far away south we could see the dim line of trees along the Gulf. We climbed aboard and began our rumbling, bumping journey. From the high seats we could look over the tops of the cane. As we got nearer the Gulf we began to see great wispy clouds of something rise and settle over the marsh against the trees. These clouds were geese, rising from the rear of the hosts on the ground and flying to greener pastures ahead of the gang.

Came the time when we could see the birds in a vast pack on the pasture and as far as we could look, both east and west. As we came near enough to see the geese as individuals, the cattle, which were grazing right in the midst of the fowl, got uneasy and began to drift away. The geese seemed to have little fear and kept at the business of feeding. Not until we were within two hundred yards did they begin to leave the ground, a few at first and then the whole lot with a tremendous roar of wings and a great chorus of their thin musical calling. A sight in itself worth all the journey from New York! Away they went to the eastward, leaving this immediate place as empty of birds as could possibly be.

"They will come back," said the guides. "Don't worry—you'll get plenty of shooting."

We dismounted with our decoys and shells, with empty ammunition cases to sit on. The decoys were silhouettes of Blues and Snows, a dozen or so in all. We selected our squats in the bushes and put out the stool on the open pasture away from the gulf side. To supplement the silhouettes we had a pack of sheets of paper, white and of typewriter size. These we spiked on reeds and low bushes so we had quite an extensive array when we retired to the bush blinds to await the promised return of the geese. We were bathed in sweat by the time we were through with all these preparations. We were right on the edge of the Gulf and what breeze there blew was south. It was so hot we had to peel to the waist.

The birds were not long in coming and they came in great twisting lines and bunches, rather high over the trees of the ridge, all talking among themselves in their melodious voices. They didn't seem much inclined to swing to the stool until they were well to the westward. As they continued to come, they were steering more to the north and getting more over our heads, so we decided to take them from below—long shots, but we reached them with number fours, chilled—good heavy duck loads which we expected to use on those smallish geese at shorter range.

The duck loads did the trick very neatly. The limit was four a day. I wanted an adult Snow Goose for a working skin model in the studio. Ditto an immature of the same species, also an adult and an immature Blue Goose for the same purpose. So, when I had these down, I relaxed and sat back to watch the superb long range shooting of my companions. It was a sight to please any gunner the way those geese came whacking down from fifty yards or more above.

The sun was getting low in the west by the time we all had our shares, and away off in the distance the tall swaying marsh buggies were beginning to move in to pick us up. We stowed our decoys, got our other equipment in a pile, together with the game, and sat watching that wonderful parade of thousands and thousands of geese across the changing sky.

X V I I

Making and Painting Decoys

BY DR. EDGAR BURKE

SOME GENERAL CONSIDERATIONS

ATTEMPTS to obtain modifications of the Federal statutes prohibiting the use of live duck and goose decoys have all failed and there seems to be little likelihood that future efforts aimed at changes in the law will have a different result. This, more than ever before, focuses the wildfowler's attention upon artificial stool. Before a duck can be bagged by even the most expert shot, that duck must be lured within gun range. The days when "any old thing" in the decoy line would suffice are gone, in my opinion. Many professional guides use rigs that belong in the same category with brass-bound, bell-mouthed blunderbusses and the enticing effect of their decoys is about on a par with the killing qualities of the weapon with which I have compared them!

Today's factory-made output is inadequate in quantity and often in quality and, if at all acceptable in the latter respect, likely to be expensive. Even the best of the factory products may be open to criticism on one score or another. The obvious remedy is to make one's own decoys.

These qualities the modern duck decoy must have. It must be as exact a replica of the resting, unsuspicious fowl as we can make. It is desirable that it be as light as is compatible with sturdiness of construction. It must be durable. In fresh-water shooting, where a relatively small number of stool are used, it is an easy matter to handle decoys with the care requisite for keeping any piece of fine sporting equipment in good order and repair. In salt-water shooting, on the other hand, where very large numbers of stool must be handled, this is a different matter and extra sturdiness and simplicity of construction are needed to withstand the wear and tear of every-day use.

My own rig, used exclusively on salt-water, is completely repainted at the end of every gunning season. Many of the decoys in it don't actually need it but the majority do, and I find that starting the new season with equipment in perfect order and condition adds much to the pleasure and satisfaction of the sport.

I, personally, wouldn't give ten cents a dozen for decoys with round bottoms. No matter how beautifully made or how fine they may look in the hand, such stool pitch and roll in a most unnatural manner on any water rougher than the proverbial millpond. Wildfowl notice these things! If anyone will take the trouble to view a rig composed of such stool a gun-shot off on a windy day, one glance will be enough to convince him of the superiority of flat-bottomed decoys. These ride, if made adequately wide, with the grace of a live duck, no matter how brisk the wind or how heavy the sea. Another point in their favor is the extreme simplicity of their manufacture.

In speaking of the ease and speed with which flat-bottomed decoys of the highest quality can be made, I have in mind stool made of pressed cork, a material superior in many respects to the more commonly employed solid or hollowed wood. Provided that all necessary tools and materials are assembled before beginning, the actual working time, including painting, required by a competent man to finish a specimen, such as is shown facing page 260 should not exceed an hour.

MAKING DECOYS

Ducks, broadly speaking, are conveniently divided into two groups, the River Ducks and the Sea Ducks. To the first named belong the Blackduck, the Mallard, the Pintail, the Widgeon and the Teals; to the second, the Canvasback, the Redhead, the Broadbills and the Goldeneyes. Representa-

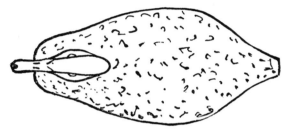

Top view of a press-cork, river duck decoy. This
illustrates the shape of the body.

tive members of both groups have certain bodily characteristics that are at once evident to even the most unobservant. Watch a captive Blackduck as it swims at your feet. Compare its lines with those of a Broadbill. They differ strikingly. In designing effective stool, regard for these differences must be had if maximal efficiency is to be attained.

To show characteristic attitudes of river ducks. The figure at the left is beginning to
manifest uneasiness. The figures at the right are indicative of contentment.

The drawings illustrate the general differences as shown in the designs of the decoy bottoms. These, in their turn, govern the shape of the entire body. A rig should imitate fowl at ease and free from suspicion, either in feeding or resting attitudes. The necks of the River Ducks are, with the exception of the Canvasback, much longer and thinner than those of the Sea Ducks. As extremes, one might cite the Pintail and the little Bufflehead.

Unalarmed, every duck carries its head more or less snuggled down into the body. The decoys should mimic this. Long necks and raised heads signify suspicion. The Sea Ducks, when at rest on water, seem almost to overflow—their bodies appear nearly as broad as they are long. Attention is called to the photograph of the resting Greater Broadbill, for which I am indebted to the kindness of my friend, Charles E. Wheeler, co-author of this book. It will repay careful study. No better model for shaping the bodies of Sea Ducks could be found than this chance snapshot. The head-on male, particularly, clearly demonstrates the broad, flattened-out, "squashy" effect given by the body of a resting seafowl. Ninety per cent of all sea duck decoys are defective in this sense. They are too narrow. Very characteristic is the low position in which the tails are held—virtually resting upon the surface of the water—which is typical for the entire group. Note the shortness and thickness of the necks of even those birds which are looking up in the picture.

In making a rig of Broadbill, Canvasback or Redhead stool, it is well to include a good many "sleepers"—birds with their heads turned, as though snuggling into the feathers of the back. It unquestionably adds to the enticing effect of the set, giving the whole an air of ease and security that is striking. I have many times watched rafts of Broadbill, as well as Redheads, in which every single bird was apparently fast asleep, all being in the position described. Such a flock will drift with the current or tide like so much flotsam.

Where Mallards, Blackducks or Pintails are being hunted in shallow water, it is equally advisable to include a large proportion of "feeders" or "tip-ups." Watch a flock of Pintail on the flats! More than half of them are "standing on their heads." Note, too, how readily and directly passing fowl decoy to these feeding birds. There is no hesitation, no circling. They come in like chickens to the farmer's call. The old market gunners who made a specialty of Brant, in the days when these geese were slaughtered in untold thousands—sometimes a hundred or more to a blind per day—were well aware of the seductiveness of "tip-ups" and every old professional rig included a goodly proportion of them.

The writer confesses to a strong preference for decoys made of so-called "press-cork," the material commonly used for insulating refrigerators. Bottoms of plywood are glued to these, one of the casein or rubber marine glues being used for the purpose. Such stool have many advantages. Among them are lightness, ease of manufacture and lack of shine when painted. It is true that the material has a certain tendency to scuff but adequate painting does much to overcome this single defect. Where a rig of limited size is planned for exclusive use on relatively sheltered fresh water, decoys made of this material deserve first consideration. My present large rig, used exclusively on salt water, has been shot over for eight seasons and every decoy in it is in perfect condition, the only replacements being made necessary by the occasional going adrift of a specimen or two.

Decoys, especially when used on open salt water, are occasionally called upon to take what is commonly known as "an awful beating." I am thinking of sudden shifts in the weather, when the set must be taken in as quickly as is humanly possible "regardless," if any portion of it is to be saved. These mishaps are a part of the sport and my own press-cork rig has had its share of rough handling while in use on virtually every gunning day of eight entire seasons. It has stood up admirably—quite as well, indeed, as have the few wooden units, both hollow and solid, which it contains. I have, therefore, in view of this material's manifest advantages, no hesitation in recommending it for first consideration to any fellow-sportsman contemplating the making of his own decoys.

Before the war, one or two of the larger dealers in decoys and allied supplies sold press-cork in conveniently cut blocks, three inches thick. It can be had of most dealers in insulating materials or of such firms as deal in natural cork. It is readily cut with an ordinary carpenter's saw and very easily shaped by means of an iron wood rasp or by coarse sandpaper.

In making a set of decoys of this type proceed as follows:

Draw the pattern of the bottom (or baseboard) on a heavy piece of cardboard and cut it out. Lay this upon a sheet of *marine* ply-board, three-eighths of an inch in thickness. Draw its outline, by means of a pencil, upon it. It is astonishing how many individual baseboards can be cut from a single piece of the ply-board if the pattern is judiciously spaced upon it. There need be but little waste. You will, of course, outline the pattern upon the ply-board as many times as you intend to make decoys. Saw them out with a coping saw. It will be found convenient to clamp one end of the ply-board in a suitable vise, if such be available, when doing this. Having sawed

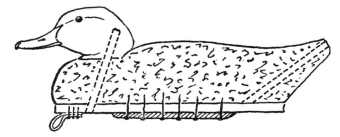

Typical press-cork Blackduck decoy. Note the overhanging stern and the dowel driven into the same for the purpose of safe-guarding this vulnerable area. The ply-board bottom, like the base of the neck, has been glued to the cork body with marine glue.

out the requisite number of bottoms, or baseboards, prepare your glue. Directions for doing this will be found upon the containers in which it is sold. A brand warranted to withstand the action of salt water should be obtained. There are many. An excellent one is "Cascamite," made and sold by the Casein Company of America. It is extremely easy to mix and has given the writer uniform satisfaction.

With a suitable brush apply the glue to one surface of the ply-board bottom and to an area of equal shape and size on the press-cork slab. In this manner distribute as many of the sawed-out bottoms on the cork slab as it will accommodate, in order to avoid wasting any of it. Before actually laying the ply-board on the cork, it is well to wait an hour, to allow the water-proof glue to thicken a little. After application, lay some heavy object on the ply-boards to fuse them and the underlying cork as firmly as possible. The writer usually employs old iron battery decoys for this purpose, but boards weighted with stones will answer, as will any other heavy object capable of exerting an equally distributed pressure. It is well to leave the weights in place overnight, at least.

By the next morning the union between ply-board and cork will be firm. The individual bodies are then roughly sawed free with an ordinary carpenter's saw. Turn each one over, bottom up, and, using the same saw, trim the projecting portions in exact alignment with the outline of the ply-board bottom. If decoys are being made for River Ducks, a considerable overhang, posteriorly, must be allowed for the tail portion. In the case of Sea Ducks the tail end comes flush with the end of the board. The reader is referred to the figure below.

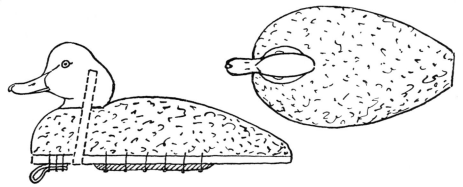

Sea duck decoy of press-cork. All contacting surfaces are glued with marine glue.

Top view of sea duck, press-cork decoy, to show breadth and general shape of body. Contrast this figure with that of a typical river duck, as shown on page 240.

Having carried the body to the point described in the paragraph preceding, we are ready to shape it by means of the wood rasp. There is no difficulty about this. It is well to check the work every few minutes, to insure evenness of workmanship on both sides. Larger areas of cork calling for removal are more quickly eliminated by careful use of the saw than by rasping. When the body shape desired has been attained, the use of coarse sandpaper here and there will smooth off any rough spots. A break or two in the press-cork may call for a trifle of filling with plastic wood. This dries

Broadbill at complete ease. Note the flattened-out, "squashy" effect of the bodies and how the heads are snuggled down into the backs of the birds. This is a splendid model for decoys.

Make a bight in line and push bight through ring. Pass end of line through bight.

Pass end of line around standing part and make single overhand knot.

TYING DECOY ANCHOR LINE

Pamlico Sound decoy anchor. Leaden weight and twisted copper shank. From Ocracoke Island, N. C.

Pamlico Sound decoy anchor. Leaden weight and copper shank. From Ocracoke Island, N. C.

Bellport decoy anchor. Leaden weight and brass rings. From Bellport, N. Y.

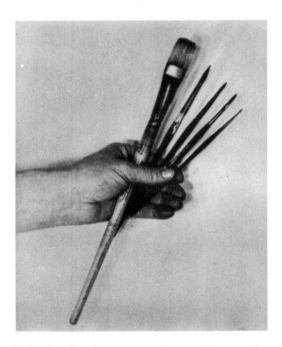

Paint brushes for decoy painting. The smaller sizes for detail painting, the largest for large flat surfaces.

rapidly and may, in its turn, be smoothed by a few strokes with sandpaper, before attaching the head.

Heads are drawn from a pattern on wood one and three-quarters inches thick. Whitewood or white pine will be found as suitable and as workable as any. In pre-war days the average sawmill charged five cents apiece for sawing out the heads. This saved an infinity of work and was well worth the money. If you must do this tedious job yourself, a heavy band saw will be found the best instrument for the purpose. After the head has been sawn

Head ready for insertion of eyes and dowel. When the hole for the latter has been bored the head is sawn off from the block, as indicated by the dotted line at the base of the neck. Leaving the excess block on the head until the eye and dowel holes have been bored is done in order to afford a convenient hold for the vise into which the whole is clamped.

out, whether by the sawmill or by your own unaided efforts, clamp it in a vise, the bill pointing toward you. Now shape it roughly with a small draw-knife. Practice and an inborn knack will lead to satisfactory results here. No one can guide you. Most makers finish the finer work with a jackknife, but skillful use of the drawknife alone will obviate the necessity for this. Finish with strips of emery cloth, held as a bootblack holds his polishing cloth, the head still clamped in the vise the while. Now, with a bit and auger drill the holes on each side designed to hold the glass eyes. Study a good picture before doing this or you will inevitably drill them far too low down on the head—sure sign of an inept workman! The depth should be little more than a half an inch. Fill the holes flush with plastic wood and insert the eyes. About a third of an inch of wire should be left on each eye. If this be bent over, in the shape of a hook, it will set in the drying plastic wood and insure against its ever being pulled out. Now drill a hole in the base of the head, extending almost to the top of the crown, for the insertion of the dowel with which the head will eventually be secured to the body and the baseboard. Fill the hole with the same glue which you used for attaching the baseboards to the cork body and push the dowel in firmly, as far as it will go. Allow at least four hours for this to dry. Next, drill a hole through the cork body, going right through the baseboard, for the reception of the head dowel. Considerable care must be exercised in these steps, in order to be certain that the dowel and the hole drilled for its reception are suitably aligned to bring the base of the head into flush and exact contact with the portion of the forward end of the body on which it is to rest. The base of the head, as well as the area of the body with which it is to contact, should first be given an application of waterproof glue before pressing the one firmly down upon the other. Don't set *all* of the heads looking straight forward, like a platoon of soldiers who have just been given the command, "Eyes front!" Vary the angles. Doing so will add life to the set. A portion of the dowel will project beyond the under surface of the baseboard. Saw it off flush with the latter. The decoy, having been allowed to dry overnight, is now ready for painting. Weights and anchor cord loops are the final touch, after the paint has completely dried.

In the case of fresh-water duck decoys, in which the tail portion of the cork body projects well beyond the end of the baseboard, there is a certain danger of breakage. To safeguard this vulnerable area, drive a short piece of dowel, well sharpened at the point, slantwise into the cork. The dowel should be accurately measured to *just* contact the baseboard when driven in. In hammering it, one feels at once when this contact has been established. Any redundancy is then sawed off flush with the end of the tail. The figure will make this point clear. (See page 243.)

A word about anchor cord loops. Rawhide or very heavy canvas will render equally good service. Avoid the use of metal eyes. They will ultimately work loose and drop out. A further defect is that they represent just one more projecting piece of metal to scratch and dent other stool with which they may come in contact when stacking. Either the rawhide or the canvas may be nailed to the bottom board with copper nails—it being well to use not less than three of these. Tie your anchor cord to the loop in the manner shown by the illustration and let no one—be he who he may—talk you into the use of swivels, snaps or other similar completely unnecessary contraptions!

Anchor cords should be heavy enough to withstand very considerable strain and much hard usage but it is inadvisable to have them heavier than actually necessary. If you use new cordage, it will pay you well to dye it a dark, olive green before shooting over the rig. Unless you do this it will be so glaringly conspicuous that fowl will notice it and shy off, causing you to lose shot after shot that you would, but for this, have had. This statement applies with particular force if your shooting is done over a rig set out in shallow water.

Tarred, heavy cod-line is a splendid material for anchor cords, especially for use on salt water. It has less tendency to snarl than any other, which is of particular advantage if the gunner prefers not to wind each individual decoy when taking in the set at the end of the day's shooting.

BALSA DECOYS

Balsa *(Ochroma lagopus)* is an American tropical wood of such extraordinary lightness that a man can shoulder and walk off with a huge log of it with no difficulty beyond the physical balancing of his unwieldy burden. Of late years considerable use has been made of it in decoy manufacture. Only the best grades, difficult for the average man to obtain, are satisfactory for this purpose. The wood is easy to work but may be described as "tricky," in so far that experience is required when working it with tools. It is so soft that it can easily be dented by pressure with the fingernails. In making solid decoy bodies of it one has the advantage that it works up into a rough-grain finish, which sucks up paint avidly and leaves no trace of shine. This also gives a peculiarly natural, feathery effect.

The general softness of this unique wood is such that solid-bodied stool made of it must have a glued-on bottom of ply-board or some substantial wood attached to them, as, otherwise, neither weights nor anchor-cord loops could be affixed. The more substantial bottom further protects the vulnerable edges of the stool from injury. Beyond this I have found balsa stool, made for me by the Wild-Fowler Decoy factory in Saybrook, Conn., eminently satisfactory. They have withstood the vicissitudes inseparable from the life of any decoy quite as well as examples made of all other materials, including hardwood, which have been constantly used with them.

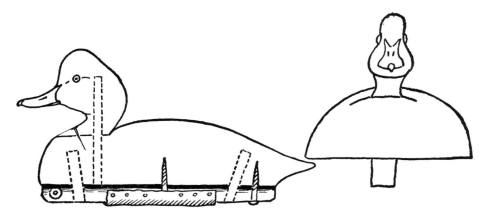

Schematic, cross-sectional view of a Sea duck decoy of either balsa or solid wood. In the case of the first-named the screws are, of course, omitted. Front view of same, to show keel.

An alternative to the plywood bottom suggested above is a wooden keel, doweled into the bottom of the balsa body by snug-fitting wooden pins, driven in slightly aslant, for better holding. The "Wild-Fowler" stool in my rig are of this construction, which has answered all demands made upon it perfectly. Heads cannot be carved from balsa, since it is much too soft.

Pine or whitewood heads must be affixed to such decoys by doweling and cementing, as nails will not hold in this material. Where lightness is the primary consideration, it is well worthy of consideration. Sea duck decoys, because of the simpler shape of the bodies, are perhaps better subjects for this wood than are river duck stool, whose elevated, projecting sterns predispose them to injury.

HOLLOW WOODEN DECOYS

The finest examples of pure craftsmanship to be found in any large collection of old decoys will usually be of this type. They are peculiar to the Connecticut shore of Long Island Sound and to the Barnegat Bay sector of the Jersey Coast, both localities, from earliest days, the home of America's best decoy makers. Good hollow wooden stool require skill, practice and much time to make. I question whether today they are worth the time and effort required to construct a sizeable rig of them. They have the further drawback of being more easily damaged than are stool of other materials, in consequence of which they demand much more care in handling than the average gunner accords his decoys. They are, of course, uniformly more expensive too.

For the man who needs but a dozen mallard or blackduck stool, for use in some small fresh-water marsh or hidden, woodland pondhole, seldom exposed to wind and never to rough water, such decoys are to be recommended. Where a more extensive set is required, the writer suggests solid wood, press-cork or even balsa, in preference to the much more fragile hollow wooden type, which, however fine they may look in the hand, have the additional defect of bobbing about in an unnatural manner in rough and windy weather. Millions of fowl have been killed over such stool since first their use began but it is believed that the foregoing fairly evaluates their field of usefulness and their defects.

NATURAL CORK BARK DECOYS

Natural cork bark, which is stripped from the trees every seventh year, cannot be obtained in slabs of sufficient thickness for making decoy bodies. Two or more pieces must, therefore, be used in building up each body. The sections are fastened by a combination of gluing and doweling. It takes a very considerable amount of practice to handle this rather expensive material. While readily sawn, it is by no means easy to whittle or shave natural cork, in consequence of which the rasp and coarse sandpaper must, to a very large extent, be substituted for the knife.

Because of its tendency to break off, the lines of the decoys made from it must be kept as simple and flowing as possible. Charred with a blow torch, it very perfectly simulates the dusky coloration of the Blackduck's plumage. It is, of course, exceedingly light, besides being impervious to water and well adapted to rough handling. If desired, it will take paint well. Natural cork decoys must be keeled, as only wood will permit attaching the necessary leaden weight and the anchor cord fastening. Keels are best attached by both doweling and gluing, as described in the paragraphs dealing with balsa decoys.

DECOY ANCHORS

Anchor patterns are legion but it is a fact that but few of them are really satisfactory. Anchors made of anything other than lead are of the devil! Iron is particularly to be avoided. Even though painted or lacquered, such anchors eventually rust and stain the decoys, ruining the painting, as well as rotting the cord, with the certainty of ultimate breakage and consequent loss of the decoy. It has the further drawback of scratching and marring the stool to which it is attached, particularly so when decoys are stacked.

It must be borne in mind that not the weight but the *shape* of the anchor really holds the decoy in place. A shallow, large-surfaced mushroom anchor

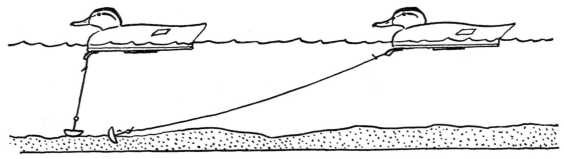

Diagram to show poor hold of anchor when cord is too short. The figure at the right indicates the hold taken by the anchor when cord is of adequate length.

is far more effective than a deep, heavier and smaller weight. Nothing is more exasperating than to have the rig drag and go adrift when the wind becomes brisk or the tide begins to run. It sometimes happens that the sportsman blames the type of anchor used when the fault actually lies solely with too short a line! The longer the line—within the bounds of reason—the more firmly the anchor will take hold.

I have had the most satisfactory service from the type of anchor shown in the photograph facing page 245. The shank of this is made of twisted, heavy copper wire. This pattern is usually referred to as a "mushroom." A year or two ago, thanks to the kindness of Mr. W. W. Worth, of Bellport, Long Island, N. Y., my attention was called to the pattern shown on the same page. This seems to me the last word and I can scarcely conceive of an improvement that could be made upon it. Having all of the advantages of the usual "mushroom," this pattern has the additional merit of being so constructed that it can be slipped over the head of the stool. Many guides are in the habit of dropping the anchor into the place where they wish the decoy which they are stacking to lie, then letting the cord settle and dropping the stool upon it.

Where one man, in a small duck boat with no one to help him, must take up a set of decoys in cold and blustery weather and stack them on the stern of a duck boat it is, of course, a matter of getting the rig in as quickly as possible. Under such conditions one does not think of winding up each individual stool. Darkness may be coming on, the boat bobs and rocks crazily and hands and fingers are stiff with cold. Under such conditions one is glad to get the last decoy safely aboard. However, when stacking stool in a decoy boat, several layers deep, it will prove well worth the trouble to wind and stack the decoys. With cords and anchors hanging loose, tangles inevitably result, delaying the placing of the set when next it is to be used. Unsnarling a mess of anchor cords in the half light of a winter dawn with numbed fingers is something of which anyone that wants it can have my share!

The Bellport pattern, because of the fact that it can be slipped over the decoy's head, is a further safeguard against snarling as the result of the anchor cord's becoming accidentally unwound.

The writer feels that other anchor patterns are so definitely inferior to the mushroom type that it is scarcely worth the time and the space to comment at length upon them. Anchors which depend solely upon their weight to effect secure holding of the individual stool are an unnecessary nuisance by virtue of that very fact. All others, regardless of shape, will drag and cause endless irritation and loss of decoys. They are best avoided.

DECOY WEIGHTS

Everything that has been said against the use of any metal other than lead for anchors may be appropriately repeated when speaking of body weights for decoys. The number of varieties of these equal the number of the types of anchors that have been devised and used since shooting over artificial stool first began. The writer has found sheet lead the most universally satisfactory material for this purpose. It can be quickly and easily cut into any size pieces desired and, if necessary, several pieces of equal dimensions may be superimposed upon one another and nailed or screwed into place. Nothing but copper nails of appropriate length, or brass screws, should ever be employed.

Sheet-lead body weights lie flat against the bottom of the decoy and so cause a minimum of scratching when coming into contact with other stool. They do not, further, interefere with neat and smooth stacking. When throwing out stool, the anchor cord slips easily over them, never catching on them, as it so often does when some projecting pattern of weight is used. In short, they have no drawbacks—which is a deal more than can be said of other types! I must except the streamlined Bean decoy weight, which is attached to the stool with a brass screw, and never causes the line to catch.

It occasionally happens that after the weight has been nailed to the bottom of an individual decoy, the same will be found, when placed in the water, to have a list to one side or the other. There is a simple and effective

Redhead, Premier Model.

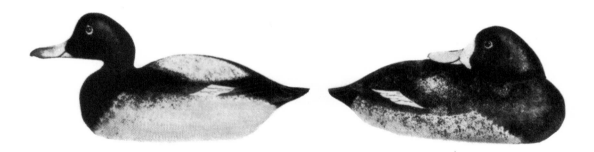

Bluebill, Premier Model.

Shelldrake, Premier Model.

FROM THE 1905 CATALOGUE, MASON'S DECOY FACTORY, DETROIT, MICHIGAN.

Blackduck, Premier Model.

Pintail, Premier Model.

Widgeon, Premier Model.

FROM THE 1905 CATALOGUE, MASON'S DECOY FACTORY, DETROIT, MICHIGAN.

safeguard against this. Before permanently attaching the sheet-lead weight to the stool, place two stout rubber bands about the body, about two inches apart. Now slip the lead under these and set the decoy in a dish-pan filled with water, observing how it rides. A slight shifting of the weight will likely enough be necessary to insure its riding evenly. Adjust the weight and try it again. When you have it placed so that the decoy floats as it should, turn it over and, without moving the lead, nail it in place.

A clever and very simple leaden weight pattern always used by the veteran wildfowler, Charles E. Wheeler, is pyriform. It is fastened by a single brass screw, so that it can be turned if sufficient pressure is applied to it. This enables one to correct any listing of the decoy by a twist of the fingers.

ON PAINTING DECOYS

The most convincing lesson in the efficacy of well-painted decoys, as opposed to scarred and long unpainted ones, that I ever received was experienced in the company of my friend Lynn Bogue Hunt, on the North Carolina coast. We had been shooting over the rig supplied by our professional guide and the results had been discouraging. The "set" was ample in numbers and the basic quality of the stool good, yet fowl sheered off from them, time after time, while still just out of gun range. Exasperated, I eyed the large and well-set raft of wooden effigies with a disgusted eye and then remarked to my shooting partner: "If *you* were a fowl, would *you* come to such decoys as these?" Lynn laughed. "If I *did,* I'd think I was a goose, indeed!" was his reply. The day was a Friday. During the daylight hours of all of the following week-end we painted that collection of blocks which had not known the touch of a brush for many years. The strict Southern Methodist family with whom we were staying looked upon our activities with thinly disguised disapproval. We were breaking the Sabbath! An inspired remark, on my part, to the effect that what seemed like work to them was play and recreation to us, reconciled them. If memory serves me rightly, we finished ninety-seven individual blocks in those two days. The practical results of our labors were impressive! Never did reward follow more promptly upon the heels of effort. The ducks that had shied off so persistently now came to our rejuvenated rig like chickens to corn.

No gunner of experience will deny that occasionally there are times and places when, even today, birds appear to be willing to come to lures of the most nondescript and battered kind but it is equally certain that these are exceptional instances, upon which no reliance can ever be placed. It is axiomatic that the better the rig the greater its attractiveness and the better, in consequence, the shooting.

In the accompanying color plates a sincere effort has been made to simplify the painting of the more usually employed decoys to a point where even the man utterly unaccustomed to the handling of paint and brush can undertake the freshening up of his own rig with confidence in the end-result. It will be noted that, with few and negligible exceptions, only plane surfaces of a single color have been employed. The plumage details are indicated entirely by dots, dashes and simple triangles, yet the final effect, when viewed at a little distance, is completely convincing. Practice, here as elsewhere, makes perfect and initial discouragements are soon overcome and forgotten. We cannot all be Lynn Bogue Hunts! Remember that it is not so much the appearance of the bird in the hand but the effect a half gunshot off that counts.

Properly chosen brushes are, of course, necessary. Without these, the most skilled of painters would be handicapped to the point of impotence. Small, flat brushes, such as are sold for varnishing household furniture, are proper for the application of the broad planes of solid color. Artist's medium- and small-sized brushes are essential for the detail painting of the feather patterns. The photograph will give a good idea of the relative sizes needed.

Flat house or marine paints that will not shine when dry should be chosen. Turpentine, and not linseed oil, is the thinning medium which should be used. Artist's colors, if used alone, will not withstand a season's use on salt water, but if mixed with house paint, are completely satisfactory and extremely useful for obtaining tints and shades for small areas, such as the specula of the wings of certain ducks. They are purchasable in collapsible tubes.

It is essential that the paint, when ready for use, be not too thin. It will run exasperatingly if attention is not paid to this detail. Priming coats had best be dispensed with. Paint right on the raw wood. A better and less shiny result will be attained by so doing. If the paint is of good quality the wood will be amply protected by one coat against water absorption.

It is not always desirable to wait until the under coating of paint has dried before applying the plumage details. A softer, more feathery effect can usually be secured by applying the finer details when the under color is half dry. The only exception to this is when applying the white stippling (see beyond) to the backs of broadbill drakes. Here the gray under color should be completely dry before applying the white.

Heads are best painted last. They afford the most convenient hold while painting the bodies. The finest detail work is usually reserved for the head and if the finished body is completely dry before this part is colored, the firm and secure grasp so necessary for accurate and comfortable head painting is afforded.

It will be found quickest and easiest to paint an entire rig of one kind of lures portion by portion. Completing the painting of each individual decoy, unit by unit, triples the time and labor involved.

Ordinary powdered, commercial lampblack, when mixed with any of the darker shades of color, will render these darker, thicker and less likely to shine. It is an especially useful admixture to black paint when painting goose and brant stool, as well as the breasts of male canvasback, redhead and broadbill. The proper amount of lampblack to be used is a matter for experiment. Stir it well into the paint, until a smooth and creamy mixture results.

In painting cork-bodied decoys the paint should be particularly thick when applied, since it is desirable that as much of it as possible adhere to the body material in order to reduce water absorption to the minimum.

MALLARD
(Male)

MALLARD
(Female)

PINTAIL
(Male)

PINTAIL
(Female)

BLACKDUCK
(Natural Cork)

BLACKDUCK
(Wood)

GREEN-WINGED TEAL
(Male)

GREEN-WINGED TEAL
(Female)

COLOR PATTERNS FOR DECOYS

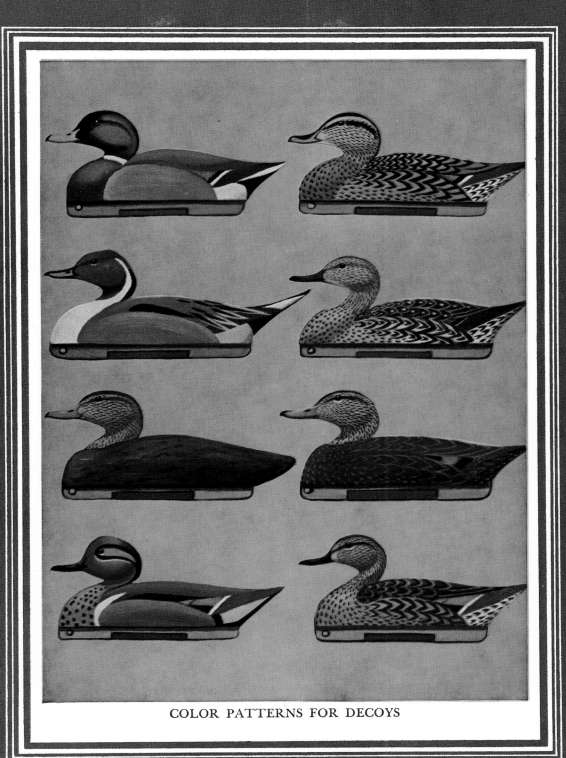

COLOR PATTERNS FOR DECOYS

This serves the additional purpose of rendering this somewhat friable substance more scuff-proof. The more coats of paint a press-cork bodied decoy has on it the better it becomes.

The three most important colors for decoy painting are black, white and brown. Of the last named the most generally useful shade is sold under the commercial designation of "Havana Brown" or "Tobacco Brown." It would be possible, equipped with only the three colors named, to paint fairly adequately a rig of any species of wildfowl subject to attraction by decoys. The addition of a very few more would be desirable, but, as a *tour de force,* it could almost be done.

The following list of colors will be found adequate for all ordinary work.

House Paint	*Artist's Colors*
Flat Black (large can)	One tube permanent Green
Flat White (large can)	One tube Prussian Blue
Havana Brown (large can)	One tube chrome Yellow
Flat Yellow Ocher (small can)	One small tube Crimson
Flat Burnt Umber (small can)	One small tube Vermilion

If a rig is painted in spring or early summer, most of the slight amount of shine will have disappeared by the time the autumn gunning season begins. The use of flat paints and the admixture of lampblack in the darker colors will virtually eliminate it, in any event. There is no type of decoy that will not show some glint when wet, natural cork not excepted. This is, to a limited extent, true of the plumage of the living fowl and need cause no undue apprehension on the gunner's part. It is an interesting fact that some of the native gunners on the waters of the upper Chesapeake paint their canvasback stool with shiny paint deliberately, in the belief that the resultant glitter will aid in attracting the attention of distant ducks to the rig. A flock of Brant, feeding afar in sunlight, send out flashes that can be seen for miles over the still water!

PAINTING INDIVIDUAL SPECIES OF DECOYS

Blackduck: The name is a misnomer! Blackducks are not black. The alternate name, "Dusky Duck," is far more descriptive. Burnt umber, mixed with lampblack, will give the proper body color for this species. The under color of the head, as well as that for the feather outlines of the body, is obtained by mixing white and a little yellow ocher with the burnt umber used for the ground color of the body itself. Be careful not to use too much of the ocher, as it is not desirable that the yellow predominate. The detail painting of the head is best done with the burnt umber and lampblack mixed for the ground color of the body. Avoid the use of black for this purpose. It is too dark. The painting of the feather detail on the body should not be obtrusive. Better omit it altogether than to overdo it. Small brushes and restraint in the painting are necessary to achieve the desired effect. The speculum is bluish purple, bordered in front and behind by black.

In the case of blackduck decoys made of scorched natural cork, no body painting whatsoever is necessary or, indeed, desirable. Burnt with a blow-torch, this material reproduces to perfection the soft, dusky sheen of the plumage. To paint it would be a case of gilding the lily. The heads, nevertheless, will require careful attention.

If the bodies be made of press-cork, they must be painted just as thoroughly as those of any other species. Unpainted, the press-cork scuffs and crumbles in time, to say nothing of its water-absorbing propensities. It is a pity that this is so, as the natural color of this material is an excellent replica of the body hue of the Blackduck. The sexes are, of course, identical in color in this duck.

Mallard Drake: Paint the entire head and neck, with the exception of the cheeks, solid black. When the paint is *half* dry, paint the cheeks brilliant green and work this color over into the adjacent black. Practice alone can guide one here. A written description is all but futile. This is no easy task, even for a skilled painter, but persistence will eventually bring about the ability to do this satisfactorily. In working the green over into the black, have the brush very dry and use light, feathery strokes. Don't smear!

For the maroon chest, mix burnt sienna, white and a little purple. This area is usually painted too light in commercial decoys. On the water, in the living bird, the maroon is very dark in appearance, except when a shaft of brilliant sunlight happens to strike it. Use a darkish shade of gray for the back (black and white) and, while the paint is still wet, run a broad line of burnt sienna along the edge where it meets the painting of the sides. Letting the two colors slightly run together at this edge will do no harm, as it will reproduce the melting effect of the plumage present in nature and very characteristic of the species. A glance at the color plate will make this clear. A little white mixed with the gray color used for the back, to lighten the shade, will be just right for the sides.

The under-tail coverts are solid black. The tail, itself, is indicated in white. The speculum is bluish purple—bluer than in the Blackduck. It is bordered in front by, first, a line of white and then one of black. At the rear margin of the speculum the order of the border colors is reversed. The buffy flank patch is painted with white into which a trifle of yellow ocher has been stirred. The bill of the drake is painted a solid, greenish-yellow, obtained by mixing yellow and white with a small amount of blue. The nail is black.

Mallard Duck: The body color of the females of this species varies astonishingly. Some examples are gray in general color cast, others definitely reddish brown. The average tone is best reproduced by mixing burnt sienna, burnt umber, yellow ocher and white. It is impossible to give precise proportional directions. Experiment! Start with white and stir in a little burnt sienna. This will be too red. Add a little burnt umber, to cut down the aggressive reddish tone. This will be better but not until a small amount of yellow ocher has been added will the desired shade suddenly evolve. Remember that the white paint must, quantitatively, far exceed the darker colors used. The plumage details are best put in with a mixture of burnt umber and black. The speculum is the same as in the male.

The bill is orange, smudged with dusky. It is well to paint the bill first with a mixture of red and yellow (this gives orange) into which a small amount of white has been stirred. When the paint has half dried, apply the dusky color. The same mixture with which the plumage details were painted (umber and black) will answer well for this. Remember that the limits of the dark and the orange on the bill are ill defined. This is one place where you can safely smear a little. This will give a very good facsimile of the natural effect. The nail is black.

Pintail Drake: The brown of the head is obtained by mixing burnt umber, white and a very little burnt sienna. Back and sides are gray. The beautiful

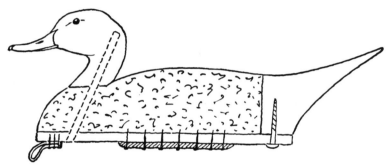

Pintail decoy of press-cork and solid wood. All contacting surfaces are glued with marine glue.

tertiary plumes, so characteristic of the males of this handsome species, are painted in only when the gray of the back is completely dry. Indeed, since they overhang the rest of the plumage, it is well to leave them until the very last. They should be made with a single, firm stroke of the brush. It is important, of course, to have the paint of just the right consistency for this, thin enough to flow freely from the brush but not so thin that it will run. White, into which a very little yellow ocher has been stirred, is the correct color.

When this has, in its turn, dried completely, indicate the shaft streaks with black, painted over the buff, as shown in the plate, using a single light stroke of the brush for the purpose. The flank patches are painted with the same creamy buff color with which the tertiary plumes were put in. The

Male Green-winged Teal.

Male Green-winged Teal.

Brant.

Female Green-winged Teal.

Female Green-winged Teal.

DECOYS MADE OF PRESS-CORK BY DR. EDGAR BURKE

Red-breasted Merganser, hollow cedar, made by Captain Parker of Parkerstown, N. J., circa 1865-70. (Bill restored.)

Red-breasted Merganser, female, hollow cedar, made by Captain Parker of Parkerstown, N. J., circa 1865-70. (Bill restored.)

Old white-winged Scoter from Lubec, Maine.

Brant, solid wood, made by Gary Bragg, Ocracoke, N. C., about 1900.

Redhead drake, solid wood, from a market gunner's rig, Ocracoke, N. C. About 1900.

other plumage markings are so clearly indicated in the plate that they will require no further explanation. The black bill has side patches of sky blue. Mix blue and white for this.

Pintail Duck: Body and head undercoloring are obtained by mixing burnt umber with a proportionately much larger amount of white. A little burnt sienna may be added to the mixture when coloring the head. All body markings to be painted with burnt umber only. In painting the breast markings it is well to lighten this a trifle by means of a small admixture of white. In most females of this species the bill is a dull bluish-slate, a shade easily obtained by mixing, first, blue and white and then adding a little black. The nail is black, as in almost all ducks.

Green-winged Teal Drake: The bill is black. The red-brown color of the head is best reproduced by mixing a little white with burnt sienna. If this appears to be too light, stir in a very little burnt umber. The green patch on the sides of the head is reproduced by stirring a small amount of white house paint into a dab of artist's color green. The edging of this patch is plain black, as is clearly shown in the color plate. The color of the chest is obtained by mixing burnt sienna, bright red and white—mostly the last-named. It is a pale shade and a good deal of white will be needed to counterfeit it with reasonable accuracy. The dark dots are black. The gray of the back and the sides is, of course, a mixture of black and white. In nature this shade of gray is a dark one, which gives the living bird an almost dusky appearance when sitting on the water and viewed at a little distance. All other details are easily gathered from the plate.

Green-winged Teal Duck: Head and body color is pale, brownish gray, obtained by mixing burnt umber with white house paint. The under-tail coverts are a dirty white in ground color. Mix a trifle of the body color with white to represent this. Plumage markings in plain black. Back, very dark brownish gray. For this use the same colors employed in painting head and body but in different proportions, with the judicious addition of a little black. For the delineation of the feather details on the back use the same mixture with which you painted the head and body, adding a very small

BROADBILL
(Male)

BROADBILL
(Female)

REDHEAD
(Male)

REDHEAD
(Female)

CANVASBACK
(Male)

CANVASBACK
(Female)

GOLDENEYE
(Male)

GOLDENEYE
(Female)

COLOR PATTERNS FOR DECOYS

COLOR PATTERNS FOR DECOYS

amount of yellow ocher to it. In nature the bill of the female of this species is more brownish than in the male but in the case of decoys counterfeiting these birds, plain black will answer every need.

Broadbill Drake: Bill pale blue. Mix blue and white for this. Nail black. While in the living bird the black head has a distinct greenish sheen, it is quite unnecessary to attempt to reproduce this in broadbill decoys. They will look equally well and prove just as effective if the entire head and chest are painted with plain black, omitting all attempts at reproducing the iridescence, which, after all, is perceptible only at closest range and in favorable light. The sides are plain white. Tail and under-tail coverts plain black. The back is dark gray, obtained by mixing black and white. The vermiculated markings so characteristic of these fowl are adequately represented by stippling the *completely dry* gray undercolor of the back with very thick white paint on a bristly, hard brush. An old toothbrush answers admirably for the purpose and, if used, should be first dipped into a small puddle of the white paint. Then, with a wooden sliver or stick, scratch off the excess paint on the brush. Having done this you are ready to use it.

Dab the brush lightly over the gray undercolor with quick, well-spaced dabs and the effect that you desire will be attained with ease. It is well to practice on a piece of wood that has been painted gray before going to work on the first decoy. If a paint brush is used, select one cut off straight across the bristles and be sure that these are stiff and not too closely packed together. An old, ragged brush is best for the purpose. Treat it just as described for the toothbrush but hold it exactly perpendicular to the plane of the surface which you are painting and apply the brush to the under color with light, quick dabs. The same effect will ensue as when using the toothbrush.

Broadbill Duck: The bill is dark, slaty blue, a shade best represented by adding a little black to the color used for the male bill. Straight burnt umber is as good a color as can be used for head and body. When painting the always slightly lighter sides add a trifle of white to the umber. The area around the base of the bill as well as the speculum is pure white. Adult females of the Greater Broadbill are very dark in color. In commercial decoys they are usually painted far too light. It will do no harm to very lightly stipple the backs of a few of your females of this species with white, exactly as in the case of the males but being much more sparing with the white than in the case of the drakes.

Redhead Drake: Bill as in the Broadbill. However, a glance at the color plate will show that the black at the tip of the bill, in most species of ducks confined to the nail, extends beyond this in this variety and is bordered, behind, by a narrow line of white. This is very characteristic of the Redhead and, while a detail, is quite noticeable in life.

The head is painted with a mixture of burnt sienna, vermilion and white —the last named color house paint, of course. In nature the heads of drakes of the Redhead have an almost purplish sheen when held in the hand. The proper shade can be gotten by referring to the color plate. Note that the neck, like the chest, is black. The red color is confined to the actual head. Back and sides are dark gray. In commercial decoys this is usually represented by too light a shade. These birds look surprisingly dark on the water. Tail and under-tail coverts are painted with plain black.

Redhead Duck: Bill as in female Broadbill but with the difference noted for the male Redhead. Head and body color is a little lighter and more yellowish brown than in the female Broadbill. Mix burnt umber, white and yellow ocher to obtain this shade. Paint the eye ring and the lighter color about the base of the bill with the same color with which you painted head and body but with the addition of a little white. Paint these areas while the ground color of the head is still wet. A more feathery effect will result.

Canvasback Drake: Bill solid black. Head and neck painted with a mixture of burnt sienna, burnt umber and white. The shade is less aggressively red than in the Redhead—more of a brick color, and the proper mixture of the colors indicated will reproduce it very convincingly. When the head is painted and about half dry, dip a soft brush into black and smear (the word is used advisedly) it about the base of the bill over the reddish undercolor. Having done this, run it over the top of the head and down the nape of the neck. A glance at the plate will make this quite clear. The chest is plain black, as are tail and under-tail coverts. The entire rest of the body is plain white.

Canvasback Duck: Bill black. Head painted with a mixture of burnt umber, yellow ocher and white. When head is half dry add a little white to the mixture used for coloring it. Dip a soft brush into this and, with a light, feathery stroke, indicate the lighter areas of the head. The chest is painted with plain burnt umber. Back dark gray (black and white mixed) while sides are lighter gray (more white mixed into the gray used for the back). Tail and under-tail coverts same as chest.

Goldeneye Drake: As the body is painted in black, white and gray, no directions will be required beyond a study of the plate. A word about the head painting may be useful. In life this has a greenish sheen so very distinct that it seems well to reproduce it if possible. After the entire head, with the single exception of the circular white area at the base of the bill, has been painted black, let the paint half dry. Then with a soft brush dipped into not too fluid artist's green color (best used just as you squeeze it out of the tube) go over the cheek areas with light, soft strokes. The problem is identical with that confronting one when painting the heads of Mallard drakes. Practice alone will achieve the proper effect.

Goldeneye Duck: Bill dark slate; tip, yellow ocher (mixed with a very little white). Head, burnt umber, burnt sienna and a little white. If you have the commercial house paint of the shade called, in the trade, "Havana Brown," use this straight. It perfectly simulates the natural shade. The entire rest of the body is painted in gray, black and white and no directions beyond a brief study of the color plate will be needed.

Canada Goose: Sexes alike. Study the color plate. Back, burnt umber lightened with a small amount of white. Don't make the ground color too light in tone. Here it is better to err on the side of darkness. Having painted in the ground color of the back, paint chest, breast and sides pure white. *While this is still wet* indicate the darker feather markings with the same mixture used for the back, working the paint into the wet, underlying white

CANADA GOOSE   BRANT

WIDGEON   WIDGEON
(Male)   (Female)

SURF SCOTER   SURF SCOTER
(Male)   (Female)

AMERICAN SCOTER   AMERICAN SCOTER
(Male)   (Female)

COLOR PATTERNS FOR DECOYS

COLOR PATTERNS FOR DECOYS

with crescentic strokes of the brush. Go over it as much as you like! Doing so will improve the effect. In completing the final painting of these areas let your strokes become lighter and lighter, especially as you approach the chest. Practice will enable you to do this better and better.

The "dirtier" the brush becomes the softer the effect of your painting will be on the still moist, underlying white paint. Take a few steps away from your work when you have half completed it and note the impression at a distance of a few yards. The result will surprise you. In indicating the plumage details on the dark undercolor of the back, use the same mixture which you employed for this but with a little white added to lighten it. Make the strokes boldly! Never mind if the crescentic markings vary a little. They do in nature and what might be termed "an irregularly regular" effect is what you should strive for.

Start at the base of the neck and let your brush strokes broaden as you approach the tail end of the decoy, when putting in these lighter feather edgings. Properly done, the inclusion of these markings immeasurably improves the final appearance of the decoy. In painting in the white cheek patch—the hallmark of the species—note that it slants backward. Attention to this detail will make the stool ever so much more lifelike.

Brant: Sexes alike. Head and chest plain black. Back, very dark brownish gray. Mix black, white and burnt umber for this. Paint sides and undertail coverts pure white. While these sections are still wet, take the brush which you used for the back, still soiled with the dark color of that area, and indicate the light, dirty gray sides by crescentic brush strokes, lightly applied. The colors will somewhat run together, which will give exactly the melting effect of this part of the natural plumage. The few plumage markings of the back can be put in with the same mixture originally used but slightly lightened by the addition of a trifle of white. As in the case of Canada Goose stool, their inclusion makes all the difference.

Surf Scoter, Drake: Scoters, or "Coot," as the native gunners of the New England Coast call them, are not particular. Anything in the shape of dark-hued decoys will usually prove effective in bringing them into gun range, so that whatever effort you expend in painting your scoter stool will be largely for your own satisfaction.

In the male Surf Scoter, the "Skunkhead" of the Yankees, the head painting is of some importance. A careful study of the color plate will enable you to reproduce it quite readily. The rest of the body is solid black.

Surf Scoter, Duck: General color cast, sooty, dark brown. Use burnt umber with a little black. In painting the somewhat lighter sides simply add a trifle of white to the mixture. The white patches on the face are a dirty white. The bill is dark grayish black.

American Scoter, Drake: Solid black, with the exception of the brilliant, orange-yellow, swollen base of the bill.

American Scoter, Duck: The darker areas of the body and head exactly as in the female Surf Scoter. For the sides, include a dash of burnt sienna. The face is gray and stands off conspicuously and characteristically against the frame of the darker top of the head and the hind neck. The bill is dark gray.

The work involved in making and painting an adequate rig of duck, brant or goose decoys is considerable and the man who has just experienced it will require no admonition to the effect that he handle the fruits of his labor with reasonable respect and regard for their preservation and continuance in a state of usability and usefulness.

Not so the average guide! Accustomed as they are to the battered and time-worn miscellaneous collection of nondescript lures which they call their "set," they will toss your finest decoys about as though they were cordwood. They will step over and on them, to the detriment of paint and the ruin of bills and heads, unless you protest loudly, emphatically and repeatedly!

When shooting with a new guide, it is well to make your wishes known in advance. It can, and should, be done pleasantly but this does not preclude its being done in a way that will leave no doubt in the guide's mind as to the exact nature of your wishes. He is there for your convenience and to enhance your pleasure and it is your right to indicate your preferences and your desires.

X V I I I

Retrievers

BY ALAN G. BAKER

THE fall migration is under way. Across leaden skies V-shaped battalions of honking geese are winging southward. From Cape Cod to the Carolinas gunners are overhauling their rigs in preparation for opening day.

The Chesapeake Bay dog, a somewhat forlorn and neglected member of the household during the long summer months, suddenly becomes an all-important factor in the open gunning season, now at hand. Necessary vitamins added to his ration are helping his coat to attain the bloom and luster which will be a valuable asset in the hard work which lies ahead. He sees you repairing decoys and painting your duck puntie, and, sensing what these preparations mean for him, is eagerly awaiting the day when he can plunge into ice-cold water and race madly after a crippled duck.

No retriever loves his work more than does the Chesapeake, and under the severest conditions of wintry gales, snow and ice, he is the dog to pin your hopes on, for he is a top performer always. Come what may he never falters.

At last the long-awaited day arrives, and three gunners huddled in their blind wait impatiently for sunrise. *Dolly,* a Chesapeake, lies curled in the sedge behind the blind. She is a veteran retriever whose ancestors for generations pursued waterfowl unflinchingly across wind-swept salt meadows, in deep tidal water, and through ice floes—a true representative of that great breed which "originated in North America and claims that country for its home. The best all-around retriever, land or water, ice or snow. They are rugged, strong, fast, faithful and smart; real dogs for the duck hunters of North America. That's the Chesapeake."

Mists swirl over the water and the surface of the bay is like glass. At dawn a breeze, freshening from the south, increases as daylight advances. The ruffling water now causes the blocks to bob about in a more realistic manner. The wind dispels the mist, visability is improved and birds commence to stir. Five Blackducks on a tour of inspection swing in quite confidently. Three remain. Guns boom along the waterfront. The season has officially opened. A cagey old "bull sprig" circles warily, then slopes for the decoys. A charge of fives slows him up, but he drops fifty yards out, a cripple.

Dolly streaks from the blind in quick pursuit. Throwing spray she dashes beyond the decoys, and with powerful strokes churns through the water in a beeline for the frantically flapping Sprig. The shore, where the three men stand anxiously watching, recedes behind her. Her head appears a brown dot bobbing among the waves, as the expanse of water between herself and the duck narrows down. The bird, struggling gamely to escape, but hindered by a broken wing and weak from loss of blood, is waging a losing fight. At times *Dolly* rears her head and shoulders above the water to gain a clearer view of the object of her pursuit. Then, sinking again to water level, she lashes out with renewed vigor. At last she draws alongside the rapidly weakening bird, and the watchers from shore see the heavy surge and swell as captor and captive alike sink for an instant from view. But *Dolly* emerges with the duck tightly gripped and commences the long swim to shore.

Mark! A single Mallard is coming toward the blind from the west. He checks his flight and starts to drop among the decoys, but suddenly flaring, towers high, directly over the blind. A gun cracks. The duck quivers, con-

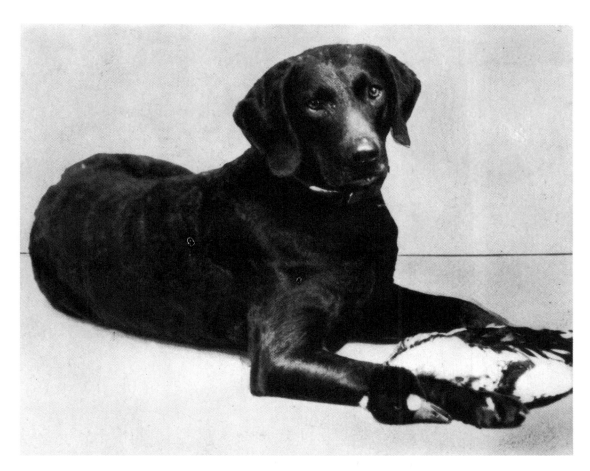

Chesapeake Bay Retriever, *Dolly*.

A fine litter of Chesapeake Bay Retrievers, eight weeks old. Owned by Paul W. Hills.

Nippy Bob, dead-grass colored Chesapeake.

King of Montauk, chocolate colored Chesapeake. J. C. Hadder, owner.

tinues on for a second, then slants into the high meadow grass behind the blind. *Dolly* has made good progress, but the gunners need her badly, so two of them pull up their boots and wade out to meet her. As soon as her feet touch bottom one takes the duck from her, and then all commence to search for the vanished Mallard. The men spread out and flounder through the dense sedge, while *Dolly* trots on ahead with head held high, testing the wind, which always carries a clear message to the keen-nosed hunting dog. She stops abruptly and plunges into high and dense cattails at her right. Her tail smacks loudly against the reeds as she proceeds. The hunters urge her on and, at last, after what seems like an eternity to them, she emerges triumphantly, carrying the Mallard and stepping proudly with head and tail erect.

All along the Atlantic Coast, on this day, many Chesapeakes, in masterful manner, are bringing in those hidden cripples which otherwise would die and furnish food only for cats, crows and other creatures.

In the year 1807 two Newfoundland pups, one black, the other a dingy red, were rescued with the crew from an English brig wrecked off the Maryland Coast. The male pup was called *Sailor* and the bitch was named *Canton,* after the American rescue ship. It is believed that these dogs were crossed with native Maryland dogs to produce the Chesapeake.

In my opinion the Chesapeake may rightfully claim Coonhound ancestry, and it is through this source that they acquire their keen scenting qualities.

When I speak of Coonhound I refer to the old southern strain of Redbone Foxhound, a hound, mostly of a dingy red color, used largely on 'coon and big game on account of its fine cold-trailing ability, staying qualities and burning desire to get away on the line. It has a tough hide and harsh coat and is lacking in the style and beauty so prevalent in other strains, but it is possessed of great bone, intelligence, stamina and tenacity of purpose.

The Coonhound and Chesapeake possess in common a high quality of sticking against seemingly hopeless odds while in pursuit of their respective game.

A racoon, when hard pressed, takes quickly to water. The hound will unhesitatingly plunge into a stream that is icy, swift and deep, while he doggedly sticks to the trail until he brings the 'coon to bay, up a tree or in a rocky ledge.

The Redbone has a drawling chop mouth, which rings out clearly as he eagerly, faultlessly and relentlessly unravels the intricate mazes of a 'coon trail, through eery swamps and across watery bottoms, under the moon's mellow glow.

The Chesapeake is a natural retriever, has a good nose and as a rule requires little training. He is used along the Atlantic Coast, and also in Minnesota and other parts of the west wherever there is duck shooting. In the west the "dead grass," a light buff or nearly cream-colored Chesapeake, is very popular. He will always be at a premium where the water is deep, rough and cold, as he has an extremely water-resistant double coat. The under coat of the Chesapeake is so dense that it is hard to part it to the skin.

THE AMERICAN WATER SPANIEL

The American Brown Water Spaniel, great favorite of the Gay Nineties, also claims this country as his home. Old legends have Columbus bringing over the first pair. As a purebreed it did not receive recognition until 1938, at which time the FIELD DOG STUD BOOK, an adjunct of the *American Field,* Chicago, Illinois, prepared and published a complete standard for the breed. It was first recognized by the American Kennel Club in 1940.

A little stream meanders through a meadow, its banks overgrown with cattails. Along this stream on a bright November day slowly and noiselessly glides a gunning puntie—a man with a gun crouched expectantly in the bow, while at the stern a man with a push pole expertly guides the craft. Amidships, the American Water Spaniel *Mike* sits, watchful and eager for action. A Teal jumps. At the crack of the gun it lurches, struggles to regain altitude and finally flutters down among the cattails.

Mike has marked the fall well. As the boat touches the bank he springs out and trots off through the cattails. The reeds bending, crackling, and swaying as he works his way through them, indicate the route he is taking, and as the boat rounds the next bend, he is there, standing on a hummock with the Teal in his mouth, ready to jump aboard. The boat continues on its slow noiseless course. With loud quackings two Blackducks burst out. A neat double sends them crashing through the cattails, and *Mike* hops out on the right bank, and in a jiffy is back with the first bird, which he holds in his mouth only long enough for the gunner to take from him. Then he swims the narrow stream, climbs the left bank, and hustles off on the trail. He is gone longer this time, for the duck, after striking the meadow, had enough life left to skulk away, back toward the stream.

Farther upstream the men can hear *Mike* splashing in the water. They hold the boat against the bank and wait for him to return. The splashing ceases. For a while there is no sound, then his brown head pokes through the cattails close to the boat, and the duck, still alive, is gently gripped in his jaws.

The American Brown Water Spaniel is an excellent hunting breed, alert, active, extremely willing, and very easily broken. They always proved their worth in heavy cover for finding game and flushing it for the gun. They are very versatile, and rank high as a retriever of waterfowl. They are not as long-legged, rugged and powerful as some of the other breeds, but they have an excellent water-resistant coat and go about retrieving with plenty of zest, because they take great pride in their work and need never to be coaxed to hunt or retrieve.

For some reason the breed at present does not enjoy the popularity it deserves.

Mr. Thomas Tyler of Rochester, N. Y., a great fancier of the breed, proclaims them to be the nearest thing to an all-around, dual-purpose hunting dog there is.

The claim that they originated in America is well founded. They somewhat resemble the Irish Water Spaniel, undoubtedly one of their progenitors, and their smaller size and similar action while hunting would make it appear quite possible that they might be of Irish Water and English Spaniel origin.

LABRADOR RETRIEVER

It is a bluebird day. The three gunners sit all morning in the blind and swap yarns. Nothing flies, and *Dina,* with no work to do, has curled up and is probably dreaming about a paradise where there is nothing but ducks.

Dina is a black Labrador Retriever. Although not of American origin, the Labrador today is the Number One choice of the American duck shooter.

The Labrador came from the St. James and White Bay region of Newfoundland, and not from Labrador. "There were two kinds of dogs on Newfoundland—the big, long-haired black dog known as the Newfoundland, and the smaller short-haired dog known as the Labrador or St. Johns breed."

The Labrador, always a great hunting and water dog, was used by the natives to haul wood and retrieve fish which had become unhooked near the surface. Their owners prized these dogs very highly and could not be persuaded to part with them even for a handsome price.

The English fishermen who came to Newfoundland in 1498, and began to build small settlements about 1522, for the most part were from Devon. Fond of hunting, they brought dogs with them. These dogs, also from Devon, were bred and schooled to meet the requirements of their owners.

"From these various breeds of dogs, bred for over a period of two hundred and eighty years under rigorous conditions, there were evolved the Newfoundland dog and the Labrador. They were the product of environment and survival and perhaps selection."

Labradors were first recognized by the Kennel Club as a breed on July 7, 1903, and in 1905 they were separately classified as a sub-variety of retrievers.

American Water Spaniels. Owned by T. L. Tyler.

Group of brood matrons American Water Spaniels. Owned by T. L. Tyler.

Three Immortals: *Shed of Arden*, Labrador; *Rip*, Golden; *Tar of Arden*, Labrador.

Le Noir (left) and F.T.C. *Gun of Arden* as a puppy, Labradors.

A quarter of a mile west of where the men are rigged, a long point extends well out into the bay. Scudding low along the water, Bluebill begin cutting by this point at frequent intervals. No one is rigged there, so while two of the men pick up the decoys, the third drives home for Bluebill stool. When he returns, the other two men are on the point building a temporary blind. They carry the stool to the blind in bags, and in twenty minutes are rigged and ready.

They want action and they get it. Whizzing, darting, and dipping Bluebill are over the blind, all in a moment. The men burn powder, but no birds fall. Ken Purdy, an experienced gunner, shouts advice: "Lead 'em, boys! Lead 'em! You're shooting miles behind 'em."

A single drake comes rocketing in, and Ken's well-placed charge catches him squarely, spins him around, and plumps him into the water. From then on all hands improve, and when a flight comes over, instead of shooting blindly into them, each man picks a bird and leads it. The birds begin to fall with greater regularity and *Dina* is kept busy. She is now almost constantly in the water, leaving the blind, or returning to it with a duck in her mouth. The birds keep on coming. *Dina's* head looks like another Bluebill to them. The flight lasts for an hour, then there is a lull. Three Teal flit by. They have a dinner date in the Gulf of Mexico, and are well on their way there, when shot rips up the air far behind them. A pair of Redheads appear from nowhere. They hover for an instant, but are gone before the men can raise their guns.

After this, singles and pairs come at frequent intervals for a half hour. It is now that the men do their best shooting. Six large ducks go by, and as they bank around to circle back, the sun glistens on their white feathers. Canvasbacks are rare. The men wait, and they come well-bunched across the decoys. Timely shooting accounts for four. Another one flares off and comes down with a splash forty yards beyond the rig.

Dina marks him down, leaves the bank with a bound and sets full sail for him. When she gets to him he dives. She treads water and waits. Up he pops thirty feet away and she races toward him. Luckily he is hard hit and not very alert, so she grabs him by the tail as he is about to dive again. When she returns the men are standing up. This shot proved a fitting climax to their memorable day and they are preparing to quit.

The Labrador is an excellent, all-around retriever, quick to mark a fall, rapid in getting to it, prompt and soft-mouthed on the return. The Labrador is also the pleasantest of all the retrievers to have beside you in a blind, as they are entirely free from that disagreeable oily odor noticeable in most of the other breeds. The Labrador, always good-natured, also makes an excellent house dog, and is a real guardian of the home and a faithful pal of small children.

IRISH WATER SPANIEL

Origin of the Irish Water Spaniel is largely a matter of conjecture. Justin McCarthy developed this rattailed, top-knotted spaniel in the early 1800's, supposedly from a blend of North of Ireland and South of Ireland strains. That the water-loving Poodle and the Irish Setter played a major part in the development, there is little doubt. But as McCarthy never enlightened the world as to what breeds he used as foundation stock, no one will ever know much about it. "He owned *Boatswain* (who lived for eighteen years), one of the first and best known of all Irish Waters."

The Irish Water Spaniel, largest of all the spaniel breeds, is the joker in the retriever pack. A clown in appearance, he is as unpredictable by nature as are the citizens of the country in which presumably he originated.

As a go-getter of waterfowl under the most adverse conditions, he is hard to beat, for the tougher the going, the more his Irish pluck and Irish luck manifest themselves.

When he goes after a cripple, no matter where the duck falls, you may be sure he will eventually return with the bird and deliver it with his expressive rattail carried very proudly.

On land his shaggy, dense, hard and heavy coat equips him well to penetrate the thickest cover, and where a thinner- or softer-coated breed might hesitate, he will boldly plunge in. His coat, a fine collector of burrs and twigs, may render him an even less pleasing sight when he comes out of the muck, mud, reeds or cattails, but come out he will, and very seldom empty-mouthed.

The work of the Irishman may be less polished and spectacular than that of some of the other breeds, but you could not want a more efficient retriever or faithful and comical pal beside you in a duck blind.

Mr. and Mrs. Charles F. Goodnow, Jr., owners of the Princess Colleen Kennels, South Sudbury, Massachusetts, claim that "the friendly and happy Irish Water Spaniel is a dual-purpose dog that cannot quite be equaled for fine performance on both waterfowl and upland birds. They are very easy to train, since they retrieve naturally, a few doing so with little or no instruction at twelve or fourteen weeks of age, so inherent is the instinct to fetch. The Irish Water is a good performer in the field at a comparatively early age."

The day before, a gale had ripped along the beach and ducks were everywhere. But today our usual bad luck had held. Just a whisper of a southerly breeze scarcely rippled the water. The motionless decoys would not even lure the most sociably inclined duck within gun range. The air was balmy and the view superb. It was a beautiful day for a landscape painter or butterfly collector, but no day for a duck hunter.

The only enthusiastic member of our party was big *Clancy,* our tousle-topped Irish canine friend. Utterly out of control, he bounded through the beach plum bushes and we watched rather disinterestedly as, racing at top speed, he disappeared from view over a high dune.

With nothing around to disturb us we immediately settled down to enjoy a quiet siesta, destined to be very short-lived, for *Clancy* came thundering back with a Broadbill. This Broadbill was undeniably high, too high even for the perverted taste of the most eccentric epicure, and the less said about it the better.

Completely undaunted, *Clancy* galloped off again and promptly returned with a beautiful Mallard drake. There was nothing wrong with the Mallard. He was plump, alive, alert, and active. We guessed that *Clancy* had taken a mean advantage of the bird and sneaked up on him when he was asleep. We believed the incident to be only a bit of Irish luck and were again on the boundaries of dreamland when *Clancy* returned, this time with a winged Widgeon in good condition.

Now fully aroused, we staggered to our feet and, deploying in a fan-shaped skirmish line, floundered along in *Clancy's* wake. *Clancy,* now under perfect control, his 'possum tail waving gaily, took complete charge of the advance. There was not a single ditch, pond, or pothole which he did not investigate thoroughly, and we collected fifteen birds, mostly Blacks. That is, we shot seven jumped birds, and *Clancy* picked up eight cripples.

Although the fates had seemed all against us, we enjoyed a successful day due to *Clancy's* choke-bore nose, the fact that a big shoot the day before had left many unrecovered ducks on the beach, a combination of both, or what you will. But in my opinion, somewhere within *Clancy's* big unlovely hairy hulk lurked the soul of an Irish conjurer, for, of a truth, where they should not have existed at all, did he not find them, and bring them in?

GOLDEN RETRIEVER

Another breed of retriever rapidly coming into prominence on account of his high degree of intelligence, is the Golden.

In the year 1860, Sir Dudley Marjoribanks visited a circus at Brighton, England, and saw there eight Russian performing dogs accomplishing some difficult feats under the watchful guidance of their trainer. Sir Dudley purchased the eight dogs and acquired thereby enough stock to carry out some interesting breeding experiments.

These performing dogs were Russian Trackers, the ancestors of the Golden Retriever. The Russian Tracker was a dog of large size, possessing a double, taffy-colored coat, together with sagacity and endurance. He had to guard his master's flocks on the slopes of the Caucasus Mountains, and was at all times a fierce and formidable fighter against the attacks of wolves and other wild animals, and faithful guardian of the flocks under his care.

It is quite possible that a Bloodhound cross was made to perfect the nose of the Golden, and this cross quickly bred out again. At one time the Golden Retriever did the work of both a setter and retriever, but now his work is purely of a retrieving nature both on land and in the water.

For an indeterminable time nothing flies, when suddenly up go the callers' necks and from their throats issue that weird clarion call of welcome to a flying flock. The men lie low in the blind and curl their cold fingers around their guns in a hard grip. A cautious peep through the tall grass surrounding the blind reveals a wavering line of Geese over the ocean and far to the east.

The callers are now gabbling goose language in lively fashion, and the line shifts its course and wavers ever closer to the blind. The leading gander has now caught sight of the decoys, honked his answer to their welcome and the entire flock, on rigid wings, is coasting straight for the rig. With pounding hearts and taut nerves the hunters keep their eyes riveted on the leading gander.

Rip, the big Golden, a statue in bronze, also watches the flock's every move. He is an expert retriever and knows fully as well as do the men that any sudden move on his part will spell disaster. Only a slight twitching of his powerful muscles reveals the nerve strain this enforced inactivity is causing him. Old white-cheeks is wary and wise. Two gun-shots off he alights on the water and most of the flock settle around him. But five eager goslings glide in with necks outstretched and feet extended. The gunners go into action, and four big birds wilt and crash to the water.

The fifth sags in sixty yards from shore and starts to swim away. A bundle of golden energy uncoils itself and goes flashing out in sudden pursuit. Ignoring the four dead birds, *Rip* goes after the cripple, and the gunners all stand on the water's edge to witness this race. Swimming smoothly, he quickly overtakes the cripple, and just as he reaches it, he makes a quick lunge which sends him below the surface. He comes up with the gosling, but with its free wing it slaps him hard across the eyes. Again they go down, but this time *Rip* has the gosling's both wings tightly held against its body and, with nothing further to hinder his vision, strikes out for shore. In popularity the Golden has gone ahead by leaps and bounds because of his beauty and tractability.

THE CURLY COATED RETRIEVER

Stories concerning the origin of this breed are somewhat conflicting. One story claims that they resulted from crosses of English Water Spaniels, Irish Water Spaniels and retrieving Setters. Another version is that the Poodle and lesser St. Johns Newfoundland were the original ancestors.

I am inclined to believe that the Poodle played an important part in the development of this breed, as he did also in the Irish Water Spaniel.

Curlies never became popular in this country, but J. Gould Remick, prominent New York sportsman, had two, *Sarona Sam of Marvadel* and *Sarona Jacob of Marvadel*. These dogs proved well able to do fine retrieving work under any condition which might arise.

Curlies are not the most spectacular type of retriever, but are excellent markers, extremely willing and intelligent, have a keen nose, and possess an excellent water-resisting coat composed of short tight curls all over. A patch of uncurled hair is not to be desired.

The Remick Curlies were always ably handled by Russell Murdock of Southhaven, Long Island.

A stiff no'theaster had churned the usually calm surface of the bay into a snarling, seething froth of high-running, angry waves, and the large rafts of ducks, unable to take this buffeting, were breaking up into small flocks and seeking the protection of some quiet lagoon, slough, cove or inland pond.

We thought the little round pond in the woods should be productive of a shoot and as we crouched tense in our brush blind with six blackduck decoys floating in front of us, we soon realized that we had, for once, been right.

Over the treetops on set wings Blackducks, Mallards, Teal and Pintail

Irish Water Spaniels from the Princess Colleen Kennels.

Princess Colleen Kennels

Two dogs retrieved sixty ducks in three hours!

Serona Shell, a good working type Curly Coated Retriever.

Ch. Noranhy Baloo of Taramar, Golden Retriever.

began to pitch for the pond. They needed the protection that this pond offered them and, dispensing with the formality of wary circling, were dropping right in.

The shooting was fast and easy, but the recovery difficult and uncertain. Without old *Jacob,* our Curly, it would have been practically impossible to collect these fine big Blacks and Mallards, and the sport is ruined for any duck shooter who can't get his birds.

We had the utmost confidence in *Jacob.* There was nothing flashy about his work, but he was calm, sure and mighty efficient. He did not disappoint us on this day, and we had every reason to be proud of his work.

His marking was uncanny. During an infrequent lull Russell Murdock would send him out to collect the difficult falls. Birds had sailed over the trees, and plunged into the woods, dead or crippled.

He was off fast downwind, and paying no attention to the easy falls, his unfailing nose would seek out the dead birds and skulking cripples as he worked back into the wind. Without *Jacob* the shoot would have been a travesty. With him it was a red-letter day, long to be remembered.

THE FLAT COATED RETRIEVER

In England, about 1850, sportsmen were vainly trying to breed a retrieving dog that would have a coat of the proper texture to withstand the ill effects of long exposure to cold water. Prior to this time many types of dogs had been experimented with for water retrieving, with indifferent success.

The Old English Sheepdog was one, also the Poodle, and various crosses with Spaniel or Setter and Collie. It was the constant endeavor of English sportsmen to produce a grade breed possessing a keen nose, a soft mouth, together with intelligence and a proper water-resistant coat. In 1850 new material was brought to light in a black-coated dog said to have been imported from Labrador. This was probably the St. Johns dog of Newfoundland, and it is reasonable to believe that they were crossed with Irish and probably Gordon Setter to produce the Flat Coated Retriever.

It is, therefore, safe to assume that the St. Johns breed of smaller, shorter-haired Newfoundland dogs was the common ancestor of the Flat Coated Retriever, the Labrador Retriever, and also, as some sportsmen believe, of our own American Chesapeake Bay dog. There is, however, a belief that the large Newfoundland dog, and not the smaller, short-haired St. Johns breed, was one of the Flat Coated Retriever's ancestors. Having seen the Flat Coat, I am inclined to favor this latter belief.

The Flat Coated Retriever, for many years called Wavy Coated Retriever, was the most popular retriever in England during the early 1900's.

It is of interest to keep in mind to what a great extent the Labrador cross influenced the early retriever. That the parent stock was a mongrel dog of distinct setter type is now known. The ultimate result proved how potent is the blood of a pure race for fixing a definite type and character, when suffused with less vital elements.

From the first, sportsmen recognized the efficiency of the new retrieving dog. Strengthened and improved by the Labrador blood, he had lost none of the Setter dignity and symmetry. He was at all times a faithful, intelligent and useful companion for the shooting man, and a reliable guard of his home.

The Flat Coated Retriever dominated the sporting scene at shoots and field trials, and was also popular on the bench. Eventually the Labrador gained favor with British sportsmen and displaced the Flat Coat, which still have their following of staunch admirers, and with proper promotion may yet regain their former popularity. In this country only a very few sportsmen ever knew much about the breed.

"Idstone" described one of the early retrievers, and the description, which admirably fits a Flat Coated Retriever, is worth quoting:

"He was black as a raven—a blue black—not a very large dog, but wide over the back and loins, with limbs like a lion, and a thick, glossy, long, silky coat, which parted down the back, a long, sagacious head, full of character and clean as a Setter's in the matter of coat. His ears were small, and so close to his head that they were hidden in his feathered neck. His eye was neither more nor less than a human eye, and I never saw a bad expression in it.

"He was not over twenty-five inches in height, but he carried a hare with ease; and if he could not top a gate with one, he could get through the second or third span, or push it through a gap before him in his mouth, and never lose his hold. And then for water. He would trot into the launching punt, and coil himself up by the luncheon basket to wait for his master as soon as he saw the usual preparations for a cruise.

"For this work he had too much coat, and brought a quantity of water into the boat; but for retrieving wildfowl he was excellent; and in the narrow water-courses and amongst the reeds and osiers his chase of a Winged Mallard was a thing to see. They seemed both to belong to one element, and he would dive like an otter for yards, sometimes coming up for breath, only to go down again for pleasure."

TRAINING

If you contemplate buying a pup of whatever retrieving breed you may prefer, it is of the utmost importance to select one that is well endowed with all the physical qualifications essential in the work he is expected to perform. Get a pup from registered parents of correct type. Do not be content with any pup just because his or her sire, dam, or both happen to be good hunting dogs but with a questionable pedigree—or none at all.

Some hunters will tell you that papers don't make the dog hunt any better. This statement is true only in rare individual cases. If you have a non-pedigreed bitch, regardless of type, who performs creditably under all conditions, your chances of getting good pups from her will be poor indeed, even though you mate her to a dog that performs as well as she does. This type of mating is hit or miss, and usually fails because you are groping in the dark and have no records to guide you along the road to sensible selection.

The advantage of registration is that it enables you to select a sire possessing in abundance those qualities in which your bitch is lacking. You then will have every reason to expect these desired characteristics to be transmitted to the offspring through your certain knowledge that the sire has them strongly stamped in him through generations of careful selection toward breed improvement.

Having procured the pup, the question of training now confronts you. Do not attempt this yourself unless you are cool-headed, and have much kindness, patience and perseverance.

It is important first to determine if the pup is worth the time, trouble and patience you will be obliged to spend on him. In an average litter of six to eight pups you will soon find that you will be working with that many individuals, and that it is practically impossible to follow any set rules of training which will work well with all of them. There will undoubtedly be a timid pup or two, which will have to be handled entirely differently from the bold type. If you are fortunate enough to have a natural retriever in the litter, you will find little trouble with him. It is then merely up to you to give him just enough work and guidance of the right kind, and never allow his interest to lag by overworking him, or giving him work too difficult of accomplishment.

When the pups are ten to twelve weeks old you will be taking them for walks away from the kennel. Even at this early age certain individual characteristics begin to manifest themselves. Some of the pups will show a tendency to investigate everything and get out on their own. This is a trait which should be encouraged, as an independent pup is often displaying early symptoms of possessing that greatest of all attributes, a keen nose. One or two pups will go off on scouting expeditions and return to you with something in their mouths. They have inherited the instinct to retrieve through generations of careful breeding and selection.

Pups of this type with real desire and natural ability often make the best. It is not necessary to go through a process of step-by-step routine work with a pup that is a natural retriever. From the start he will want to retrieve birds, and because he has a keen nose will take no interest in a pad, cork

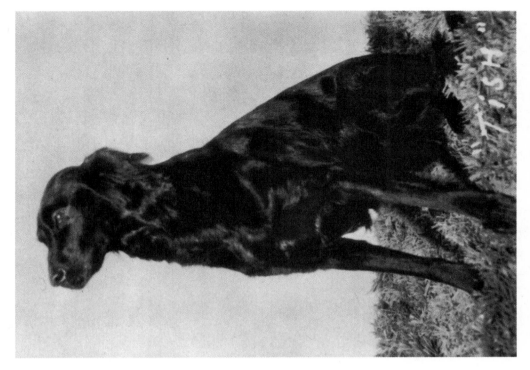

English-bred Flat Coated Retriever, *Tish of Paxcroft*

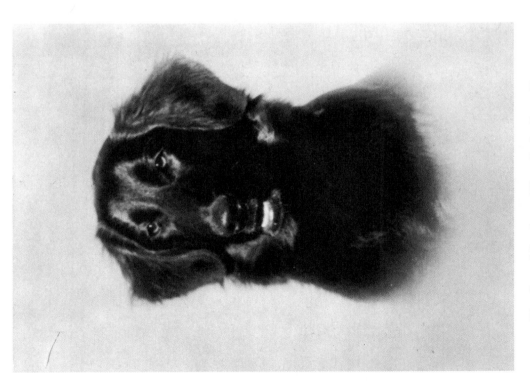

Flat Coated Retriever, *Waac Lady*. Owned by
Mrs. Peter Engelhart.

Goldwood Tuck, a Golden Retriever. Owned by H. J. Kaufman.

Use of dumbbell in training dog to hold object evenly balanced.

dummy, or any such contraption. Use a Pigeon or Mallard for him and watch him go to work. He soon will be bringing the bird right to hand with not a feather ruffled. Continue to school the pup with short, frequent lessons. Be firm yet kind, insist on prompt and correct work on his part, never punish him in a fit of temper and he will reward your every effort by ultimately becoming the full-fledged, thoroughly trained retriever you will be proud to have beside you in a duck blind.

Now we come to the problem pups—the timid ones, those that are indifferent and the headstrong type. Timid pups which cower away at every strange sight or sound are luckily the exception in a normally healthy litter. There might be one, however, that seems a little afraid of noise. You can overcome this fault by introducing a firearm at the correct time. Fire it when the pup is preoccupied, when he is eating, or when he is interested in retrieving an object, or watching a trained dog work. Use a cap pistol, as it does not make too much noise, and do not stand too close to him.

A few lessons of this kind, gradually substituting firearms that are louder, will usually cure the gun-shyness. Indifference may mean that the pup has no nose, and therefore no interest. Try to arouse some spark of interest in him by working him with an older dog. What he sees he will probably try to imitate. He may also be a somewhat slow starter and may improve as he grows older. Do not spend too much time with him but work with more promising prospects; then try him again when he is a little older and more mature.

The headstrong pup may be the best in the litter, but will require stern handling. He will have to be taught to mind perfectly, even if you have to resort to a choke collar. Don't let him get away with anything. When you order "sit" or "hup" see that he obeys. If he displays signs of a hard mouth, run wires through the bird or object he is to retrieve. Make him retrieve promptly. If he runs away from you, don't chase him, but teach him to come quickly by means of a whistle and a reward, and if that does not work, use a thirty-foot cord and a choke collar.

Be just a little more determined and stubborn than the pup. Insist on obedience, but don't break his spirit. If you persevere and show him that you are the boss he will reward you by becoming a fast, hard-driving retriever, the kind with the pluck and fortitude to face any problem and come out on top.

It should always be remembered that kindness and patience in the handling of retrievers pay big dividends.

Dolly, my Chesapeake, received her early training under the gentle, quiet, and watchful guidance of Fred Mühs, veteran Blackduck and Goose gunner of Shinnecock Bay, at Hampton Bays, Long Island. At that time live callers were legal and all the guides used them.

Dolly at first was somewhat confused by the live birds in the rig, but she learned in a surprisingly short time to differentiate between the live geese and duck callers and a dead or crippled wild Blackduck or Goose.

The birds also soon got used to her and would not lunge on their hobbles when she stepped carefully among them in pursuit of crippled wild birds.

Every morning *Dolly* would make her rounds of the goose pen, and any caller that might have escaped from the pen during the night would be promptly located by her on the meadow and quickly brought back to the pen.

The best training for any hunting dog is to give it as much of the kind of work it is fitted for as possible. *Dolly,* being intelligent and willing, learned very rapidly, and Fred was always there with a quiet word or gesture to guide her over the rough spots.

Today Fred is still shooting Geese and Blackduck at Shinnecock, and he has *Lady,* a nice-working Chesapeake bitch. She is a fast retriever in the water, but, to quote Fred, "There just isn't another *Dolly.*"

Dr. Gilbert A. Chandler of Natick, Mass., writes the following concerning the training of his big Irish Water Spaniel pup *Dinty.*

"I had only a limited time to teach my Irish Water Spaniel pup *Dinty,* because the open season was close at hand.

"He had a swim in the lake every day and seemed to enjoy both this and retrieving a stick with feathers wound around it, and we slowly learned each other's likes and dislikes. Gunfire did not cause him to flinch, and I felt encouraged.

"Then came opening day! Heavy fog, cold wind and an unfamiliar kind of water confronted six-months-old *Dinty*. Never before had the pup seen or scented salt water. Flock after flock of Bluebill swung over the decoys. We got our share, but no amount of coaxing or cussing could tempt *Dinty* to place a foot in that salt water, or touch one of those ducks, the sight and scent of which caused the hair along his hackles to rise.

"The next night we were picking ducks in our cellar when *Dinty* sauntered in. He took a few sniffs, then retired to a corner and lay down. Without paying any particular attention to the pup I tossed a bird on the floor. After a time he got up, nudged the bird with his nose, then tried to pick it up. I at once took the bird away from him and placed it upon the pile of dead ducks. When he had settled down again I threw another duck.

"*Dinty* got up, picked up the duck and started out the door. I called him back, led him to the pile with the duck in his mouth, saying "Fetch" all the time, and placed that duck with the others. For an hour I threw ducks all over the cellar. This served to tenderize the ducks, and also give *Dinty* a rough idea of what he was supposed to do. Like all intelligent pups he caught on quickly. This was a game that made sense, and there was no salt water to bother him. As quickly as I could toss a duck *Dinty* would pick it up and bring it back eagerly, hoping and expecting me to throw it again.

"The next Sunday, as we pulled the boat up on the grass island, a crippled Black floundered off the sedge into the water. *Dinty* was on him in a flash. Ten feet out he captured the duck and soon had him back on shore. Before sundown he had retrieved seven ducks shot over the decoys, and in addition nosed out a crippled Broadbill, with which he came proudly trotting in, and promptly placed it on the pile of dead ducks.

"The season of 1946 *Dinty* retrieved a total of twenty-five ducks and four cock Pheasants. A very creditable record for a pup of any retrieving breed less than eight months old."

X I X

Waterfowl

BY LUDLOW GRISCOM

ONE of the outstanding events of the conservation year of 1946 was the sharp decline in the continental supply of waterfowl. Moreover, the proved decline came on the heels of widely publicized releases that the duck restoration program had been so gloriously successful that many hunting restrictions should be removed. To put it mildly, ignorance and prejudice of an amateurish kind exist among both sportsmen and bird-lovers. The hunters are not the menace to the ducks some bird-lovers think. The bird-lovers are not the menace to sport the hunters think. Actually a decline in ducks is far more serious to sportsmen than to bird-lovers. It takes far more ducks to furnish fun for gunners than for opera glass wielders! In arguing over minute details of fact and opinion, fundamental biological principles have been forgotten or ignored. An effort to emphasize them would appear timely.

I take as my premise that sound conservation is an applied science based on biology, and must consequently accept and reckon with certain fundamental biological principles. You may call them laws of nature if you will, or think of them as the acts of God. The time element involved is infinitely longer than normal human patience.

1. Every duck has always had a limited breeding range and a definitely limited winter range. The total number of individuals can never be greater than the number that can find favorable breeding habitats, nor can it be greater than the carrying capacity of the winter range.

2. It follows that the total number of individuals in existence will be based on whichever of these two factors *is the lesser*.

3. The total number of individuals is also a balance which has been struck between many other favorable and unfavorable factors. In addition to habitat there are climate, pressure from enemies, food supply, disease, strain and loss from migration, reproductive fertility, an unbalanced sex ratio, to mention some only of the more obvious.

4. In a primeval wilderness, none of these factors ever was or ever will be static. Minor variations in temperature and rainfall cause immediate fluctuations in plant crops, the number of small fish and invertebrates. Major climatic variations result in droughts and "dust bowls," or severe freezes of marshes and ponds in the winter range. Peak populations inevitably decline, and are suspected of starting a new cycle of epidemic diseases.

5. It is inconceivable that *all* favorable and unfavorable factors remain absolutely static two years in succession. Nature is cyclic, climate is cyclic, all living things are subject to cyclic increases and decreases. Once every so often, thanks to the arithmetical principles of the least common multiple, many favorable factors in combination result in a peak of abundance. Inevitably another major cyclic swing will produce years with a *maximum number and development* of unfavorable factors. The population "crashes" to a "low," which certainly causes a decline of 50 per cent, and possibly up to 75 per cent of the total number of individuals in existence during the boom years. These population swings went on centuries before the first gun was fired in the New World, are taking place in our time, and will surely continue should the firing of a gun be made illegal forever.

6. Over most of these factors *man at present has no control whatever.* It is, therefore, silly for interested men to shake hands and congratulate themselves on their supposed prowess, after two or three "good" years have seen a gratifying increase in the population. Their happy assumption that they deserve all the credit, and that this gain will be permanent, is doomed to disappointment.

7. It is equally unrealistic to set up a howl of grief and anger, when the inevitable decline takes place, and to blame the government or any human organization or agency. It is not necessarily due *solely* to hunting.

8. The historical period of research, study and conservation management is far too short to warrant placing any ceiling on the maximum possible number of waterfowl the continent can support under present conditions. We simply do not know whether the greatest possible combination of favorable circumstances has occurred in our time or not. It would appear most improbable.

9. We positively do know, however, the maximum possible combination of unfavorable factors has *not* occurred. Every fifty thousand or so years there is an Ice Age. When the fifth will arrive we do not know, but when it does, not only the ducks but our human civilization will disappear from much of North America like chaff before a hurricane.

10. There is great need for realism in another direction. Nature appears both prodigal and wasteful. We must accept an annual mortality which reaches truly astronomical figures. If a population is remaining constant, one pair of birds starts the breeding season, they lay X number of eggs, a smaller number of fledged young start south with the adults, and *only one healthy pair* need survive to start next year's breeding season. The very great majority of all individuals in existence perish annually, in the natural order of events, in the primeval wilderness.

Let us then force ourselves to consider realistically what these normal annual losses actually are. To prove it requires simple arithmetic only, based on the figures supplied by the U. S. Fish and Wildlife Service. The accuracy of the figures does not affect the argument or the principle involved.

a. In 1944 there were 125,300,000 ducks.
b. Let us call it 60 million pairs in round numbers.
c. Ducks lay 10-16 eggs.
d. Which makes a potential of between 600 million and a billion birds.
e. In a static population, only 125 million return to the breeding area.
f. Therefore, a potential of 475-875 million birds have been lost.
g. The kill of 1944, 20 million birds, is mere chicken feed, as it is about four per cent of the lesser figure.
h. It becomes vitally important, however, if too few eggs are laid, too few hatch, or too few downy chicks are raised to maturity.

I know of no more interesting illustration of the clash between sentiment and biology. I have every respect for the many Americans who feel a pang when a duck is killed by hunter or hawk. They are much more philosophic about the downy chicks which never grew up, completely calm over the eggs which did not hatch, and ice cold over the eggs which might have been laid but were not. They are also philosophic about all losses of grown birds from all other natural causes combined during fall, winter and spring. Unfortunately sportsmen are equally uninterested.

Nevertheless, birds are sure to become extinct, which fail signally in *any one* of *these three early stages* too many years in succession. As far as the biology of survival is concerned, it makes no difference at which one of the six stages of the year's life history the death of the individual occurs.

Bird-lovers who accuse naturalists who advance this view of being cold-blooded forget that human vital statistics are compiled in exactly the same way. If we wish to show that the population of New York City is increasing, all we have to do is to prove that the annual birth rate exceeds the death rate. It is immaterial at what ages the various deaths occurred. France has been alarmed for years at her declining birth rate. There was a slow, steady population increase in western Europe during the Dark and Middle Ages in spite of the mortality caused by constant strife, violence and wars, with epidemics of smallpox, cholera, and typhus thrown in, which caused sharp temporary decreases in the population. The fundamental biology of ducks and humans has much in common!

It would appear to be of relatively small consequence under primeval conditions just which unfavorable factors caused the mortality in any one year, or in what proportion. In an undisturbed state of nature they automatically cancel out and strike a normal balance. If peak numbers of predators cause a decline, the decline causes the starvation of the predators, whose number in turn decreases to par. No one ever heard of parasites and epidemic diseases exterminating themselves by exterminating their hosts! The decline caused by a series of hard winters is certain to be made up by the survival of unusual numbers in the series of mild winters sure to follow sometime in the future.

It is, consequently, my earnest conviction that some people interested in conservation must take a longer view and learn these fundamental propositions in the natural history of animals. Bird-lovers as well as sportsmen should benefit by education, and each group must give up some cherished illusions, and adopt a more realistic attitude.

1. No amount of success in conservation will ever make possible an unlimited hunting season, and no closed season will ever produce an unlimited supply of ducks. The biologists of the U. S. Fish and Wildlife Service are well aware of these propositions, but usually fail to mention them except when fate forces them to apologize for a decline in ducks. Moreover, they have no appropriations for a real educational program.

2. Under certain conditions, the size of the kill would be of no consequence whatever, and a closed season could not prevent a decline from natural causes. For instance:—Let us assume that the carrying capacity of the winter range is only two-thirds of the ducks leaving the breeding grounds after a signally successful season. Let us further assume that hunting regulations, which would have produced a kill of 20 million birds, are replaced by a closed season. Obviously 20 million birds would be "saved." But if the winter range will only carry two-thirds of the summer crop, how in the name of common sense can it carry two-thirds plus 20 million!

3. It is an equally serious illusion of certain sportsmen that more breeding habitats will create a large surplus which can be killed, because the

winter range will not support them. In the first place, a *permanently closed* season *throughout the winter range* would be required. And who, pray, can calculate the percentage of the surplus, or predict in advance the losses from natural causes of the winter and ensuing spring migration?

Now let us try to apply some of these propositions more specifically to our North American ducks. We are anxious to conserve them, by which we mean not only that we wish to maintain their present numbers, but if possible restore some percentage of their former numbers. The chances for success are best discovered by an appraisal of assets and liabilities.

There are very real assets furnished by the birds themselves. They are hardy, tough, wary in danger, increasingly adaptable under protection. More and more they are accepting civilization, nesting in the immediate vicinity of man and wintering in places and under conditions which were inconceivable in my boyhood. Their reproductive fertility is one of the highest of any bird group on earth.

The liabilities may be divided into two categories, the ones over which man has virtually no control, and those few remaining, where he has.

First and foremost of these latter is the question of habitat. Our waterfowl have very definite and restricted habitat requirements, and let us say that 75 per cent of the continent does not interest them in the least. They must have marshes and ponds in which to breed. Their decrease in the last 300 years, to their present numbers, is primarily due to the loss of a large percentage of their former breeding territory and the destruction of portions of their former wintering grounds. The national slogan of all unselfish sportsmen and bird watchers should be "No marsh, no ducks, no sport."

The second great liability, unrestricted market gunning throughout the year, which seriously cut the surviving population *below* the carrying capacity of the remaining favorable territory, has been illegal for over a quarter of a century. Its virtual elimination made possible an immediate and permanent increase in the total population.

One of the outstanding generalizations about our waterfowl, beautifully brought out by Dr. Frederick C. Lincoln of the U. S. Fish and Wildlife

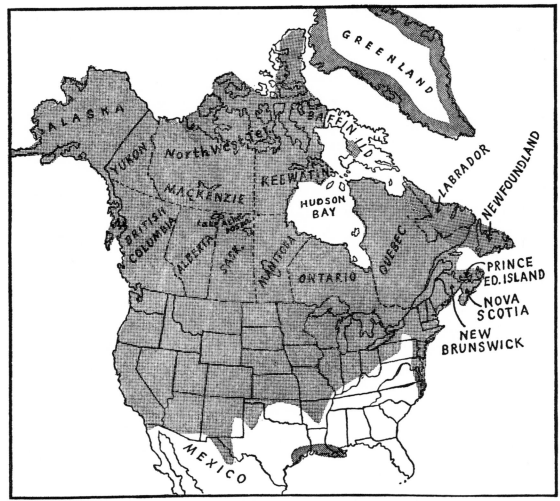

BREEDING GROUND

Service, was that the winter range of most species was enormously compressed in total acreage as compared to the breeding range.

It follows that the carrying capacity of the *remaining winter range* is possibly *the critical factor,* which places a definite ceiling on our total waterfowl population. My conviction that this is so has been steadily growing in recent years. The evidence is as follows:

The cycle of drought years in the 1930s, which produced the "dust bowl" era, affected the breeding grounds primarily. Interest and most competent

WINTERING GROUND

effort turned to a restoration of breeding areas. Not only were these efforts successful, but the drought broke, and a series of good years produced the greatest swarm of ducks to move south in 1944 in a quarter of a century. There was some astonishment that this great surplus could not be found by the end of the following winter, and everyone admits that it had evaporated in 1946. Again, the breeding season of 1945 was not a serious failure, and everyone with adequate field experience is impressed by the amount of possible breeding territory in the northern states and Canada which is unoccupied, or not fully occupied. Finally everyone knows that civilization has developed by leaps and bounds in the last quarter of a century in what were pre-eminently rural southern states.

One may well ask the rhetorical question—Of what use is it to raise a large crop of young on the breeding grounds if the winter range will support two-thirds of them only?

We are now in a position to comment sensibly on the hope expressed earlier that some percentage of the former numbers of waterfowl could be restored.

In biological terms there is only one way in which it can be done. To recapture a former range, any reduced species must be able to develop a surplus population in its surviving range. This surplus population will inevitably be produced on the breeding grounds as the result of a succession of good years. Unless this surplus can survive on the winter range, there will be no birds to extend the breeding range or occupy it more fully. Two different sets of favorable environment are consequently prerequisite. While mere protection from hunting is not alone sufficient, the production of this surplus population might easily require a closed season in poor years.

It follows that the federal government's wildlife refuge program is of fundamental importance. The so-called advance of civilization has always involved the draining of marshes and ponds, the pollution of rivers, estuaries and bays. In the long range view the total number of waterfowl will be limited to the acreage of favorable habitat which can be preserved, intact and unspoiled, and the number of birds it can support. A permanently closed season could not possibly increase this number.

There cannot be less than three million Americans genuinely interested in our waterfowl. They are really concerned for various reasons whenever there is a decline. Most of them blow off steam in quarreling about the proper hunting regulations of the particular year. Some bird-lovers are convinced that every decline is due to too long a hunting season the year before! Almost every effort of the government to acquire a new refuge is bitterly opposed by local sportsmen. They reason that if 10,000 acres of duck marsh become a refuge out of a total of 20,000, their shooting has been cut 50 per cent forever. But they forget that some years later, population increases and the march of civilization may have drained all 20,000 acres; then there will be no ducks in that section of the country, never again, absolutely never. Moreover they refuse to learn the easily proved fact that federal management has always increased the ducks 5-25 fold in a reasonable number of years and enormously improved the local shooting.

To continue the method of approach originally adopted, the toll of ducks killed in the hunting season is one more unfavorable factor for them, and constitutes the third liability over which man has control. This annual kill is not one of the many natural factors which produce the prodigious annual mortality, which is the lot of all living animals, the tenth of my original propositions. Sportsmen must face the fact that it is a *relatively new* and *additional strain* in the struggle for survival. Those who wish sport to continue must consequently take whatever steps are necessary to see that this strain is *compensated for*. In return for the bad, some good must be done the ducks.

While I have tried to show that the preservation of favorable environments and habitats is of fundamental importance in conserving our waterfowl, it does not follow that there is no point in properly restricted hunting regulations. I hasten to reaffirm my conviction that they too are absolutely essential. I have no intention of entering into a discussion of the technical details of any one year. No private individual or organization has the necessary knowledge of detailed facts. Even the officials of the federal government are forced to exercise their best judgment, based on estimates. But proper restrictions will be better appreciated if the people interested see more clearly what restrictions cannot accomplish and why.

Again, there is a human element. People do not like to be restricted, and will not obey restrictions which they do not understand. There are practical problems here with which I am not directly concerned, but of which I am sympathetically aware. But I must urge ever more scientifically sound and ideal hunting regulations, as research increases our knowledge. An educational program to sell these ideas to the public is badly needed. This seems to me a more constructive policy than the mere criticism of each year's regulations.

I consequently venture to close these remarks by suggesting certain general propositions. It is my hope that they may correctly apply to hunting the fundamental points of natural history just discussed. In no case is criticism of current regulations intended or implied.

1. The degree to which hunting is liberal or restricted should depend (a)

upon the carrying capacity of the environment because that determines the supply and (b) whether the amount of suitable territory is shrinking or expanding. Neither of these factors remains static for very long.

2. Those species of waterfowl whose breeding or winter ranges have been the most seriously destroyed by civilization should be given special protection to the degree required.

3. Those species which show marked inability to adjust properly to civilization should receive some extra protection. Outstanding examples are the Redhead and Ruddy Duck.

4. Hunting should be closed in those sections of the winter range where a failure in food supply occurs, where disease breaks out, or severe drought conditions exist.

5. Further research and improvement in techniques is possible in estimating the plant and animal food crop on the winter range; in other words, its carrying capacity. This would be more important than a mid-winter census.

6. The results of the breeding season and the carrying capacity of the winter range furnish the ideal criteria for the open season, whichever is the lower.

7. The annual kill should never exceed a minor percentage of the total annual losses.

8. The annual kill should never reduce the total population below the carrying capacity of the winter range.

9. There is no ground for abandoning hope that our waterfowl can be restored or increased as well as conserved. An extension of the wildlife refuge program particularly in the winter range, is a prerequisite for a permanent gain.

10. More liberal hunting must not kill off the surplus population which must be created.

11. An increase in hunters must be compensated for by a corresponding decrease in the permissible take.

12. If this surplus population has additional preserved or reclaimed territory in which to breed and winter, a permanent gain will have been made.

Sportsmen and bird-lovers will both gain in the long run, and our duty to conserve our natural heritage of wildlife will have been more than well done.

Index

Admiral Beatty Hotel, St. John, New Brunswick, 43

Albemarle and Chesapeake Canal, effect on Currituck shooting, 191

Allen, Capt. George, 62

alligator gars, Louisiana, 231-233

ambushing, Connecticut shore, 68

American Field, 272

American Kennel Club, 272, 274

Atlantic flyway, 3, 6, 7, 16, 17, 20

Audubon Magazine, 95

bag limits, 16, 18, 71, 169, 183-185, 200, 298

baiting, artificial vs. natural, 173

Baldwin, Clark, 62

Baltimore, Lord, 178

banding records, 4

Barbour, Joel, 94

Bartlett, James, 130

batteries, early Connecticut shore types, 66, 67

  Great South Bay, 92, 93

  Pamlico Sound, 206

battery rigs, Currituck Sound, 194, 195

Bean, L. L., 101

Bellport Bay, Long Island, 86-88

Bellport Gun Club, Inc., 89, 94

Bellport (Long Island) Coast Guard Station, 86, 87

Bergen, Judge H. A., 94

Bigelow, Dr. Henry, 154

Black Beard, 190

blackduck, preference for woods, 79, 80

  range of, 8

  wariness of, 78

blinds, Army camouflage material for, 40

  Back Bay, Virginia, 182, 188

  Barnegat Bay types, 108, 109

  Chesapeake Bay, 117, 128

  Currituck Sound, 193, 195, 196

  "dry land," Pamlico Sound, 207

  early Connecticut shore types, 67

  eastern Long Island, 80

  eastern shore of Virginia, 137-139, 146, 158, 159

  Louisiana, 232

  New Brunswick, 33, 34, 40

  "rolling," North Carolina, 210, 211

  stake, Pamlico Sound, 202-204, 208, 216

boats, early types in Connecticut, 63-66

  early types in Maine, 48, 49, 52

  Great South Bay, 91-93, 103, 104

  Susquehanna Flats, 119

Bond, Anson, 62

Bragg, Capt. Gary, 206-208, 212, 215

Bragg, Capt. Tom, 212

brant, decline and recovery of, 12, 107, 209
differing response to decoys in old and young birds, 208, 209
not attracted by decoys of other species, 206

breeding grounds of waterfowl, 3, 5-8, 289, 292-296, 298, 299
effect of drought years on, 294, 295

Brookhaven Town, Long Island, 87, 88

Browne, Erle, 52

Brown, Everett, 96, 99

Bureau of Biological Survey, 177

Burritt, Commodore Francis, 62

bushwhacking, Chesapeake Bay, 125

Campbell Club, Little Inlet, upper Smith's Island, Va., 158

Canaveral Club, Banana River, Fla., 225

carp, destruction of waterfowl food plants by, 15

cattail, 14

celery, wild, Potomac River, 176, 178
Susquehanna Flats, 10, 118

Central flyways, 5

Chadwick Hotel, Chadwick Beach, N. J., 106

Chandler, Dr. Gilbert A., 286

channel bass, eastern shore of Virginia, 146, 158

Chesapeake Bay Country, The, by Swepson Earle, 113

Chesapeake Bay place names, 117, 118

Chincoteague, Va., people and customs, 147

Cleveland, Grover, 106, 107

closed seasons, when and where to apply, 298

clothing, 40-42, 205

Cobb family, eastern shore of Virginia, history of, 148-157

Cobb, Messrs. Lucius and Arthur, 148

Connecticut shore, pollution on, 64

Conservation, 3, 16-20, 44, 69-71, 81, 82, 185, 288-293, 296-299

Co-ordination Act, 19

Cornwallis, Thomas, 178

Corwin, Capt. Frank, 103

Corwin, Capt. Wilbur R., 89, 90, 94

Corwin, Ed, 95

Corwin, John, 95

Corwin, Wilbur A., 87, 89, 90, 92, 94, 95

Crumb, Capt., collection of rare birds, 156

Cully, Nelson, 115

Curles Neck Club, Turkey Island, Va., 173

Currituck Club, 190, 192-194

Currituck Sound, formation of, 190, 191
historical lore, 189, 190

Cushman, Larrimer, 144

customs officials, 29, 30

cycles, in nature and climate, 289, 290

dead-rise bateau, 139

decoy anchor cord loops, 246, 247
anchor cords, 101, 247, 251
anchors, 250-252
body weights, 252, 253

decoys, balsa, 247-249
Barnegat Bay, 109, 110, 249
blackduck, simulated by sods on ice, 131
coaxing ducks into, 129
Connecticut shore, 249
cork, 239, 255
difference in quality unimportant, 131, 132, 159, 254
eastern shore of Virginia, 139, 140, 159
essential qualities of, 239, 240
factory made often inferior, 238

decoys (Cont.)
  "feeders" or "tip-ups," 241, 242
  Florida, 226
  Great South Bay time-saving Rig, 91
  goose, best lure for pintail, 205
  goose, live, 215
  goose, profile, 208, 216, 237
  heads, how to make, 245, 246, 248
  importance of coloring, 100
  importance of unalarmed attitude in, 241
  Indians', of stone, 62, 72
  in New Brunswick, 35
  iron, 92, 187, 243
  live, 58, 59, 72, 185, 186, 215, 238, 286
  natural cork bark, 249, 250, 257, 258
  painting, 253-255, 257-261, 263-265, 267, 268
  Pamlico Sound, 205, 206, 215-218
  picking up, 104, 242, 247, 251
  placement of, 101, 119, 128, 129
  press-cork, 240, 242-244, 249, 257, 258, 260
  press-cork, how to make, 242-246, 260
  profile, mounted on lath triangles, Long Island Sound, 74
  repainting, 239
  shape of, 240, 241
  "sleepers," 241
  surf scoter, 267
  two groups of, 240
  typical rig, Bellport Bay, Long Island, 100
  wariness of, as shown by various duck species, 102
  well painted, advantages of, 72-74, 253, 354
  wooden, hollow, 249
  wood keels for, 248, 250
deer, upper James River, Va., 162

Delaware Bay, oil pollution in, 13
Dixon, Thomas, 155
dogs, in New Brunswick, 24, 25, 26, 32, 37
  in Nova Scotia, 26
Dominy, Kellogg, 99
drainage of duck waters, 5, 7, 296
duck calling, 129
duck calls, 174, 183, 205
Duck Decoys, by Joel Barbour, 94
"duck depression," 16
duck population in 1944, 291
Ducks Unlimited, 71, 99, 161
duck trappers, eastern shore of Virginia, 157, 158
Dvorachek, William H., 178

Earle, Swepson, 113
eelgrass, chief winter food of Canada geese, 209
  effect of its decline on shooting, Pamlico Sound, 209
  effect on edibility of brant, 86, 136
Eno's, Forked River, N. J., 111

Federal Aid to Wildlife Restoration Act, 69
Federal Duck Law, 185
federal sanctuaries, 18, 19, 69, 106, 109, 188, 296, 298
Field Dog Stud Book, 272
field glasses, advantages of, in blinds, 206
fish and wildlife, Louisiana marshes, 233, 234
Fiske, John, 190
Fitchett, "Hard-time," 149
Florida, duck hunting waters of, 226, 227
  types of duck shooting, 223
food of waterfowl, 10, 11, 20, 176, 298

food plants destroyed by salt water, 11, 106, 181, 191
formula for estimating number of ducks in flock, 95
Fredericton, New Brunswick, 42
French, Dr. Ralph W., 60

geese, blue, winter home in Louisiana, 235
    Canada, domesticated flocks on Ocracoke Island, N. C., 214
    Canada, hunger-weakened birds summer in Pamlico Sound, 210
    Canada, lice infestation of starved birds, 210
    increasing numbers in lower James River, Va., 173
    snow, survival of, Back Bay, Va., 184
Gerrard, Thomas, 178
giant cutgrass, 14
Goodnow, Mr. and Mrs. Charles F., Jr., 277
goose calls, 174, 205
goose shooting, Currituck Sound, 197-199
    in corn and wheat fields, 173, 174
    lower James River, Va., 173
Gould, Henry, 90, 92
Great South Bay, 87-89
Green, Capt. George, 62
Green Island Club, Pamlico Sound, 212, 222
guides, Back Bay, Va., 182, 183
    Barnegat Bay, 110
    Currituck Sound, 192-194
    Florida, 225
    Great South Bay, 90, 94, 100
    Long Island, 81
    Louisiana, 231
    New Brunswick, 21-23, 31, 32, 35, 36, 39, 40
    Pamlico Sound, 212, 217, 218

guides (Cont.)
    rough handling of decoys by, 268
gunning clubs, lower James River, Va., 173
    sanctuaries and conservation measures of, 173
gunning "dink," 153, 154, 158, 159
guns, early types, Connecticut, 63
    early types, Currituck Sound, 192
    early types of market gunners, Maine, 48
    flintlock, 192
    four gauge, 154
    muzzle loading, 62, 63, 192

Hallock, Benjamin, 103
Halloway Point Club, Potomac River, 177
Hamel, Richard B., 94, 95
Hamill, J. S., 177
Hammond, J. H., 37
Hardy, Charles, 59
Harrison, Benjamin, 175
Harrison, William Henry, 175
Harvey House, Harvey Cedars, N. J., 112
Hawkins, Capt. Charles S., 94
Hine, Capt. George, 62
Holland, Ray, 162
Houdlette, Capt. Harold, 49
Howell, Lewis, 103
Hudson, Ira, 139, 140, 147
hurricane of 1938, effect on game covers, 27

Ice Age, 290
infections of wildfowl, botulism organisms, 7
Izaak Walton League, 177

Jones, Samuel, 222
jump shooting, Florida, 227

kill of ducks in 1880s, Back Bay, Va., 183, 184

kill of wildfowl, 16, 291, 292, 296-298
King, Barney, 95

Lacey Act, 69
Laing, Edward, 62
lead poisoning of waterfowl, 18
Lee, Richard, 179
Leopard's Spots, The, by Thomas Dixon, 155
line shooting, Connecticut shore, 64, 74-76
Long Island Sound, Connecticut shore, early gunning methods, 61, 62, 64, 65, 67, 68, 72
Louisiana marshes, character of, 230
lower James River, Va., character of, 173, 174
   historical lore, 174, 175

Madison, James, 179
Maine Fish and Game Department, 48
mallards, decline of, Back Bay, Va., 184
  meat affected by various foods, 10
man's part in destruction of waterfowl, 15, 16, 157, 296
Marjoribanks, Sir Dudley, 278
market gunners, Back Bay, Va., 186-188
  Chesapeake Bay, 124-127
  Pamlico Sound, 211, 212
market gunning bags, Great South Bay, 94, 95
market gunning, Currituck Sound, 191, 192
marsh buggy (Louisiana), 236
marshes, how formed, 9
Mattamuskeet National Wildlife Refuge, N. C., 19
McCarthy, Justin, 276
McLean, Senator George P., 70
McWilliams, Charlie, 212

Merrymeeting Bay, Me., early history of gunning, 48
  food for waterfowl, 48
  formation of, 45
  intersection of waterfowl flyways, 46
  unwritten "scull" law, 53
migration of waterfowl, 4, 7, 38, 204
Migratory Bird Conservation Act, 19
Migratory Bird Hunting Stamp Act, 69
Migratory Bird Treaty Act, 69, 71
Miles, "Jimmie Lew," 62
Miner, Jack, 199
Mississippi flyway, 5
Monkey Island Club, Currituck Sound, 193
Monroe, James, 179
Moore, Capt. Harry O., 120-126
Moore, Capt. Will, 120
Moore, "Uncle Charley," 120
Moss, Judge, 116
Mother of Waters, by Capt. Charles W. Wright, 113
Mühs, Fred, 286
Murdock, Russell, 280, 281
Murray, Henry, 62, 68

Narragansett Bay, pollution in, 13
New Brunswick, Fourth of July open season, 21

Ocean House, Toms River, N. J., 111
Ocracoke Village and Island, N. C., history and legend, 212-214
Oil Pollution Act of 1924, 13
Old Virginia and Her Neighbors, by John Fiske, 190
O'Neal, Ike, 212
O'Neal, Walter, 212
outboard motors, legislation against, 55

Pacific flyways, 5

Pamlico Sound shooting, 216

Parker River National Wildlife Refuge, Mass., 19

pass shooting, Connecticut shore, 68
    eastern shore of Virginia, 135
    Florida, 226

Pattersquash Gunners Association, Inc., 87, 88

pet goose decoy, 155, 156

Petty, Bob, 90

Petty, Dan, 90

Petty, John, 95

Phillips, John, 39

Phillips, Dr. John C., 59

Pine Island Club, Currituck Sound, 193

pintail, the prevailing species in Pamlico Sound, 204

pirogues, Louisiana, 232

"Pittman Robertson" funds, 5, 20

pollution, 12, 13, 14, 64, 296

ponds, 8

pond shooting, Currituck Sound, 195
    Florida, 226, 229

Pope's Creek, Va., 179

Porter, Dr. Charles, 68

Potomac Landings, by Paul Wiestach, 179

Potomac River, character of, 176, 178
    historical lore, 179

Potomac River Water Chestnut Eradication Commission, 177

Poyner, T. J., 192

Princess Anne Club, Back Bay, Va., 183, 188

Princess Colleen Kennels, 277

Purdy, Ken, 275

Quanch Life Saving Station, Long Island, 89

Ragged Island Club, Back Bay, Va., 188

Raleigh, Sir Walter, 189

rapids, favorite hangout of river ducks, 169

redheads, stooling characteristics, 187

Remick, J. Gould, 280

Rennert Hotel, Baltimore, 127

retriever, Chesapeake Bay, 26, 269-272, 282, 286
    curly coated, 280
    flat coated, 281-283
    golden, 26, 278-280
    Labrador, 26, 274-276, 282

retriever pups, importance of registered parents, 283, 284
    training of, 284-287

retrievers, kindness in handling, 286

Ripley, Sydney Dillon, 95

Robbins, A. & M., 150

Rockefeller, John D., Jr., 175

Roosevelt, Franklin D., 177

Rowe, Eben, 192

Rowe, Lewis, 192

sanctuary, natural, formed by impenetrable marsh, 144, 145

Sanford, Dr. "Len," 62

Sasscer, Representative Lansdale G., 177

scientific names of waterfowl, 46, 47

scooters, Great South Bay, 93, 94, 96

scows, eastern shore of Virginia, 154

seaside, eastern shore of Virginia, terrain of, 142-145

Seelinger's Marsh, Back Bay, Va., 182, 183, 188

Selleck, J. W., 62

Shattuck, George, 155

Shepard, Eugene, 62

shore birds, eastern shore of Virginia, 146

sinkbox, Back Bay, Va., 186, 187

sinkbox (Cont.)
early Connecticut shore types, 65, 66
Maryland type, 118, 119, 128
Smith, "Bull," 87
Smith, Capt. Burr, 62
Smith, Capt. George, 62
Smith, Capt. Ike, 90, 91
Smith, Capt. John, 174, 175, 179, 189
Smith, Col. William "Tangier," 87
Smith, Jean, 87
Smith, Representative Howard W., 177
sneakbox, Barnegat, 107, 108, 110
Snow, Judge William S., 177
spaniel, American brown water, 26, 272-274
Irish water, 276-278, 286, 287
Sportsman's Paradise, Cobb Island, Va., 152
Squan House, Barnegat Bay, 111
stool, mixed, 131
stools, dark and light, 131
storms of 1896, eastern shore of Virginia, 157
Sunset Hotel, Barnegat City, N. J., 111
Swan Island Club, Currituck Sound, 193
Sweeden Point picnic area, Potomac River, 177

Thorne, Ltd., St. John, New Brunswick, 43
Titus, Joseph Henry, 89, 94
Tuckerton House, Tuckerton, N. J., 112
Turrell, George B., 88
Tyler, John, 175
Tyler, Thomas, 273

Uhler, Francis M., 177
upland and shore birds of Cape Cod, 57, 58
upland birds, New Brunswick, 23, 24, 30
upper James River, Va., 162, 171

upper James River, Va., character of, 165-168, 172
U. S. Fish and Wildlife Service, 7, 14, 17, 18, 20, 210. 290, 292, 293

Van Slack's Tavern, Poplar Branch, Currituck Sound, 193
Virginia, eastern shore, country and people, 134, 135

Wakeley, Ephraim, 62
Walker, George, 155
Walter, Ralph, 130
water chestnut, 13-15, 176-178
waterfowl, adaptability to civilization, 293, 298
as economic resource, 16-18
decline and recovery, Currituck Sound, 191
decline of, Back Bay, Va., 182
decline of, eastern shore of Virginia, 157, 158
decline of, in 1946, 288
diversity of, in west as compared with east, 4
losses from natural causes, 290-293, 297
mortality, factors of, 289-294
reproductive fertility, 293
waterfowl population, 16, 291, 296
Long Island areas, 70, 71
waterfowl species, Back Bay, Va., 183
Barnegat Bay, 106, 107
Chesapeake Bay, 114-116
Currituck Sound, 195
eastern shore of Virginia, 135, 136
formerly common to Connecticut shore, 63
Florida, 224, 225

waterfowl species (Cont.)
    Louisiana, 233-235
    Pamlico Sound, 203, 204
    Potomac River, 176
    upper James River, Va., 166
water hyacinth, 13, 14
weather, effect on shooting, 98, 102, 130, 131, 204, 208, 216
Weeks-McLean Law, 69
Weeks, Secretary of War John W., 70
Wheeler, Charles E. (Shang), 100
Wheelock, Jeffries, 155
Wicks, Charles "Cappy," 62

widgeon grass, staple food of Canada geese, Pamlico flats, 209
Wiestach, Paul, 179
Wildfowler Decoy Factory, 248
Wimbrow Brothers, 139
Winsor Hotel, Fredericton, New Brunswick, 41
winter range, carrying capacity of, 294, 295 of waterfowl, 7, 8, 106, 113, 202, 224, 235, 289, 292-296, 298, 299
woodcock shooting, Nova Scotia, 24
Worth, W. W., 251
Wright, Capt. Charles W., 113